AMERICAN HISTORY
at a Glance

The Lenox Collection, The New York Public Library

A woodcut made from an illustration that accompanied Columbus' first letter announcing the discovery of America.

AMERICAN
HISTORY
at a Glance

Fourth Edition

MARSHALL SMELSER
JOAN R. GUNDERSEN

Harper Perennial
A Division of HarperCollins*Publishers*

First BARNES & NOBLE BOOKS edition published 1975

ISBN 0-06-463475-2

91 92 93 94 95   20 19 18 17 16 15 14

AMERICAN HISTORY

at a Glance

Contents

Maps

The Opening of a New World

The discovery of America was not an accident which occurred outside of the main current of human affairs. It was the logical result of a series of happenings which began centuries before. The leading Continental powers that participated in the exploration and occupation of the New World were England, France, Holland, Spain, and Portugal. England was to prove the most successful.

THE BACKGROUND OF EUROPEAN EXPANSION

The Crusades had taken European men to strange lands on the western edge of Asia and had introduced them to previously unknown material goods. This contact encouraged a trade in oriental wares. Spices and fine fabrics were especially desired in Europe to relieve the sameness of coarse foods and clothing which were then in common use. Nevertheless, the existence of many middlemen and monopolies, and the vast distances and difficulties of overland shipment from places farther east, kept supplies limited and prices high. It was almost inevitable that men would some day look for an all-water route to the sources of the staples of the Asiatic trade.

European business activity increased and profits accumulated in the hands of merchants and bankers. This surplus could be invested in new businesses; thus, credit could be made easier and business practices more flexible. Without credit and "investment capital," new overseas ventures could hardly have been undertaken.

The growth of seagoing trade required geographical knowledge, ships, and seamanship. These were steadily improved during the late Middle Ages. From ancient geography and from astronomy, men knew the shape and approximate size of the earth, and they had had thousands of years of experience in sailing in European waters. In the late Middle Ages they colonized several Atlantic islands and they eagerly read Marco Polo's book on China. Marco Polo and several missionaries reported that China was bordered by the sea—an important fact. The work of shipbuilders gave sailors new confidence by making available new types of ships, notably the Portuguese "Caravel," which could sail against the wind faster and more efficiently than ever before. The wider use of the "astrolabe" for finding latitude and the magnetic compass for steering made easier the work of finding one's way over the unmarked face of the mysterious ocean. New charts, based on facts instead of legends, came into use.

The expansion of business was not the sole motive of the wandering medieval mariners. To them the Crusades were fairly recent in time, and the dream of freeing the Holy Land from the Mohammedans was not yet dead. Exploration might yield great treasures to finance new Crusades and perhaps could discover mighty Christian kings who would serve as allies. Columbus had exactly such hopes.

Another religious idea was to be important in the occupation of the New World. Europe was about to be swept by a great religious contest, the Protestant revolution. Not many of the earliest Protestants came to America, but in later generations the quarrels and wars promoted the notion of going to America to escape the turmoil and turbulence of Europe.

There was at the same time as these economic and religious changes a great political revolution which was of more immediate significance. That was the rise of national states, of independent nations somewhat as we now know them. Kings who had been, in name at least, vassals of the Emperor of the Holy Roman Empire, now emerged as heads of their own countries, in practice responsible to no superior in this world. In this rise they usually had the help of their own merchants and bankers, who provided the money (through taxation) for royal armies and navies which overawed or defeated local rivals among their nobility. In return the kings provided that peace without which international trade could not flourish. The most important of these national states that greatly influenced early American history were Portugal, Spain, France, and England.

Thus the changing ways of material life, of business, of navigation, of religion, of politics, all made clear the way for great seamen to steer for unknown havens beyond the curve of sea and sky.

THE DISCOVERY OF AMERICA

First of the western peoples to search the Atlantic were the Portuguese. Directed by Prince Henry (1394–1460), called "the Navigator," founder of a school of navigation, the Portuguese searched for African wealth and for an African route to the silks and spices of the East. Decade by decade they mapped the coast of Africa; they rounded the Cape of Good Hope in 1488, and at last reached India in 1498 led by Vasco da Gama. This century of Portuguese experience was part of the story of the discovery of America. Portuguese sailors used the new equipment, tested the new ships, raised chart-making to a science, and gained great and valuable experience in long passages. All these things were necessary to the art and science of navigation which made the discovery possible.

But no Portuguese discovered America. That was reserved for Christopher Columbus, an Italian in the service of Spain. Columbus was convinced that he would come upon Japan at about the place where later explorers found Florida, and after many unsuccessful attempts elsewhere he finally secured adequate outfitting and financing from the Spanish King and Queen, Ferdinand and Isabella. He hoped to find a sea route to Asia, to carry missionaries there, and to gain wealth and honors for himself and family, as "Admiral of the Ocean Sea." In three ships his expedition steered west, pushed by the southeast trade winds and found land on October 12, 1492. But it was not Asia, although Columbus died thinking that it was. He had found a grand, lush New World that in centuries to come was almost to surpass the highest flights of man's imagination.

There have been more than a dozen claims that America was discovered by explorers who had sailed earlier than Columbus. The only claim supported by positive evidence is that of

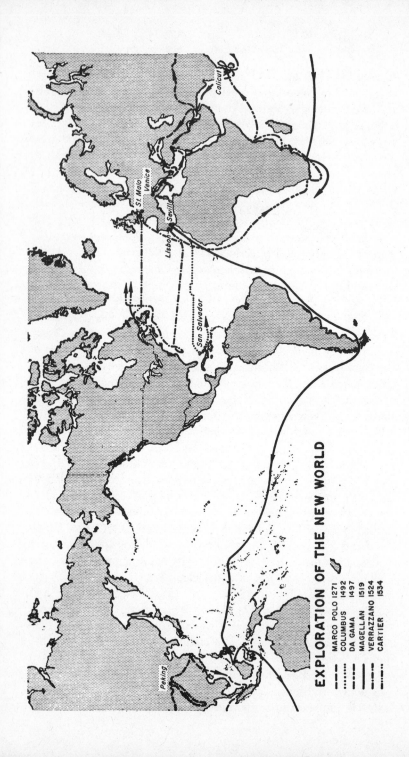

EXPLORATION OF THE NEW WORLD

- — — MARCO POLO 1271
- ········· COLUMBUS 1492
- ———— DA GAMA 1497
- ———— MAGELLAN 1519
- ─·─·─ VERRAZZANO 1524
- ·········· CARTIER 1534

Peking

Calicut

St. Malo
Venice
Lisbon
Seville
San Salvador

the Norsemen of Scandinavia who probably found the mainland of North America in the tenth century. But their voyages led to no permanent results, and history is more concerned with the contemporaries and successors of Columbus who unveiled and populated the New World.

EXPLORATION AND EARLY DEVELOPMENT

Within a half-century of the discovery, the shores of North and South America were traced by men who, usually, regarded them as obstacles in the sea road to the far Indies and who were trying to find a way around or through the strange new continents. John Cabot, of Florence, sailed for the English King Henry VII and in 1497 reached some part of northeastern North America. A Portuguese captain, Pedro Cabral, accidentally found Brazil in 1500. Other Portuguese explorers probably visited Newfoundland in 1500 and 1501. A Florentine businessman, Amerigo Vespucci, unintentionally gave his first name to the new continents when his report, in 1507, of a voyage with the Spaniard Ojeda gave the idea for the name to a German geographical scientist. In 1513 Balboa crossed the Isthmus of Panama, saw the Pacific, and made clear the fact that America was not Asia. In 1519 Ferdinando Magellan led the expedition which gained timeless glory by sailing around the world for the first time in man's record. Magellan was killed on the way, but one ship survived to complete the circuit. Verrazano, in 1524, and Jacques Cartier, 1534–41, sailed for the King of France. They explored the eastern coast of the present United States and revealed the St. Lawrence Valley. In 1609 the Dutch sent Henry Hudson to explore the present Hudson River around Manhattan Island, which later became the province of New Netherland.

The Portuguese and Spanish Empires. Untiring were the Portuguese. With skill and vigor they built up trade with the parts of Africa and Asia which they had explored. In those places they did not usually "colonize" in the American sense because wherever they went they found able businessmen with whom to deal. Hence, they established trading posts in little forts, protected by armed guards. But in Brazil they promoted permanent agricultural settlements.

By far the most successful early New World enterprises were

those of the Spanish. Making use of the earlier experiences of the Portuguese and Genoese, and using the skills gained from their own colonization of the Canary Islands of the Atlantic, the Spaniards shaped a colonial empire in America based on mining and on agriculture, which was conducted on great, self-sufficient and almost self-governing farms called "encomiendas." The Indian aristocracy was replaced by a Spanish ruling class. Sometimes the Indians were abused, but the king and the Church protected them to some extent. Business affairs were conducted by monopolies under government direction. From Columbus's first colony of Hispaniola (now Santo Domingo) settlements expanded to other islands and to the mainland of Central and South America, under the leadership of hardy conquerors—the "conquistadores"—such as Cortez in Mexico and Pizarro in Peru. Spanish explorers also marched vast distances through the southern part of the present United States; the best remembered were DeSoto in the Mississippi Valley and Coronado in the Southwest. By 1600 Spanish America had been founded, Spanish in culture and Catholic in religion, with 150,000 Europeans leading a society of millions of Indians, and able to boast of scholars, artists, scientists, and saints.

The parallel expansion of Portugal and Spain might have caused ill-feeling and war, except that Pope Alexander VI, in the Papal Bull of 1493, had drawn a "line of demarcation" between their spheres of operations—a line later adjusted by the Treaty of Tordesillas (1494) so as to give Brazil to Portugal. Of course, non-Catholic nations did not later feel bound to observe such an arrangement.

In the seventeenth century, Spanish holdings in the New World were enlarged; Northern Mexico and Lower California were occupied and new missions were established in Florida where, already in 1565, St. Augustine, the oldest city of the United States, had been founded. North of Florida, Spanish expansion was blocked by English settlements, while West Indian islands not occupied by Spain were taken, one by one, by English, French, Dutch, and Danish colonists. After 1700 Frenchmen penetrated the lower Mississippi Valley and the coasts along the Gulf of Mexico, including Texas. The founding of Georgia and Louisiana by the English and French, respectively, further limited Spain's northward movement, but, in the Southwest, Spaniards pressed into Arizona and New Mexico and consolidated their holdings in Lower California. In the Great War for Empire (Seven Years' War), 1754–63, Spain lost Florida but was compensated by the grant of all French territory west of the Mississippi River and by cession of the city of New Orleans. On the Pacific Coast the Russians were moving south from their colony of Alaska to the vicinity of San Francisco. (How different our later story might have been if they had made good in that venture!) As a countermeasure the Spanish moved north into California and settled continuously farther north until they reached San Francisco in 1776.

The Founding of New France. Unlike the Spanish and Portuguese overseas empires, the French colonies started as modest ventures based on slender resources. They had no Columbus, nor any sudden discovery of great wealth. Most of the earliest work for France was done by little-known fishermen or fur traders who came in small groups to fish on the Newfoundland banks or to barter for furs with wild Indians gathered in misty coves.

The first settlements by Frenchmen in the Western Hemisphere were failures. French Protestants were ejected from their quarrelsome little colony in Brazil by the Portuguese in 1560. Four years later, others settled in Florida. Because this settlement overlooked the Gulf Stream and the regular routes of the Spanish treasure fleets, the French were butchered in 1565 by Spaniards led by Menéndez, who excused the deed on religious grounds. To prevent a recurrence of French occupation and to protect the treasure ships from French and English raiders, the Spanish promptly founded St. Augustine, nearby.

More fortunate were the French ventures in Canada. One of the many little trading companies, that of the DeMonts, had the good luck to secure the services of Samuel de Champlain, a whole-souled, hardy, and vigorous man who may properly be called "the father of Canada." He continued the exploration of the St. Lawrence Basin which had been begun by Cartier, and in 1608 he founded the city of Quebec. Quebec became the political, religious, and military center of New France and the base used by "woods-runners," "black robes" (missionaries), and soldiers in extending the sway of France over a forested empire stretching across half a continent. The economy of New France was intended by the home government to be agricultural,

OWNERSHIP OF THE CONTINENT, 1682-1783

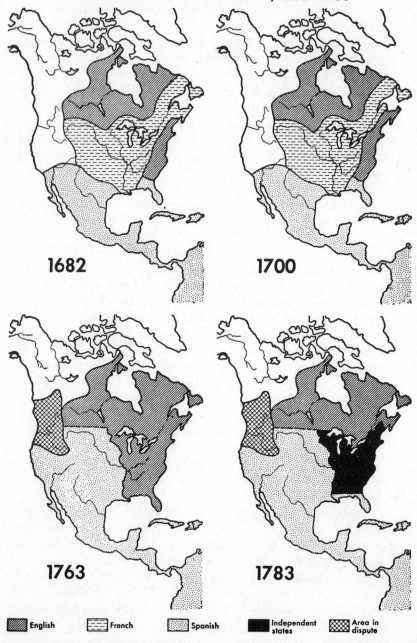

1682

1700

1763

1783

English French Spanish Independent states Area in dispute

but the *habitants* often preferred to trade for furs with the Indians, and, in reality, this trade became the economic backbone of New France. The fur trade was given to licensed monopolists until the 1670's, but a brisk, illegal traffic was carried on by forest rovers who relied on brandy as currency. This "black market" was vigorously opposed by the Catholic missionaries, who saw their edifying work undone by debaucheries and by swindling of the Indians. The work of the missionaries was earnest and even heroic, but they apparently made little impression except upon children and the aged among their uncultured charges.

French expansion westward was swift. In less than fifty years after the founding of Quebec, the adventurous French roamers had found a canoe route over white waters and through silent forests between Lake Superior and Saskatchewan, at a time when a French settlement in Wisconsin was twenty years old. The French had almost reached the Rocky Mountains before the British had founded half of the "old thirteen" colonies of North America. By the first quarter of the eighteenth century, the lily banner of the kings of France floated securely on the shores of the Gulf of Mexico and at every strategic strong point inland, from the mouth of the Mississippi to the mouth of the St. Lawrence.

When the English colonies began their slower but more massive growth, Canada and Louisiana loomed as serious threats. If the forest empire of France were to be secured and consolidated, the French needed to confine the English to a strip along the Atlantic Coast.

COLONIZATION BY THE ENGLISH

The English were among the latest to adventure to the New World. Internal difficulties, both political and religious, followed by a long war with Spain, distracted the nation from dreams of imperial grandeur, and it must be remembered that England was a relatively poor country. There were, however, advocates of expansion who, by books, example, or financial sponsorship, hoped to lead their fellow countrymen to colonize abroad. Best remembered of these men were Sir Walter Raleigh and Sir Humphrey Gilbert. They argued that England should rival Spain by acquiring quantities of gold and silver; that various raw materials might be secured for English manufacturers from their own colonies instead of relying for supplies on doubtful foreign friends; that savages might be converted to the Church of England's version of Protestant Christianity; that England was overpopulated and might drain her surplus people into colonies. The ideas of economic self-sufficiency and relief of overpopulation were probably the strongest motivations that were offered. England was changing from a feudal, Catholic, and agricultural country into a capitalist, Protestant, trading state. Through familiarity with trading corporations which did business with most parts of the known world, the minds of businessmen were being prepared for speculations in companies formed to open up the previously unknown world to the west.

That the New World could be a great source of wealth was dramatically shown by the capture of treasures from Spanish colonial towns and ships. Two Elizabethan Englishmen drew much attention by their anti-Spanish exploits. Sir John Hawkins traded illegally in the Spanish American Empire. Sir Francis Drake looted Spanish ships and settlements along the Pacific coasts of the two Americas, sailed on around the world, and brought home a great treasure, for all of which he was knighted by Queen Elizabeth, his silent partner. Sir Humphrey Gilbert tried to colonize Newfoundland but drowned on his return passage. His half-brother, Sir Walter Raleigh, carried on his projects and planted the colony at Roanoke, now North Carolina, in 1587, from which the settlers totally disappeared, leaving behind only the mystery of the "lost colony."

The Spaniards regarded these and similar activities of the "Elizabethan sea dogs" (the sobriquet of the English marauders) as criminal, hence a cause for war. In 1588 a powerful fleet, the Spanish or "Invincible" Armada was sent against Britain only to be roundly beaten by superior English gunnery and tactics. Storms which followed the long battle completed the temporary disarming of Spanish sea power. This engagement was the beginning of the long rise of the British navy to first rank on the seven seas, a position achieved by the time of the eighteenth century. More immediately, it kept Spain and England at war for another fifteen years.

Meanwhile, extensive changes were occurring in the religious and social life of England. Queen Elizabeth and her advisers reorganized the Church of England along "moderate" or "broad" principles, completing the change begun by her father, Henry VIII, from Catholicism to Protestantism. Her middle-of-the-road approach left both Catholics and rigorous Protestants unsatisfied. Their unwillingness to accept the Elizabethan settlement led to suppressions and persecutions and consequent refugee movements which were to provide colonists for America in the next generation. Another group which later provided emigrants was the growing body of landless farmers who were deprived of their ancient rights to farm the common fields (as farmers had done in the Middle Ages) by the growth of modern agricultural practices based upon the enclosure of previously open fields. English life was growing harder for many. To them the assured existence of an American farmer (perhaps surrounded by neighbors of like religious convictions) was to be a vision capable of inspiring them to great exertions.

But the transfer of the peoples waited on the correct organization of colonial projects. Unlike the rulers of the other western kingdoms, the monarchs of England had no uncommitted funds for extraordinary projects. Hence, all the English settlements in America began as private enterprises, although launched with the approval of the government. Investors had to be persuaded that profits could be made. It seemed to some that sufficient returns could be made by selling land; by subletting land subject to a fixed, perpetual charge, called "quitrent"; by trading with the Indians for furs; by extracting forest products such as tar and turpentine for shipbuilders; or by raising exotic agricultural produce, such as silk or spices. It was not incredible that they might duplicate the Spanish experience of finding gold and silver. Some investors had strictly commercial ambitions Others dreamed of holding vast estates in land and founding noble families after the medieval manner. These latter founders often wove medieval ideas into their schemes of colonizing, and we call their colonies "proprietorships." The other group, the more modern, business-minded colonies we can best call "commercial" colonies.

Virginia: The English Beachhead. The first permanent colony founded in America by Englishmen was Virginia, an enterprise of the Virginia Company, chartered by James I and given a monopoly of the exploitation of much of the Atlantic Coast of the present United States. The first settlement was in 1607 at Jamestown, an unhealthy site. Owing to the high mortality rate, it is doubtful that Virginia would have survived except for the forceful leadership of several founders, including Captain John Smith, who compelled the demoralized colonists to do what was necessary to survive. John Rolfe's improvements in growing tobacco in 1612 assured financial survival by creating a source of income from European sales. In 1619 the company furthered the cause of permanence by urging recruitment of women for the colony. The company, however, was not a financial success for its stockholders and was dissolved by the king in 1624. Virginia was henceforth directly under the Crown, as a "royal colony." Probably the most valuable gift of the Virginia Company to this country was the House of Burgesses, a representative assembly and the first such body in America which was capable of becoming an organ of free and representative self-government. It was founded in 1619.

It was in Virginia—also in 1619—that Negro laborers were first introduced into the British colonies of North America. Before the end of the century their status had crystallized into hereditary, chattel slavery. By mid-eighteenth century their labor was thought to be "indispensable" to southern agriculture.

Early Virginians were troubled by their neighbors, red and white. After Pocahontas allegedly saved John Smith's life, there was peace so long as her father, Powhatan, lived. But in later years there were serious Indian wars. As for their white neighbors, neither Spaniards nor Frenchmen admitted the legality of the occupation of Virginia. The colony was never seriously threatened by either, but there were occasional armed clashes on the coast and the menace of attack was always there.

The success of Virginia taught several lessons: A colony must provide its own food and not expect to rely on rations from home. A colony must be based on family living, not on the work of transient prospectors and adventurers who produced nothing for sale abroad. A colony prospers under the system of individual enterprise.

New England. After Virginia, the next successful settlement was that of the venerated "Pilgrim Fathers," in 1620, at Plymouth, now a part of Massachusetts. The original Pilgrims were Protestants who could not accept the Church of England and therefore migrated to the Netherlands. Not wholly satisfied there, they decided to go to America. After forming a commercial trading corporation, they sailed on the *Mayflower* in 1620, landing on the bleak coast of New England early in the winter. Before going ashore, knowing themselves outside the limit of any government, they drafted and signed the "Mayflower Compact," an agreement to be bound by their own rules. By careful diplomatic work they remained at peace with their Indian neighbors for half a century, but they drove out any white neighbors whose conduct they thought ungodly. Their direct influence on later American life has been slight, but their days have been movingly recorded by their leader, Governor William Bradford*, and their fortitude has been, to succeeding generations, an American ideal.

Larger and much more influential was the neighboring settlement of Massachusetts Bay, organized as a religious refuge for Puritans, on the basis of the American experience of an earlier company, the Dorchester Adventurers. The leading stockholders of the Massachusetts Bay Company, unhappy about "Romish" tendencies in the English Church, agreed in the "Cambridge Agreement" to migrate to America. Their migration, which began in five ships in 1629, was skilfully organized and backed by adequate funds. In the next twelve years almost twenty thousand persons came to this settlement, as the "high Church" movement in the Church of England was strengthened by royal support, and Puritan hopes of "purifying" the Church steadily dwindled. The company charter was commercial in form but over a period of years was slowly adapted to be the basic instrument of a self-governing commonwealth.

Massachusetts had legal difficulties for a time with Sir Ferdinando Gorges, the leading man of the Council for New England, a body with a prior claim to the land. Since the early days of the Virginia Company, Gorges and several associates had been trying to develop New England. He never assented to the Massachusetts project. He sought in vain to persuade King Charles I to dispossess the colonists; indeed, his colony of Maine was later annexed by Massachusetts.

---

*See William Bradford, *Bradford's History of Plymouth Plantation, 1606–1646*, ed. W. T. Davis (New York: Barnes & Noble, Inc., 1908, reprinted 1952).

The colonists of Massachusetts settled compactly, carefully preserved their culture and religion, in a "Christian commonwealth", and prospered by agriculture from the first. If any one man were to be credited for the success of this remarkable group, it would be the conscientious and prudent English squire, John Winthrop, who served as governor many terms.

Excepting Plymouth, the rest of the seventeenth-century New England was settled by colonists who used Massachusetts as a base. Many congregations followed their able, strong-minded pastors to new sites. Others sought to plant new settlements on rivers or harbors rather than to penetrate the hilly, forested back country. Connecticut, which was settled from Cambridge, Massachusetts, in 1636, was one of the most thriving and successful of these. Its founders were strongly attracted by the trade and soil of the Connecticut River Valley. They were shortly followed by a group of London Puritans who came to New Haven via Boston. Connecticut annexed New Haven in the 1660's. The government of Connecticut was much like that of Massachusetts, although not based on a commercial charter. Instead, the founders drafted a series of statutes, together called the Fundamental Orders of Connecticut, which served as a political basis for thirty years. In the 1660's it was clear that their holdings would be more secure under a legal grant; a charter was successfully sought from King Charles II, a charter so satisfactory that it served as a "state constitution" after the American Revolution. Part of the same movement, but involving land not within the same boundaries, was the founding of Springfield, Massachusetts, on the Connecticut River. Men of the colony of Connecticut provided most of the manpower in the Pequot War of 1637, during which the Pequot tribe of Indians was practically exterminated.

A less orthodox foundation was that of Rhode Island, settled by exiles or irreconcilables from Massachusetts. Best known of these was the tolerant but contentious Roger Williams, keenly interested in religion but, unlike most men of his century, unwilling to coerce people into religious conformity. For his theological and legal views Massachusetts banished him in 1635. The colony of Rhode Island was formed by the union of four towns: Providence (which was founded by Williams in 1636), Portsmouth, Newport, and Warwick. The inhabitants were strongly individualistic; it required real qualities of leadership in Williams to hold them together. The colony secured successive charters from England in 1644 and 1663. The second charter explicitly guaranteed liberty of conscience, a freedom legally unknown in England.

Maryland. All of the colonies mentioned thus far were founded in the reigns of James I and Charles I. In the same period the first proprietary colony, Maryland, was founded. George Calvert, the first Lord Baltimore, a Catholic peer, was granted Maryland in 1632 and planned to establish a religious haven and a great family estate. The first settlement was made in 1634. Despite a campaign to persuade Catholics to go to Maryland, not many did, and they were soon outnumbered by Protestants. The government of Maryland was established on a feudal principle, with the proprietor possessing, in Maryland, much the same power that the king wielded in England. The representative assembly consciously imitated the English Parliament. Maryland had many difficulties with both Indian and white neighbors. Of the latter the most troublesome was the anti-Catholic William Claiborne, a Virginia squatter on Kent Island in Chesapeake Bay, whose party was evicted by force. In line with their intentions of founding the colony, the Catholic Calverts provided religious toleration, which was enacted into law in the Toleration Act of 1649. Later the Church of England was legally established and Catholics were occasionally penalized.

New Netherlands. Between New England and Maryland a contemporary colony, New Netherlands, was established (1626) by the Dutch, the first settlement being in the Hudson Valley. The colony was only a side interest of its founders, the Dutch West India Company (which was formed primarily for privateering against the Spaniards in the Caribbean), and its population was mixed in origin and unhappy about their misgovernment. The English merchants found New Amsterdam, the chief port, a cause for irritation in that it was planted between English colonies and was a base for Dutch shipping competition. In 1664 an English expedition was sent against it. The colony was taken without a fight, from its frustrated and tactless governor, Peter Stuyvesant, and given to the younger brother of Charles II, the Duke of York, who called it New York. Certainly no brother ever gave a potentially richer gift.

New York, under the Duke, was a proprietary colony. The proprietor's chief, but not sole, interest was profit. However, he made little from it. The population was very mixed in national origins. Those from England or from neighboring English colonies wished for an assembly. In 1683 one was established, but its laws never received the Duke's assent.

The Closing of the Seaboard Gaps. The original settlements did not make a completely settled strip along the Atlantic Coast, but between the 1660's and 1732 the gaps were filled.

In 1664 the Duke of York gave as a subgrant that part of his proprietorship between the Hudson and Delaware rivers to Lord John Berkeley and Sir George Carteret who sold to an ever increasing number of other proprietors. The area was called New Jersey.

Farther south, at about the same time, another proprietorship, the Carolinas (now North and South Carolina), was being founded. English national policy favored southern expansion to compete with Spain, and the Carolinas were the result. The chief promoter was Anthony Ashley Cooper, Lord Shaftesbury, who assisted in the Restoration of Charles II. Since the state of the royal treasury could afford no other reward, the king gave Shaftesbury and eight others this great grant. The chief aim of these gentlemen was to establish grand estates and live on the rents, but their "sales talks" made much of enlarging the empire and of producing tropical crops for England. A few settlers already lived near Albemarle Sound. The first permanent settlement, near present Charleston, was made in 1670. For years the Carolinas remained a weak, isolated outpost, always threatened by the Spaniards of Florida.

Shaftesbury believed that the feudal age had been a golden age and tried to recreate feudalism in the Carolinas by means of an elaborate, artificial structure of government embodied in a document called "The Fundamental Constitutions of Carolina." It was never more than partly effective. The development of the Carolinas brought disappointment to the proprietors. Small farmers, great planters, and the British government were all dissatisfied, and the royal government bought out the proprietors in 1719.

Pennsylvania was a remarkable experiment in idealism, combined with real promotional skill. The liberality of its founder attracted people of several nationalities and many religions. In a sense, one can say that Pennsylvania was the most "American" of colonies. The proprietor was William Penn, a Quaker, who received his great province in 1681 from James II in satisfaction of a debt owed to his father. The land was partitioned off from the old New York grant. Penn was a gentleman and a practical idealist who believed in brotherly love. The charter of this new proprietorship gave the owner less kingly power than was given to earlier proprietors and knit the colony into the fabric of the British Empire. But Penn was free to draft the first laws on a consciously moral plan which provided liberty of conscience for all. The assembly gradually developed into a miniature British House of Commons. Penn himself spent little time in America and profited little from the colony.

Penn's colonists found the lower Delaware Valley already inhabited. Swedish interests had planted a small and unsuccessful colony there in 1637, as "New Sweden." The neglected, indeed, practically ignored, colonists offered no resistance when, in 1655, they were annexed by the Dutch of New Netherlands, who had their own post competing for the fur trade upstream near the present site of Trenton. Included in Penn's grant, they were given a separate assembly, as Delaware, in 1704, but continued under the governor of Pennsylvania.

Scattered individuals lived in present New Hampshire from 1608. They were brought under Massachusetts in the 1640's but by order of the royal courts in 1679 were designated as the royal colony of New Hampshire.

Last of the "old thirteen" continental colonies was the proprietorship of Georgia, founded by a philanthropic board of "Trustees of Georgia" in 1732, to provide new starts for English bankrupts. The colony did not begin to prosper until the Trustees' charter expired in 1752.

English colonizers had many other interests, from the arctic to the tropics, which concern us less directly. During the entire colonial period the English sugar plantations in the West Indies seemed to many Englishmen more important and valuable than the continental colonies. Barbados and Jamaica were the richest of the West Indies islands. The fur trade of the Hudson Bay watershed was also continuously pursued after 1670 by the Hudson's Bay Company.

Great Britain was not the only nation which tried to colonize in the sparsely settled temperate zone of the New World, but the British alone succeeded. Several reasons suggest themselves. Their settlements were relatively compact and defensible. They did not restrict migration to their own kind; hence they increased in population more rapidly than their rivals. Although the home government tried to influence their economic life in its external relations, it never controlled their local economy and its problems could be solved by men familiar with local circumstances. Perhaps the most important reason was that British colonists, almost from the first, came "family style," husbands, wives, and children, and were therefore wholly committed to the adventure. Following the first bands of seekers after gold and glory came these farm families who put down deep roots and were never after blown away by the storms of war or hard times. Compared to them the trappers, soldiers, and wandering missionaries of the rival powers were as transients in a strange hotel.

2

The Colonial Period

The early colonists lived concurrently under two governments —their own local units and the imperial rule of the British. In a new land, 3,000 miles distant from the motherland, it was natural that they would develop a way of life distinctly their own; yet, they were inextricably tied to and involved in the affairs of the British Empire, which, at this time, had focused on a struggle with France for world supremacy.

THE PROVINCIAL SOCIETY

Migrants coming from Europe (especially Germany and Ireland) and from Africa made the Americans a more diverse people than the British. Land practices were equally diverse, but the availability of farm land was the overriding consideration. The land was available only after the primal owners, the Indians, were bloodily displaced or exterminated. But Indian ways shaped settlers' life styles. In the 1600's labor in America included mostly temporary and voluntary servants, but after 1700 most were in permanent slavery.

Although men far outnumbered women in the early stages of settlement, the American population grew as much by natural increase as by immigration. The first generation may have married late, but the second, marrying earlier, averaged seven children to a family, most of whom survived to adulthood. The family was the basic unit for education and work. About 95 per cent of the colonists supported themselves by agriculture, and most of the others produced raw materials (fish, furs, lumber) for direct sale or for processing abroad. The distinctly American social life was rural, family-centered, and "provincial." Nearly all people were seriously religious, although differing greatly in doctrine, from the conservative theology of Catholicism to the "advanced" views of the Quakers. The course of American religious life was generally in the direction of "toleration," because there were so many creeds that no one of them could be supreme and compel conformity. The culture of the people, despite their various origins, continued, especially in language and literature, to be British. The law of colonial America was derived mainly from England. Although culture tended to decay in the rough surroundings of a raw country, there were serious and often successful efforts to maintain high standards in the arts, letters, and sciences.

Every colony had a governor and some sort of representative body. Eight of the governors were appointed by the Crown, two by proprietors, and two were elected locally (Delaware shared a proprietor's appointee with Pennsylvania). In each representative body at least one House was elected. Vigorously contending for local interests, and thereby schooling themselves in self-government, these assemblies, for one reason or another, were often in conflict with royal administrators. They were not "democratic," because universal suffrage was as yet unknown, and property or religious qualifications barred many from voting or holding office. But they were more fairly representative than was the English Parliament. In quarrels with governors or other crown officials the assemblies' chief strength lay in their purse power, that is, their practical monopoly of internal taxation. Without agreement on taxes and budgets, the executive had a hard time governing. This contentious spirit should not be interpreted as an early surge toward national independence. Independence was never an issue before 1775.

BRITISH COLONIAL POLICY

Most of the British colonies in North America were founded in the "Stuart Age" of English history, when the Stuart family contributed four kings to the throne. The first two, James I and Charles I, exerted little control over the colonies, leaving them, for the greater part of the time, free to develop in their own way. The reign of the Stuarts was interrupted by Civil War and "the Commonwealth" and the "Protectorate" established by Oliver Cromwell—the period from 1642 to 1660. The colonists generally held themselves aloof from the turbulence and continued their independent growth. With the "Restoration" of Charles II, they began to receive more attention from England. When New York's proprietor, the Duke of York, ascended the throne as James II his unpopularity as a Catholic was stimulated by a fear that he intended to become an absolute monarch, and he was expelled in the "Glorious Revolution" of 1688. His expulsion was cause for celebration in America because of his centralizing of colonial administration in the "Dominion of New England," an enforced union of all the northern colonies, with Boston as its capital, which, had it succeeded, would probably have destroyed local self-government in the colonies. Americans this early had become wary of interference in the internal government of their home provinces. The empire in which they lived was unsystematically organized and had never been planned for imperial purposes. As long as they had home rule in local affairs, the colonists were content to live under the dual system of government.

Until the 1760's the imperial government interfered very little with the concerns of local government in the colonies. It reviewed colonial legislation and heard appeals from colonial courts. Otherwise, its attention was limited to matters of empire-wide concern. Such matters were chiefly economic, involving the regulation of imperial trade and commerce by means of a body of laws which, taken together, enacted an economic theory called "mercantilism." This doctrine stated that business should be so regulated as to make the nation strong in world affairs, by the encouragement of shipping, agriculture, British industry, and the use of a gold currency; the mercantilists tried to avoid dependence on foreign businessmen. As far as American colonists were concerned, the promotion of the use of empire-built, empire-owned, and empire-manned ships, by the enactment of the several Navigation Acts, was the aspect of mercantilist policy most noticed. But all the other mercantilist objects were also sought through the passage of laws regulating trade by monopolizing the British market for colonial raw materials (and the colonial market for British manufactures) and by promoting the use of hard money.

The trade laws were not generally disapproved in America, although there was grumbling at the restrictions on paper money.

The chief pinch came from restrictions on trade with the **French West Indies**; to avoid these, recourse was had to smuggling (although probably not as often as it has been alleged).

THE ANGLO-FRENCH RIVALRY

From the late seventeenth century until a few years before the declaration of the independence of the United States, Great Britain and France were formally at war four times. The expansion of New France had made the British colonists feel that they were deliberately encircled. Frenchmen and English colonials had rival land and trade claims west of the Appalachians, and each courted Indian allies. The home countries were also fierce competitors in India, Africa, and the West Indies. Thus, the American scene was only one theater of a global struggle.

King William's War (1689–97) was an American expansion of the War of the League of Augsburg between William of Orange and Louis XIV. Indian fighting in the forests and on the frontiers was savage, especially in New England. So far as the colonists were directly concerned, the war had no great result.

Queen Anne's War (1701–13) was the colonial phase of the War of the Spanish Succession. Fighting in America raged from the Gulf of Mexico to the St. Lawrence River. At its finish the powerful Iroquois Indians were recognized as under British protection. Acadia, Newfoundland, and the Hudson Bay region were acknowledged to be British.

King George's War (1745–48), in Europe called the War of the Austrian Succession, was equally bloody in America but indecisive. New England men were proud to have taken the great fortress of Louisbourg but were disappointed by its return to the French at the time of the peace, which both sides seemed to consider an armistice rather than a true peace.

The crisis of colonial rivalry was the French and Indian War, better known as the Seven Years' War, perhaps most properly called the Great War for Empire. As a result of this conflict, the French were expelled from North America.

Basic claims of the two empires overlapped. Through their wards, the militant Iroquois, the British claimed the Ohio Valley and the headwaters of the St. Lawrence River. By discovery, the

French laid claim to much of western New York, Pennsylvania, and Virginia. Great and fertile tracts of land, along with bales and bales of peltries, were in issue. In any war the French had the advantage of unitary government and military command. They held key forts on all important western lines of communication. They had most of the Indians on their side. But their population was small, widely scattered, and composed in too large part of transient elements, not of families. The British colonies were many differing political units which were held together and loosely governed in military affairs by a king who lived three thousand miles away. These colonies had no record of co-operating in a common cause, and each had to be coaxed and persuaded separately to contribute men and money. This lack of unified control was their gravest weakness in a military sense, but who shall say that the experience in self-government was not worth the cost? Another probable defect of imperial defense was the fact that British officers tended to be contemptuous of colonial soldiers and did not take full advantage of useful American traits in warfare. Offsetting the weaknesses was the large number of British colonials; they outnumbered the French colonists by twelve or fifteen to one. The royal navy of Britain was a prime asset, being then the best in the world. The Iroquois allies were worth many times their number of pro-French Indians. And lastly, the civilian leadership of the British Empire was literally great.

In the New World there were four areas where politics and geography combined to designate theaters of operations: the northeastern boundary of New England, the Lake Champlain corridor, the headwaters of the Ohio River, and the West Indies. These places saw most action.

The war might have started in Asia, Africa, or Europe. It happened to begin in the upper Ohio River system, when the governor of Virginia sent his senior militia officer, George Washington, to warn the French away from the present site of Pittsburgh. They refused to go—one thing led to another—and the war started in 1754 with two small clashes in the neighboring forest. It soon became a world conflict, and it went badly for the British everywhere, except in India. Best remembered, but not necessarily most important, of the early British defeats was the slaughter of Braddock's army in America. Elsewhere in

America, as well as in the Mediterranean and in Europe, the British endured crushing, humiliating defeats.

More important than any other single cause in turning the defeats into a parade of victories was the genius of one man, William Pitt, who came into the British government in 1757 and took full, direct charge of foreign relations and the war effort. As much as any one man could be, he was responsible for victory. He established a unity of command by which he personally directed the commanders in the world-wide field of battle. To twentieth-century readers his orders still seem wise and forceful. He also chose able, young commanders who had reputations to gain, not to protect. His practices had a healthy effect on the spirit of responsible officers.

His plans, his policies, and his bright aggregation of able generals and admirals brought the most brilliant procession of military victories known to modern history before the rise of Napoleon. The Union Jack flew in triumph in every corner of the world. In America, Wolfe's victory at Quebec destroyed the French Empire in North America forever.

The British military victory was confirmed in the Treaty of Paris of 1763 and in related negotiations. France vacated North America: her lands east of the Mississippi went to Britain; those west of the Mississippi to Spain, her bedeviled ally and sharer in her ignominy. The British Empire became the first power of the world.

3

The American Revolution

The day of American independence was precipitated by the passage of laws of the British Parliament to establish a strong imperial organization in the colonies. Instead of advancing this goal, the new policy united the colonies, hitherto an unaccomplished feat, in militant grievance against the British Empire.

IMPERIAL REORGANIZATION

Although the Great War for Empire removed the French and Spanish threats, it accented the lack of colonial unity. Earlier attempts to form a colonial union had invariably failed, and the Albany Plan of Union, chiefly drafted by Benjamin Franklin at an intercolonial congress in 1754, had likewise failed of adoption. During the war the importance of the colonial assemblies had been magnified by the empire's need of money which only they could grant. The antiquated government of the empire had been seriously strained by the war. Pitt had made the imperial government work, but he had left office in 1761. The war had doubled the national debt. Could not the Americans help by paying more of the cost of colonial government? The mercantile Navigation Acts had been poorly enforced—perhaps their enforcement would be a good place to start making reforms.

With the removal of the French from the West, the frontier required effective government, and the relations of the Indians with white traders and settlers needed to be regularized. This problem became an emergency with the outbreak of a far-flung frontier uprising (led by the Indian chief Pontiac in reprisal against British Indian policy and in hope of promoting a French

revival) which required two years and much blood and treasure
to quell. As an emergency measure to separate whites and
Indians temporarily until a permanent solution could be reached,
a Royal Proclamation in 1763 barred whites from all lands west
of the Appalachian divide. This naturally angered traders and the
speculators in western lands. Constant tinkering with the location
of the dividing line and steady pressure from special interests
caused the breakdown of the policy. That the old disorder had
returned was shown by the outbreak of an uprising at the
headwaters of the Ohio River and named for the Virginia governor who put it down, "Lord Dunmore's War," in 1774. In that
same year the boundaries of Quebec were extended to the Mississippi and Ohio rivers by the Quebec Act, which provided a
government but encroached on lands claimed by colonies from
Virginia to Massachusetts. Its grant of quasi-freedom for the
Catholic Church also aroused heated protests from colonial
Protestant leaders. These changes emphasized the need for in-
telligent imperial policy but did not meet that need. This was
partly owing to the make-up of the English political system which
produced many ministries made up of factions that combined
and recombined to secure the support of the limited English
electorate but were neither well informed nor keenly interested
in American affairs.

British Policies and Colonial Opposition. At the close of the
Great War for Empire, Parliament, under the ministry of George
Grenville, began a conscious program of imperial government.
The first objective was to raise customs revenues by enforcing
the Revenue Act of 1764 and to levy internal taxes by passing
the Stamp Act of 1765. The use of colonial paper money was
prohibited by the Currency Act of 1764, and the colonists were
required to pay for housing troops by the Quartering Act of 1765.
Colonial resentment promptly initiated the first great debate
on British imperialism. James Otis and others had argued that
a law to take money without consent was unconstitutional. The
argument was used against the Revenue Act and reiterated in
the Stamp Act Congress of 1765, where nine colonies condemned
that law. Many merchants signed Nonintercourse Agreements,
that is, they agreed not to buy from Britain until the Stamp Act
was repealed. A new organization, the Sons of Liberty, enforced
the agreements and terrorized royal Stamp Tax collectors. As a

matter of expediency Parliament repealed the Stamp Act in 1766 but simultaneously passed the Declaratory Act which asserted that the colonies were subordinate unto and dependent upon the Crown and Parliament of Great Britain and that the king and Parliament could bind the colonies in all cases. The colonists celebrated the repealer but did not seem to see the full implications of the Declaratory Act.

In London a new cabinet came into office in 1767, pledged to reduce land taxes in England. To regain the lost revenue, Chancellor of the Exchequer Charles Townshend introduced his famous Townshend Acts—customs duties on tea, paper, paint, glass, and lead—which (or so Englishmen argued) met the objections to the Stamp Act since they were external, not internal, taxes. But the colonists protested just as they had done before. The Massachusetts legislature issued a *Circular Letter* stating that the colonists could be taxed only by their own assemblies. The Virginia Burgesses expressed sympathy with the *Circular Letter* through resolutions agreed to by George Washington and Thomas Jefferson, among others. John Dickinson, a Philadelphia lawyer, in his popular *Letters of a Pennsylvania Farmer* convinced many that external taxes to regulate trade were acceptable but if intended to produce a revenue were unconstitutional. And once again, merchants combined to boycott the British businessman. Violence flared sporadically, and in Boston the civilian antipathy to the soldiery was climaxed in 1770 by the Boston Massacre. Because the Townshend Acts were antimercantilist they were repealed, except for the tax on tea. For the next two years, 1770–72, relations between colonies and homeland were friendlier.

The 1760's had been depression years but conditions had improved, at least for the business classes, who were now less interested in making political protests. Samuel Adams, a principal leader of Boston "radicalism," thought the calm was dangerous to liberty, and he moved to organize a "committee of correspondence" to circulate "grievances." The example was widely copied in the colonies and every Anglo-American friction was thus given intercolonial publicity.

None of the frictions excited many people until the British Cabinet, now under Lord North, gave the disaffected leaders a ready-made issue in the Tea Act of 1772, a "clever" scheme to dispose of the East India Company's surplus tea by means of bypassing the American wholesalers. Instantly the wholesalers, this powerful and conservative group of business leaders, had a burning grievance. The Tea Act was opposed everywhere, but most theatrically in Boston where men disguised as Indians threw a shipload of tea into the harbor—the Boston Tea Party. The conservative American merchant was repelled, the Sam Adams type of "radical" was gleeful, and the member of Parliament was exasperated. The Bostonians were promptly punished by the passage of the "Intolerable Acts" (1774) which closed the port (until compensation should be made), royalized the government of Massachusetts, re-enacted the Quartering Act, and provided for trial of accused royal officers outside the colony. But the British government, in its anger, had overreached itself. More than anything which had gone before, these acts united the colonies, and the Virginia Burgesses issued a call for a Continental Congress to convene in Philadelphia in 1774 to discuss their grievances.

The Continental Congresses. The colonists were in a new mood. James Wilson and John Adams published pamphlets denying the authority of Parliament over the colonies. When the First Continental Congress met (1774) three factions were present: those who expected to use force ultimately; moderates who hoped for a peaceful solution; and conservatives who thought some softening of British policy was advisable but who would never approve of using force or declaring independence.

In Congress the colonies made a united constitutional protest which practically proclaimed dominion status. They did not argue that they should have it, but that they already had it. They continued to recognize the Crown as the cement of the empire and petitioned King George for a redress of grievances. They appealed to the French Canadians to join them and once more adopted an economic boycott of Britain. They endorsed the Suffolk Resolves of Massachusetts, which declared the "Intolerable Acts" void and which advised the training of a militia force. The British government remained immovable. The colonists must submit or resist in a more lively way.

Massachusetts was the scene of the explosion. Its local government was meeting outside the British lines, inasmuch as its assembly had been dissolved by the British. General Thomas

Gage resolved to seize the provincial governments' leaders—John Hancock and Samuel Adams—as well as the ammunition which was being deposited in Concord. On "the eighteenth of April in '75" British troops set out to raid Concord via Lexington. The Massachusetts "minutemen," having been alerted by the now famous rides of Paul Revere and William Dawes, met the British, and the war was on. In America the response was electric. The Second Continental Congress, which had long been scheduled to meet in May, adopted the growing, ill-organized New England army outside Boston. One of the most fortunate decisions of the Congress was its choice of a commanding general. The members chose George Washington. In spite of these preparations, the Congress was uncertain about complete independence; a conciliatory gesture was evident in its petition to King George III to restore peace.

THE WAR FOR INDEPENDENCE

Before General Washington took command, the colonials were pushed off Bunker Hill,* near Boston, at terrible cost to the British, who evacuated Boston nine months later. During the siege of Boston, reflective Americans began, reluctantly, to conclude that independence from Great Britain offered the only safety for their liberty. A pamphlet by a newly arrived English radical (*Common Sense,* by Thomas Paine) expressed this common sentiment in uncommonly good prose. It sold a hundred thousand copies and helped Americans to know how widely their feeling was shared. As they saw it, and as Paine said it, the corrupted British Parliament, led by the king, was steadily encroaching on the ancient rights of life, liberty, and property, and ignoring all remonstrances.

The Declaration of Independence. In July of 1776 the Congress finally declared independence, basing the assertion on the natural law of human equality, the right of revolution, and the transgressions of the king. The Declaration of Independence, the work of five men led by Thomas Jefferson, committed the patriots to resistance and gave the loyalists something to oppose.

---

*Properly "Breed's Hill." The colonials were ordered to fortify Bunker Hill but, once on the spot, they chose rather to dig in on Breed's Hill, a little lower and to the east.

General Considerations. It was impossible to classify rebels and loyalists by outward signs. All kinds of people were on both sides. Generally, however, loyalists tended to be older, richer, and longer schooled. They were more likely than the rebels to live near the seacoast and to have a social position to keep up. Perhaps forty thousand to one hundred thousand loyalists emigrated during the war, some to England but most of them to Canada, especially to the present province of New Brunswick.

Always in difficulties for lack of money, the patriots financed their war effort by requisitions on the states, domestic loans, foreign loans, and, most of all, the issuance of quantities of "printing-press" money.

The patriots raised a small but dependable regular army of state regiments—the Continental Army—which provided the hard core of resistance. They also used state militia when necessary and available. The men were never adequately supplied and equipped, and most of what they had came from European nations. They did not fight in Indian fashion, as legend has it, but tried to copy the best European tactics, which were based on the "shock power" of the smooth-bore musket at close range. Their numbers fluctuated from three or four thousand to ninety thousand. In the later years of the war, they were joined (but not outnumbered) by thousands of French troops.

The British, unable to raise enough men at home, relied on additional strength secured by hiring German troops from their princeling masters and on the aid of Indians and loyalists (who were not wholly dependable). Apparently strong, the British forces were weakened by governmental financial difficulties, by the unfamiliarity of the American climate and terrain, and by the difficulties of supply across the broad Atlantic Ocean. The royal navy out-gunned American ships a hundred to one. But despite the "paper" strength of the British Empire in ships, population, and established government, the Americans had a higher morale, based on political convictions.

Military Operations. Before the evacuation of Boston the British attempted to occupy the Carolinas but were repulsed at Charleston. A similar defeat met an American force which invaded Canada in two columns after taking Ticonderoga and Crown Point. After leaving Boston, William Howe (successor to Gage) seized New York City and most of New Jersey, being repelled only at his farthest advance post, Trenton (Christmas, 1776), a defeat he made good by taking Philadelphia the next summer. Major General John Burgoyne proposed to lead the British army which was idle in Canada to join Howe by an overland march to New York. Burgoyne never stated the strategic purpose he had in mind, but his superiors in London probably saw the expedition as an opportunity to separate New England from the other embattled states. When Burgoyne's forces in Canada attempted to join Howe, however, they were cut off and captured at Saratoga by Horatio Gates—a great victory for the Americans (October, 1777). But, despite the victory, Washington's army suffered and dwindled that winter at Valley Forge.

The French, happy at the embarrassment of their ancient foe, Britain, gave secret help to the Americans from the beginning. When Burgoyne surrendered, the help became open. In the expectation of preventing a reconciliation of America and Britain, France made an alliance with the American states early in 1778. Spain, a long-time ally of France, made no alliance with the Americans but gave valuable help in the South and the West. Britain was further embarrassed by the French-promoted and Russian-initiated League of Armed Neutrality, and also by another open enemy, the Netherlands. Thus, at one time, she fought America, France, Spain and the Netherlands and was on bad terms with the other chief maritime powers of Europe.

The presence of these new enemies in the field was particularly irksome on the high seas where Britannia had ruled the waves for decades. Now her fleet was actually outnumbered in ships of the line, and her resources were seriously strained to guarantee the safety of the British Isles themselves. There were no decisive naval battles in European waters, but privateers harassed British merchant shipping, exasperated the navy, and drove insurance rates up. In America any British army was now likely to have its retreat temporarily cut off, and, indeed, that is what happened when Washington's army and the French navy trapped the British at Yorktown.

After an indecisive clash at Monmouth in 1778, there were no great battles in the North, but only the cold-blooded treason of Benedict Arnold, who unsuccessfully tried to sell West Point to the British in 1780. In the West, George Rogers Clark defeated small British forces and enabled the infant settlements of Kentucky to survive. The South was the most active theater, where the British won victories but lost a war because they could not hold conquered areas nor protect their loyalist helpers. In disgust at the indecisiveness of his campaigns, Lord Cornwallis settled at Yorktown, Virginia. There he was besieged by Washington and Rochambeau; a French fleet under De Grasse blocked his escape, and he surrendered (October, 1781). There was no subsequent important fighting in America.

The Peace Treaty. There had been occasional attempts earlier by the British to reconcile their angry ex-subjects, but none came close to success. Now, negotiation began in earnest. The American negotiators (Benjamin Franklin, John Adams, and John Jay) were supposed to collaborate with the French but had justifiable suspicions that the French would hope to compensate Spain at American expense. In separate negotiations with the British, the Americans achieved a diplomatic triumph in the Treaty of Paris (1783), a generous treaty recognizing the independence of the United States and stating its boundaries. In an eight-year struggle the American free spirit (augmented by French ships, musketeers, and materials) had humbled the greatest empire and had introduced a new sovereign people into the family of nations.

THE COMPLETION OF INDEPENDENCE

During the long war the Americans saw their social and economic life change. It may be disputed whether there had been a true "social revolution," or displacement of classes, but the economy certainly required readjustment to function under a new independent nation, which, in turn, had to learn to function under a new political structure.

Social and Economic Changes. British restrictions on business were gone, and there were a few changes made in the land system, also. Some landed estates were broken up, but not many. Feudal restrictions on the method of inheritance were dropped. Manufacturing was theoretically unrestricted but in practice lacked technology, risk capital, and labor. Sea trade—no novelty—was ready to expand if materials and markets were open.

There was a general movement to separate church and state

and a number of churches severed their European connections—for example, the Methodist and the Protestant Episcopal. By and large, the war slowed cultural development. Primary schools suffered in the theaters of operation. Colleges and academies lost most of their students, then recovered quickly. New colleges opened as plans began for state universities. The first law professorship and American medical schools date from this period. To the existing American Philosophical Society other learned societies were added, chiefly in New England. The arts and letters were still the domain of a few gifted men patronized by the rich. The art most successfully practiced by Americans was painting, as represented by Gilbert Stuart. Jedidiah Morse's geography textbook and Noah Webster's spelling book and dictionary were noteworthy. The advance of science was hindered by lack of training and financial support, but the beginnings of specialized studies were made.

Although there was a rapid growth of population, it was a natural increase. The rate of immigration was relatively low from 1775 to 1825. This "homogenized" the population. Among major social changes was the humanization of punishment for crime. Slavery practically disappeared in the North but remained in the South, where leaders expressed regret at its persistence.

Political Change. There is a good deal more to tell about the political revolution which skilfully built new governments, something which few revolutionaries in world history have been able to do. In the first place, acting as an independent nation, each state wrote a constitution or remodeled its old charter. Early in 1776 the Congress told the states to suppress royal governments and set up their own. Constitutions were written by all except Connecticut and Rhode Island, which kept and adapted their generous Stuart charters. By the end of the revolutionary era, it was customary to submit constitutions for popular approval. Unlike the British constitution, the constitutions of the states were in written form, for the colonists wanted the limits of government spelled out in writing.

Many state constitutions reflected the popular conception of religion and government as linked, requiring religious tests for public office. Seven states wrote bills of rights, with special care to guarantee freedom of speech and press. (In practice the rights did not extend to opponents of independence.) The significance attached to property rights was shown by property qualifications for voting and holding office. The separation of powers—executive, legislative, and judicial—was usually stated as a desirable principle. Governors were given less power than the royal governors had possessed, and legislatures were made more powerful. The growth of a peculiarly American system of law was assured when courts began to publish their court reports.

These constitutions governed the states individually, but there still remained the problem the British had failed to solve: how the states could be brought to co-operate in a common cause. A temporary answer, framed in wartime, was provided by the Articles of Confederation, which knitted the states together loosely though well enough to finish the war and make peace. The Articles gave responsibilities to the Congress, but no real power. Congress could only cajole or persuade the states and was helpless if defied, unless it warred on a delinquent state—a remedy which nobody wished to use. The vote of nine states (each state had one vote) was necessary for decisions, and a unanimous vote was required for any change in the Articles. The Congress had no income or tax power. Any successes it had were the fruit of the working of public opinion on its side.

4

Development Toward a Federal Union

The role assigned to the "central government" under the Articles of Confederation was one which purposely lacked conviction. Although Congress had responsibilities, it had no power to enforce its actions. It was the intention of the designers of the Confederation that ultimate power be vested in the states, as a precaution against the emergence of an all-powerful authority similar to that of the British King-in-Parliament.

The postwar years of a country are necessarily those involving social and economic readjustment. In addition to meeting these changes, America had to cope with her new political status. The time has been called "the critical period" for the new nation, which experienced difficult situations both at home and abroad. In the late 1780's it seemed apparent to many leaders that the Confederation, as so devised, could never efficiently preserve the gains of the Revolution; consequently it was decided to convene to revise the Articles of Confederation. Instead, however, this momentous convention wrote the Constitution of the United States of America. The thirteen colonies had successfully completed another period of transition—the passing from a weak Confederation to a federal Union which could be made strong.

THE CONFEDERATION

In the era of the Confederation, although most publicized as a period of disorder and dissension, was scored one great achievement—the devising of a new plan for the settlement of the country's western lands.

The Western Land Policy. The Confederation could have treated its wild West as a dependency but chose instead to plan for its proper organization and eventual equality. The ratification of the Articles of Confederation had been delayed by Maryland until she was assured that the West would be pooled for the common good. Seven of the states claimed boundaries extending to the Mississippi River, but, yielding to Maryland's insistence, New York and Virginia gave up their claims in 1780 and 1781. The others followed suit, ceding one hundred and fifty million acres to the United States. Now, the Congress needed to decide how to regulate and dispose of this grand quantity of real estate. The answer was written in the Land Ordinance of 1785. The ordinance provided for survey before settlement, for division of the land into rectilinear blocks (for ease of survey and recording), and for the reservation of one section in each township for public purposes. This system reduced the confusion and litigation so rife earlier. The ideas were not new. Prior survey and the approximately rectilinear township were New England practices, as was the reservation of public land. The size of sections (640 acres or one square mile) came from Virginia and North Carolina grants.

Having provided a land system for the ungranted lands of the West, the Congress soon had to think about the political organization of the region. The Ohio Company, organized in Boston, proposed to buy land in the Muskingum Valley, using revolutionary Congressional I.O.U.'s for payment. When joined in the request by the Scioto Company (in which several Congressmen were interested) the grant was made, and a government was provided in the Northwest Ordinance of 1787. The most striking provision is that these colonies, called "territories," were eventually to be promoted to equal statehood. In the Old Northwest not less than three nor more than five states were to be created. While a territory was small in population, it was to have executive government (as in a "crown colony"). When there were five thousand free adult males (i.e., freemen over 21 years of age) they could have a territorial legislature and a nonvoting member of the Congress. As soon as the population reached sixty thousand, the territory was to become eligible for statehood. This was the American novelty which solved the "colonial" problem—a "colony" raised to equal status when properly prepared. The Northwest Ordinance also prohibited slavery in that area, a prohibition re-enacted by the new Congress in 1789.

The story of the Old Southwest is quite different, mainly because all desirable Kentucky land was already in private hands when ceded by Virginia, and the more southern lands were not ceded until after 1790. The most attractive areas of the Old Southwest were the Bluegrass region of Kentucky, the Nashville basin of Tennessee, and the fertile lowlands of the Great Kanawha, Cumberland, and Tennessee river valleys. This country was heavily forested with hardwoods. By the end of the War for Independence there were fifteen or twenty thousand settlers in Kentucky and almost as many in the Nashville basin and along the upper tributaries of the Tennessee. By 1790 there were a quarter of a million people in the Southwest. Land practices in the region were advantageous to speculators. State governments sold land in their western claims cheaply, gave tracts to encourage settlements, and awarded land as soldiers' bonuses. Speculators bought up these rights at low prices and accumulated gigantic tracts. There was much long-lasting litigation, owing to the overlapping boundaries of lands, which had been granted before survey, were laid out in irregular forms, and used natural markings for boundaries.

The chief early settlements were the Watauga in northeastern Tennessee, Nashville, and Boonesborough. Several early settlements governed themselves at first under self-made compacts not unlike that of the Plymouth Pilgrims.

Another frontier was northerly, not westward. That was Vermont, which carried on as a self-constituted state from the War for Independence until it became the fourteenth state of the Union in 1791.

Difficulties of the Confederation. Weaknesses of the "government" under the Articles of Confederation led to a growing dissatisfaction throughout the country. Foreign trade, currency, international relations, public finance—all seemed to pose problems which were insoluble by means of the existing Confederation.

To a nation dependent upon extractive industries, the revival of foreign trade was especially urgent. Before the Revolution, the West Indies had been the best outlet for exports from New

England and the Middle States. After the Revolution, Britain barred the Americans from renewing that trade. While English merchants "dumped" goods in America, Americans were allowed to sell in Britain only what the English could not get elsewhere, principally tobacco and various products of the forest. The French hoped to replace Great Britain in the American economic system but were unable to provide the long-term credit American business apparently demanded, nor did the Americans like to deal with the legalized French monopolies. The only innovation in foreign trade which promised well for the future was the opening of a traffic with China in the 1780's.

Freed from Parliamentary controls, the states tried various currency devices to solve their problem. Those states which used paper currency made creditors unhappy. "Hard money" states plunged debtors into deflation and despair. In Massachusetts the burden of debt, incurred during inflation but payable during a depression, precipitated the uprising called "Shays's Rebellion" after its leader, the war veteran Captain Daniel Shays. The revolt failed, but its occurrence shocked many into a realization of the need for a stronger government.

The Congress had no assured income but only an unenforceable state-requisition system. Interest on United States promissory paper fell steadily in arrears, and revenue amendments to the new Articles failed of enactment. New Jersey threatened to stop paying its requisitions in 1786. Some states added to their load of taxation by assuming the national debt owed to citizens within their boundaries.

Nowhere did the Confederation weaknesses appear more plainly than in the field of foreign relations. Its impotent government had nothing to bargain with and no navy to command the respect of the great powers.

Relations with Britain were especially unhappy. The British held six posts on American soil and barred merchants from trading with the West Indies. Furthermore, they refused to send an envoy to the United States until 1791. The British had promised in the Treaty of Paris of 1783 to evacuate the western posts but stayed, justifying the occupation with the charge that the United States had violated the treaty. The real motives (since violations were simultaneous on both sides) were, probably, to retain control of the western Indians, to profit from the fur trade, and to be handy to pick up the pieces if the United States fell apart.

In the case of Spain there were difficulties in the Old Southwest, which concerned the Spanish boundary in that region, and the use of the Mississippi River by the Americans. The Spaniards were in no mood to be generous toward the United States. They had hoped the western boundary of the United States would be well east of the Mississippi, and they had failed to get Gibraltar, their prime aim in entering the war against Britain. At the end of that war they closed the lower reaches of the Mississippi to American traders, in accord with their mercantilist policy of keeping the Gulf of Mexico a Spanish lake. The Americans wished to navigate the river, to have a "right of deposit" of goods in New Orleans in order to transship them to ocean-going vessels, and to be free to sell in the Louisiana market. An attempt by John Jay and Gardoquí, a Spanish agent, to come to agreement was defeated by the Congress in 1786 because Jay consented to closing the river to the United States. By this time westerners were beginning to think that Spain might have more to offer than the United States, an attitude encouraged by Spanish agents.

In addition to strained relations with Britain and Spain, the Congress had other diplomatic business to attend to—promotion of trade treaties, suppression of piracy, and Indian problems. Six nations made commercial treaties with the United States, but Britain was not one of them, and our natural economic partner was Britain. As for piracy, the Americans could only pay blackmail to Morocco, stay out of the way of the other corsairs of North Africa, and take calculated risks in their now almost obliterated Caribbean trade. The Indians of the Old Southwest were under Spanish influence. Four treaties with important tribes were made in the years 1785–89 in which the United States promised to protect the Indians from the settlers, but it was impossible to keep the promise and the Spanish won them back. In foreign relations the prevailing spirit of the United States was one of isolationism, an idea with roots deep in the Colonial period when men said they came here to avoid the turbulence of Europe. Temporarily suspended during the War for Independence, the idea of isolationism rebounded to its earlier strength thereafter. Nothing in the diplomatic history of the 1780's encouraged any other attitude.

THE CONSTITUTION

The political incompetence of the Confederation was accented by increasing radicalism (as in the Shays Rebellion) which alarmed people into re-examining the problem of union. All attempts at reform from inside the Congress had failed miserably. But another approach was available. In 1785 at Mount Vernon, delegates from Virginia and Maryland amicably discussed differences between their states. Encouraged, five states met at Annapolis in 1786 to propose commercial reforms for the Union. The delegates, among them Alexander Hamilton, decided they were too few for such momentous decisions and petitioned the Congress to invite all states to Philadelphia in 1787 to revise the Articles of Confederation. The Congress did so.

Accomplishments of the Convention (May-September, 1787). An excellent representation attended at Philadelphia despite the comparatively long distances to travel. Eleven states sent fifty-five delegates. The leading "radicals" of the Revolution were absent. The most influential Americans present were Washington, Franklin, James Madison, and Alexander Hamilton. Madison, "Father of the Constitution," assumed the burden of floor leadership. The best-known and most admired member, George Washington, was a delegate from Virginia. Because of the universal respect he commanded he was a very fortunate choice for chairman, helping by his presence, no doubt, to calm any fears in the minds of the general public, outside the locked doors of the hall.

The Constitution has been called a bundle of compromises, a description which clouds the fact that the delegates had more agreements than disagreements. The delegates were uniformly committed to the British tradition in political philosophy, with American deviations caused by the experience of vigorous local home rule, by a relatively larger electorate than Britain's, and by the recent intense study of political principles during the Revolution. All agreed that government must protect private property. Such protection involved questions of taxation, currency, public debts, and the regulation of business. The Confederation had shown itself unable to solve these problems; hence the delegates were able to agree to give the responsibility to a more effective central authority. They also agreed with little difficulty that the new government should be a republic, that its powers should be separated, that there should be a single executive, and that the legislature should have two houses. A more surprising agreement was the one to establish a separate system of federal courts. They took it for granted that the Constitution should be in writing. This latter point has surprised some Europeans, but it should be remembered that the Americans were used to government based on written instruments. This accorded also with the popular idea that governments are formed by written contract among the people.

Before the delegates convened, several plans had been prepared for discussion. The Virginia delegation offered the "Virginia Plan," which proposed a true national government, beyond mere repair of the Confederation. Among other details, it provided for a federal judiciary and a power of amendment to be lodged outside the legislature. Thus it would elevate the United States above the states. Because Virginia's plan would give the more populous states more seats in the legislature, a "New Jersey Plan" ("small-state plan") was introduced. It provided for election of a one-house Congress by the legislatures, not the people, with each state having one vote. It strengthened the Confederation by adding an executive and a Supreme Court. Charles Pinckney of South Carolina presented a plan, but no copy has survived. (Later attempts to reconstruct his plan have convinced some people that he was the chief author of the Constitution.) Alexander Hamilton presented a plan also; it would have subordinated the states completely and would have established a life-tenure President with an absolute veto. It was ignored by the Convention, and Hamilton became a strong supporter of the Constitution as written because he thought it much better than the Articles it superseded.

Despite harmony in philosophy, and in many specific applications of their commonly held political theories, there were grave disagreements which had to be compromised. In the plan known as the "Great Compromise" the question of the representation of the states was decided by having them equally represented in the Senate and represented in proportion to population in the House. Whether or not to count slaves for representation was settled by counting three-fifths of them. The election of the President was settled by establishing the electoral college. On the issue of the slave trade, the delegates compromised by forbidding Congress to abolish it before 1808.

Although the Constitution does not specifically mention the balance or separation of powers, the document is written so as to provide the three classically separated powers: the executive, the legislature, and the judiciary. The delegates easily agreed on a single executive, but twelve ballots on five ways of choosing him were taken. The office, as created, sets up a strong executive officer, with a limited veto, who shares some of his power with the legislature. The provision setting up two houses of the Congress was not debated. The lower house (the House of Representatives) was to be elected by the people, and the upper house (the Senate) by the state legislatures. The qualifications of voters for the lower house were left to state law simply because the delegates could not agree. The unique, separate judiciary was to be appointed by the President with the consent of the Senate. Whether or not the courts were to pass on the constitutionality of laws was not stated, but it is hard to see where else the people could go for protection against legislative tyranny, if not to the courts.

As for the relation of the states to the federal government, the United States was made a true Union. In a league or loose confederation the central authority operates on the member states, whereas the United States uses the "coercion of law" by operating directly on individuals. Both state and national officers were to swear to support the Constitution. The Constitution was not a "democratic" document. Only one house of the Congress was an organ of the people. The President was not thought of as the people's choice, but the choice of elite electors, and he and the Senate could muffle the voice of the people as expressed in the House of Representatives.

Having devised what eventually became the oldest and most cherished Constitution, a majority signed it and departed for home to enter the battle for ratification. For the Constitution to become effective, it was necessary to secure the approval of popular conventions in at least nine of the states.

The Ratification Controversy. The process of ratification was to be by popular conventions elected in each state for that purpose. This technique at once by-passed local leaders with their vested interests and justified the preamble, "We the people . . . " In the conventions and the press the new Constitution was criticized severely. We cannot know for sure, but it seems probable that if there had been a referendum on it, by universal suffrage, ratification would have been defeated. Provincialism, sectionalism, and fear of new taxes were important to the objectors.

Many feared that the rights and even the existence of the states were in danger. It has always been a problem where to draw the line between the Union and the states. Although the new government was to have only those powers enumerated in the Constitution, many of these people were unreconciled to it. Others charged the Constitutional Convention with going beyond its powers. Called "to revise the Articles of Confederation," it had discarded the Articles and produced a wholly new instrument of government. Ergo, the Constitution was "unconstitutional." If true, eleven states (those whose delegates participated in the framing of the Constitution) seceded from a thirteen-state Confederation! It was argued that civil liberty was not secure from the central government unless a Bill of Rights guaranteed it. Both friends and foes insisted on this point. A Bill of Rights had been deliberately omitted by the Constitutional Convention, not because the delegates were foes of liberty, but because they thought liberty sufficiently guaranteed without it. Still another group of opponents of the Constitution were those who recognized that the Confederation had been but loosely bound together and provided no true, energetic government, but who liked it that way. They had striven for local home rule, had won it with the Articles of Confederation, and wished for nothing more.

Among the most active supporters of the constitution were the men who collectively had written and approved it. They had the advantage of knowing practically all the arguments against it, in advance, because they had sat through and participated in the debates of the Convention itself. Most of these men, no doubt, thought a better document would have been written if their own ideas had prevailed; but each had submerged his own thinking for the sake of agreement and now, with few exceptions, they joined in the battle in their respective states to secure ratification.

A series of letters written to New York newspapers in 1788, by Alexander Hamilton, James Madison, and John Jay, since collected in one volume as the *Federalist Papers,* urged the ratification. To read this admittedly partisan series is probably the best way to come to an understanding of the issues of the debate. In refuting the antifederalists the authors emphasized the inadequacy of the Confederation, the need for a stronger government, and the safeness of the new Constitution.

They argued that men grouped themselves into factions in the state because of conflicting interests. The regulation of their conflicting claims was the business of the government, and the federal Union had been specifically drafted with this purpose in mind. To those who feared that the new government would encroach on popular liberties they explained that the judiciary was the warden of liberty, and a safe one, for it had neither money nor armies. In one of the last of the letters (No. 78), "judicial review," as we call it, was explicitly stated to be a function of the courts. As for a Bill of Rights, it was unnecessary for four reasons: the states had their own Bills of Rights; the Constitution had several guarantees (such as the prohibition of *ex post facto* laws); the Congress had only those powers specifically delegated to it; and there was no reason to fear, in a republic, that the people would oppress themselves. This last argument ignored the fact that majorities can and do oppress minorities. It was unnecessary for the authors to argue that separation of the powers of government was desirable as a system of checks and balances. Everybody believed that and the job of the *Federalist Papers* was to convince people that it had been done.

The authors argued against limiting the number of terms of the President on the grounds that it would dampen his incentive to retain public favor, would confine his plans to short-range views, might encourage him to use force to prolong his tenure, could deprive the country of needed experience, and might turn a President out of office in the middle of a national crisis.

They also explained the modern idea of "federalism," comprising not a confederation, not a league, but a novel harmony and reconciliation of local and national sovereignties. Federalism is the chief American contribution to the art of government.

The *Federalist Papers* conceived of "democracy" as direct government by the people, a system which could be used only in small places. They also regarded democracy as dangerous because it could not resist fads of the moment and could easily degenerate into mob rule. Much better was a mixture of the three classic principles of government: monarchic (the President), aristocratic (the Senate), and democratic (the House of Representatives).

In the actual voting on ratification, the small states generally approved. The large states were divided, and bitter quarrels occurred. Eleven states ratified the document in less than a year. Rhode Island and North Carolina waited until the new government was functioning: North Carolina joined after the Bill of Rights went to the states and Rhode Island after being threatened with trade disabilities as a foreign nation.

5

The Federalist Period

The years 1789–1801 saw the United States emerge as a national entity. Governmental precedents were carefully established and international diplomacy prevented all-out wars with European antagonists. Responsibility for thus securing the foundations of the young republic goes to the Federalists, but their methods of doing so were not without opposition. This opposition formed itself into a new political group, which was soon to get the opportunity to make its own contributions to American history.

THE ESTABLISHMENT OF A FEDERAL GOVERNMENT

When the necessary number of states had ratified the Constitution, the old Congress set the dates for elections. Under the new electoral-college system each elector voted for two men for President, the candidate receiving the second highest number of votes being thereby Vice-President. Every elector voted for George Washington. Since more voted for John Adams than for any other second choice, he became Vice-President. At the same time, Representatives and Senators were being chosen.

When the new officers had been installed, they proceeded (with a cautious care for the importance of the precedents they were establishing) to lay tonnage and customs duties, to create the great executive offices, and to establish the judicial branch. In the same first session of the Congress, James Madison assembled all of the proposed features of a Bill of Rights, most of which was approved by the Congress and sent out to the public for ratification, thus quieting the fears of many people.

To head the new executive departments President Washington

appointed Thomas Jefferson, Secretary of State; Alexander Hamilton, Secretary of the Treasury; Henry Knox, Secretary of War; Edmund Randolph, Attorney General. Of all of these men Hamilton was to have the most immediate influence on legislation.

Hamilton's Financial Program. Hamilton proposed that the United States "fund" its national debt, which was sadly in arrears, by exchanging new bonds for the old obligations. There was opposition to the method (but not to the goal of re-establishing national credit) because it would profit speculators. However, the measure was adopted by the Congress. Next, he asked that the federal government assume the debts of the states, on the ground that they were incurred in a common defense in the Revolutionary War. The states whose debts were paid (mostly southern) opposed the measure until Hamilton's friends agreed to vote to put the national capital on the Potomac. The bargain gained the abstention of several Virginians, enough to carry the legislation. The Treasury's next step was to request the incorporation of the Bank of the United States, modeled on the Bank of England, with most of the stock being in private hands. The Bank was to be the fiscal agent of the nation. The controversy over this bill centered on the interpretation of the Constitution. Jefferson, an advocate of states' rights, applied a "strict construction" with his argument that incorporation of a national bank was not a power delegated to the Congress in the Constitution. Hamilton, an ardent nationalist, countered with a "loose construction" of interpretation in his assertion that the legislation was necessary and "implied" in the constitutional powers of the Congress. (The doctrine of implied powers in the Constitution was upheld in a Supreme Court decision of 1819.) President Washington signed the bill. Hamilton capped his program with an excise tax on whiskey, by the gallon, partly to bring in revenue but, also, to distribute the tax burden so that elements of the population not otherwise taxed would feel the existence of central authority. Furthermore, Hamilton issued a *Report on Manufactures* which expounded the case for a protective tariff as well as it has ever been put, but the Congress did not enter fully into the program. However, a mint was established, and the present decimal system of currency was enacted.

DEVELOPMENT OF POLITICAL PARTIES

	1796	1800	1804	1808	1812	1816	1820	1824	1828	1832
Elected President	Adams Fe 71	Jefferson D-R 73	Jefferson D-R 162	Madison D-R 122	Madison D-R 128	Monroe D-R 183	Monroe D-R 231	J.Q. Adams NP(A) 84	Jackson JD 178	Jackson JD 219
Alabama							D-R 3	NP(J) 5	JD 5	JD 7
Connecticut	Fe 9	Fe 9	Fe 9	Fe 9	Fu 9	Fe 9	D-R 9	NP(A) 8	NR 8	NR 8
Delaware	Fe 3	Fe 3	Fe 3	Fe 3	Fu 4	Fe 3	D-R 4	NP(A) 1 Ca(C) 2	NR.3	NR 3
Georgia	D-R 4	D-R 4	D-R 6	D-R 6	D-R 8	D-R 8	D-R 8	Ca(C) 9	JD 9	JD 11
Illinois							D-R 9	NP(A) 1 NP(J) 2	JD 3	JD 5
Indiana						D-R 3	D-R 3	NP(J) 5	JD 5	JD 9
Kentucky	D-R 4	D-R 4	D-R 8	D-R 7	D-R 12	D-R 12	D-R 12	NP(C) 14	JD 14	NR 15
Louisiana					D-R 3	D-R 3	D-R 3	NP(A) 2 NP(J) 3	JD 5	JD 5
Maine							D-R 3	NP(A) 9	NR 8 JD 1	JD 10
Maryland	Fe 7 D-R 4	Fe 5 D-R 5	Fe 2 D-R 9	Fe 2 D-R 9	Fu 5 D-R 6	D-R 8	D-R 11	*	NR 6 JD 5	NR 5 JD 3
Massachusetts	Fe 16	Fe 16	D-R 19	Fe 19	Fu 22	Fe 22	D-R 15	NP(A) 15	NR 15	NR 14
Mississippi							D-R 2	NP(J) 3	JD 3	JD 4
Missouri							D-R 3	NP(C) 3	JD 3	JD 4
New Hampshire	Fe 6	Fe 6	D-R 7	Fe 7	Fu 8	D-R 8	D-R 7 IR 1	NP(A) 8	NR 8	JD 7
New Jersey	Fe 7	Fe 7	D-R 8	D-R 8	Fu 8	D-R 8	D-R 8	NP(J) 8	NR 8	JD 8
New York	Fe 12	D-R 12	D-R 19	D-R 13 IR 6	Fu 29	D-R 29	D-R 29	**	NR 16 JD 20	JD 42
North Carolina	Fe 1 D-R 11	Fe 4 D-R 8	D-R 14	Fe 3 D-R 11	D-R 15	D-R 15	D-R 15	NP(J) 15	JD 15	JD 15
Ohio			D-R 3	D-R 3	D-R 7	D-R 8	D-R 8	NP(C) 16	JD 16	JD 21
Pennsylvania	Fe 1 D-R 14	Fe 7 D-R 8	D-R 20	D-R 20	D-R 25	D-R 25	D-R 24	NP(J) 28	JD 28	JD 30
Rhode Island	Fe 4	Fe 4	D-R 4	Fe 4	Fu 4	D-R 4	D-R 4	NP(A) 4	NR 4	NR 4
South Carolina	D-R 8	D-R 8	D-R 10	D-R 10	D-R 11	D-R 11	D-R 11	NP(J) 11	JD 11	ID(F) 11
Tennessee	D-R 3	D-R 3	D-R 5	D-R 5	D-R 8	D-R 8	D-R 7	NP(J) 11	JD 11	JD 15
Vermont	Fe 4	Fe 4	D-R 6	D-R 6	D-R 8	D-R 8	D-R 8	NP(A) 7	NR 7	A-M 7
Virginia	Fe 1 D-R 20	D-R 21	D-R 24	D-R 24	D-R 25	D-R 25	D-R 25	Ca(C) 24	JD 24	JD 23
Losing Parties Votes	Jefferson D-R 68	Adams Fe 65	Pinckney Fe 14	Pinckney Fe 47; G. Clinton IR 6	DeW Clinton Fu 89	R. King Fe 34	J.Q. Adams IR 1	Jackson NP(J) 99; Crawford Ca(C) 41; Clay NP(C) 37; †	J.Q. Adams NR 83	Clay NR 49; Floyd ID(F) 11; Wirt A-M 7

Fe = Federalist   NP(J) = No Party (Jackson)   JD = Jacksonian Democrats

D-R = Democratic-Republican   NP(A) = No Party (J.Q. Adams)   NR = National Republicans

IR = Independent Republican   Ca(C) = Caucus (Crawford)   ID (F) = Independent Democratic (Floyd)

Fu = Fusion   NP(C) = No Party (Clay)   A-M = Anti-Masonic

* NP(A) 3, NP(J) 7. Ca(C) 1   ** NP(A) 26, NP(J) 1, Ca(C) 5, NP(C) 4

† Inasmuch as no candidate received majority of electoral vote, J. Q. Adams was chosen president by House of Representatives

Development of Political Parties. As the slim, boyish, nervous Hamilton scored success after success in getting his program written into law, an opposition began to take form. In time this split developed into our two-party system of politics. The first two parties were the Federalists and the Republicans. The Republicans enrolled in their ranks the defenders of states' rights, city workers, small subsistence farmers and, generally, those who were suspicious of what are now called "big business" and "big government." The Federalists drew support from financiers, the great merchants—that is, importers and wholesalers—and the retailers they supplied, land speculators, professional men who served the merchant leaders, journalists dependent on seaport advertisers, shipowners and builders, the great farmers who exported their surplus crops, and, generally, those who appreciated the value of a strong, centralized government to preserve a common market in America, a common policy in foreign affairs, and the rights of property. The Republicans showed more trust in the good sense of the average man; the Federalists thought of "democracy" as mob rule, and they trusted in the superior political talents of a natural aristocracy. It may be added that when the Republicans put their leader Thomas Jefferson in the White House he found that the extreme devotion to states' rights was more useful as a political slogan for men out of power than as a working principle for a responsible national administration. The economic views of Hamilton were congenial to the Federalists, who wished to assure stability by attaching the business interests to the new government. The Republicans were led by the long, gangling, freckled Thomas Jefferson and the short, erect, precise James Madison who thought businessmen were too powerful in the Hamiltonian design of government. A kind of one-man third party was the nominally Federalist John Adams. Stout, honest, and quick-tempered, he opposed the domination of any one interest in the affairs of state and wished monarchy, aristocracy, and democracy thoroughly mixed in the United States.

Hamilton's group drew their strength from the public creditors, bank shareholders, the exporting farmers, and the importing merchants. Jefferson and Madison led the subsistence farmers, the workmen, and men who feared that liberty was not safe under a business-minded government. Each side had its press, and it was not long before a heated press-war broke out, full of vituperation and invective. Washington, who held aloof from the conflict, generally favored Hamilton and disliked the animosities of the press. The quarrel should not obscure the real achievements of Alexander Hamilton: the establishment of national credit and financial honor and the securing of an adequate public revenue. The outbreak of the French Revolution sharpened the differences between parties—Republicans admiring it as a continuation of their own, Federalists detesting it as subversive of decency—but it did not become a national issue until the French and British went to war several years later.

A symptom of discontent with Federalism was the outbreak in 1793 of the Whiskey Rebellion in Pennsylvania, where farmers resisted the excise tax on the product of their stills. It was promptly put down, but some Federalists blamed it on the Republicans and on their new network of political clubs, the Democratic-Republican Societies. Although these groups reminded Federalists of the Jacobin Clubs of France, they were the "homegrown" organs of farmers and laborers. In time they were to become the chief strength of the Jeffersonian political party.

FOREIGN AFFAIRS

The guillotining of the King of France and the outbreak of war between France and Great Britain sharpened the American cleavage over the French Revolution and precipitated a series of events that tested the new national fabric.

The most immediate problem for the young republic was how to avoid participation in the Anglo-French war. The United States had a treaty with France, made in 1778, whereby the French possessions in the West Indies were to be protected, if necessary, by the United States. No more certain road to war with Great Britain could be taken than to interpret this treaty broadly. President Washington wished to avoid war. Alexander Hamilton thought the treaty no longer binding because its co-maker, the king, was dead. Thomas Jefferson did not wish to go to war, but he was also anxious to avoid any action which could conceivably hurt the French and the cause of liberty, equality, and fraternity, which (he supposed) would be the outcome of the French Revolution. The upshot of many cabinet discussions was the President's Proclamation of Impartiality (Jefferson was successful in keeping the word "neutrality" out of the document), in which the world was told that the United States would stand aloof. Generally, the Federalists were pleased and the Republicans angered. The arrival of a brash Minister from France, Citizen Edmond Charles Genêt, complicated the problem of the war when he insisted upon using the United States as a base from which to attack British and Spanish colonies and British shipping. Rebuked by the executive branch, he threatened to appeal to the Congress and, amid resulting partisan uproar, was dismissed by the prudent, slow-to-anger but now furious President Washington.

Relations with Great Britain. Having suffered from French insult, the United States had now to endure British injury. Great Britain, enforcing a blockade of France, began to seize American ships carrying French property. Several members of the Congress moved to penalize British shipping in the American trade and to confiscate British property in the United States. To Federalists this policy seemed likely to provoke a war with Great Britain, which would be both a military and an economic disaster since American shippers were making money despite the losses from seizures. They proposed, and the President agreed, to send Chief Justice John Jay to London to try to negotiate a settlement of all outstanding Anglo-American differences. Jay brought back a treaty by which the British agreed to evacuate the frontier forts, to compensate for ships seized, to arbitrate the debts owed to British subjects, and to admit small ships to the West Indies. The United States was required to stop competing in the shipment of tropical products. This treaty so little favored the United States that President Washington sent it to the Senate in 1795 without recommendation. The Senate narrowly ratified it. By this time the text was made public and the Republicans, who had publicly doubted Jay's ability, honesty, and patriotism before reading the treaty, now exploded with imprecations. Money was needed to carry the provisions into effect, which meant the House of Representatives had to act. The appropriation was narrowly carried after an oratorical set piece by Representative Fisher Ames in which he warned of a British war if the treaty was not fully implemented.

The Treaty with Spain. More agreeable to all was the treaty negotiated by Thomas Pinckney with Spain in 1795 whereby Spain yielded on all the points the Americans had raised, granting the United States the use of the Mississippi and the right of deposit of merchandise in New Orleans, and defined the boundary of Florida. Spain was so pliant only because she had unsuccessfully tried all other policies.

Conflict with France. Having come to a rather frigid peace with Britain, the United States next discovered that the Jay Treaty had annoyed the French, who suspected it of being an Anglo-American alliance. In hope of resolving matters, President Adams sent a new Minister to France, Charles Cotesworth Pinckney, but he was not received by the French government and had to withdraw from the country.

Diplomacy had come to a stop. Perhaps war would follow. Special missions to Britain and Spain had preserved peace with those nations. The same expedient was tried with France. John Marshall and Elbridge Gerry were sent to join Pinckney in a commission to negotiate on the mutual Franco-American grievances. In Paris no official notice was taken of them, but after humiliating delays an unofficial delegation (referred to as Messieurs X, Y, and Z in the published reports) called on them and suggested a way of getting their business done, to wit, bribe the officials of the French Foreign Ministry and promise a public loan to France. The disgusted Marshall and Pinckney broke off their visit and left France. Gerry lingered awhile in the unfounded hope of making a peaceful settlement. This "X Y Z affair," the name by which it was announced early in 1798, caused a feeling of outrage in the United States. The Navy Department was founded, the army was enlarged, and ships were launched. American ships were authorized to take armed French vessels and—to the distaste of the French government—an undeclared naval war was begun. In the next two years United States ships scored a number of solid victories.

The 1796 Election and Action at Home. The Federalists not only provided external defense, but also established a system of internal security, part of which temporarily nullified the free speech and free press guarantees of the Bill of Rights. In 1797, after two unanimous elections to the presidency, George Washington returned to private life and was succeeded as President by John Adams. Adams had defeated Thomas Jefferson in the election of 1796 by only three electoral votes. The tone of the politics of the day was heated. Republicans were convinced that the Federalists were pro-British and monarchist. The Federalists accused the Republicans of being pro-French. Each suspected the other of traitorous tendencies. The Federalists were in control of all three branches of government and, therefore, in a position to take steps against their allegedly treasonable opponents.

Fearing that French revolutionary ideas were being spread throughout the country by immigrants, the Federalists took advantage of the excitement over the "X Y Z affair" in the spring of 1798 and passed a law requiring a fourteen-year residency period for citizenship (the Naturalization Act) and two laws to control the movements of unnaturalized foreigners (the Alien Acts). These laws may have been impolitic, but they were certainly constitutional. The last step to complete what a sober scholar has described as their "authoritarian system" was the Sedition Act, which punished oral or printed remarks intended to bring the government or its officers into contempt. This law has been defended by pointing out that the truth of the remarks was allowed as a defense, but in practice that merely meant the defendant had to prove his innocence, an idea repugnant to the American tradition of personal liberty. The prosecutions under the act were partisan and vindictive. Most of the defendants were Republican editors who were critical of the administration. All were convicted and "punished." Prosecutors and judges were partisan and malicious. Federalist editors shortsightedly applauded the suppression of rival presses.

The temporary answer of the Republican political minority was the adoption of critical Resolutions by the Kentucky and Virginia legislatures. Although the fact was not public at the time, the authors of the two sets of Resolutions were, respectively, Thomas Jefferson, author of the Declaration of Independence, and James Madison, "Father of the Constitution" and compiler of the Bill of Rights. These distinguished patriots were not so much concerned with defending themselves and their party against false and cruel accusations of treason as they were with seeking a solution to the problem of what to do when the Congress passes a law which violates the Constitution. Their Resolutions declared that Congress had trespassed the limits of the Constitution and that the states should act together in setting limits to such action. The Resolutions were circulated to all other legislatures. To the disappointment of the authors and their supporters, not a single state joined them in the protest. The Kentucky and Virginia Resolutions were either ignored or condemned. Some Federalists professed, indeed, to see them as the signal for a civil war. Hamilton thought the newly enlarged army should be concentrated on the border of Virginia for national security. The only permanent, ponderable effect of the "states' rights" Resolutions was to provide material for later promoters of secession, the propriety of which Madison, in his old age, vigorously denied.

THE ELECTION OF 1800

The presidential campaign of 1800 occurred in this atmosphere of doubt and fear. Adams and Jefferson were the candidates. The first decisive event of the campaign was the New York election of state legislators (who were to choose the state's presidential electors). By the "modern" techniques of careful precinct organization and listing of favorably inclined voters, Aaron Burr, the Republican Vice-Presidential candidate, led the New York Republican party to a victory which assured that he and Jefferson would carry the state.

All would not have been lost for Federalism even then except that a ruinous split developed in the Federalist party. President Adams had expelled the Secretaries of State and War, Timothy Pickering and James McHenry, from his cabinet. They were Hamilton's men. Adams had "inherited" them when he succeeded Washington. Adams also muttered that Hamilton (now long in private life but still very influential in the party) was pro-British. Adams infuriated Hamilton when he undermined the move toward war (and military command by Hamilton) by responding to the first opportunity to negotiate with the French.

As the election proceeded, the Jefferson-Burr ticket won. But a new, unforeseen complication occurred. Under the then electoral system, each elector voted for two men for President, the second highest becoming Vice-President. As the Republican electors of 1800 followed their party interest, each voted for both Jefferson and Burr. The Constitution provided that in case no candidate received a majority the election would be determined in the House of Representatives, where each state would have one vote. When the issue reached the House, certain Federalists put party above country and resolved to support Burr, who was they believed, a man of no principle and, therefore, one with whom they could "do business" in the future, unlike Jefferson who was regarded as a dangerous doctrinaire. In the House more than thirty ballots were taken before a few less bigoted Federal-ists decided that Jefferson could be trusted not to rip the national fabric and elected him just in time to be sworn in on the constitutional date.

A grand calm settled on the country as, by good fortune, peace with France was ratified at about the same time, and a concilia-tory Jefferson took over the direction of the republic he loved.

6

New Times, New Lands

During the years 1801–24, the United States doubled her size, entered a war of little consequence, and turned her endeavors homeward in tune to a rising, but temporary, spirit of nationalism.

THE JEFFERSONIANS

When Thomas Jefferson walked across the street from his boarding house to the Capitol in Washington (to which the government had moved from Philadelphia in the previous year), to take the oath as President, the Federalists lamented the coming of the Jacobin. Campaign falsehoods had convinced some that he was a physical coward, an atheist with lax morals, and a fierce partisan with subversive leanings. But Jefferson's inaugural address was wise and mild, and the Federalist listeners were agreeably surprised. On constitutional powers, on public finance, and on the relations of states to the federal government, he was careful to avoid alarming his recent opponents. Limited government, economy, and harmony were the Jeffersonian themes.

The Administration. The accession of the new administration put a damper on capital social life. Where Washington and Adams had put a certain amount of courtly glitter into their public appearances, Jefferson, a widower, practiced a studied austerity in social life, as an encouragement of republican simplicity and democratic procedure.

Jefferson did not make wholesale replacements of Federalists in office; of course, any vacancies were usually filled by loyal partisans, and by the end of Jefferson's first administration the majority of the federal officeholders were Republicans.

Among the newcomers to policy-making posts were James Madison, Secretary of State, and Albert Gallatin, Secretary of the Treasury. Madison had been a close collaborator with Jefferson in national politics for ten years. In the House of Representatives, Madison had led the Republican minority. When he left the Congress, his position of leadership had been assumed by the scholarly, Swiss-born Gallatin, at the time a resident of western Pennsylvania.

The new Secretary of the Treasury worked out a system of public finance whereby economy was achieved even though the detested excise tax was repealed and the national debt paid off. His principal economies were made in the army and navy departments. Proof that his financial program worked was the fact that the national debt was substantially reduced despite the necessity for naval action to chastise Mediterranean pirates.

The Federalists now retained power only in the judiciary. Early in 1801, foreseeing the end of their reign, they passed a Judiciary Act which created new judges and officers for lower federal courts while cutting the size of the Supreme Court, though Adams was able to appoint John Marshall to the conveniently vacant Chief Justiceship. The new positions were filled with Federalists, some (the "Midnight Judges") appointed on John Adams's last day of office. The Republicans, still angered over the conduct of federal judges in cases under the now-expired Sedition Act and feeling that the new Judiciary Act represented an attempt by the discredited Federalists to retreat into the judicial branch (as a defeated army takes refuge in a fortress), declared war on the judiciary by repealing the Judiciary Act and impeaching two Federal judges: one an alcoholic, and the other, Samuel Chase, the most vindictive of the Sedition judges. The former was convicted, but Chase was acquitted because he could not be proved guilty of an indictable offense.

The Republicans also turned to amending the Constitution. The Eleventh Amendment, ratified in 1795 (a direct reaction to a Supreme Court decision), protected the states against lawsuits: the electoral system was revised by the Twelfth Amendment (ratified in 1804) to elect President and Vice-President separately, thus preventing a repetition of the Jefferson-Burr tie.

In May of 1803, Jefferson, who had long resented paying tribute to the Barbary pirates of North Africa, dispatched a naval force against Tripoli, which ended the practice so far as that state was concerned. It is ironic that Jefferson took this measure, as he had a reputation for being both antiwar and antinavy.

The Louisiana Purchase. The single most influential event of Thomas Jefferson's administration was the purchase, from Napoleon Bonaparte, in 1803, of Louisiana, an area of more than eight hundred thousand square miles; the acquisition more than doubled the size of the United States

The Louisiana region, bounded by Texas and the Rockies on the west, Canada on the north, the Mississippi and Lake Pontchartrain on the east, and the Gulf of Mexico on the south, had been ceded to Spain by France at the close of the Great War for Empire in 1762. In the late 1790's Napoleon planned to revive the French New World Empire. He hoped to regain the French West Indies. It was essential to this plan that a mainland food supply be secured. Therefore, by the Treaty of San Ildefonso in 1800, he reacquired Louisiana from Spain. The price paid to Spain was Napoleon's promise of an Italian kingdom to be given to one of the members of the Spanish royal family. (Characteristically, he never "made delivery.") His next step was to send an army to reconquer the self-freed slaves of San Domingo, but the project was a failure. Foreseeing further war with Britain the French Emperor decided, unknown to the Americans, to forego transatlantic adventures. At the moment he was in need of cash.

American reaction to the retrocession of Louisiana from Spain to France was bound to be sharp. Spain was weak and no threat; but France, under Napoleon's driving power, was everything that a neighbor should not be—noisy, vigorous, demanding, and truculent. With a dreamer after world dominion at her back, the United States would be in trouble.

President Jefferson had usually favored France over Britain in their interminable wars but, when France occupied New Orleans, he wrote to Robert R. Livingston, the American Minister in Paris, that "we must marry ourselves to the British fleet and nation." Even before the French took possession, the Spaniards, in 1802, closed the Mississippi. By this time Kentucky and Tennessee were states, and Ohio was on the verge of statehood. The Mississippi River was the only vent for their surplus meat and grain. The problem, as quickly shown by western anger, had become an emergency.

GROWTH OF THE UNITED STATES

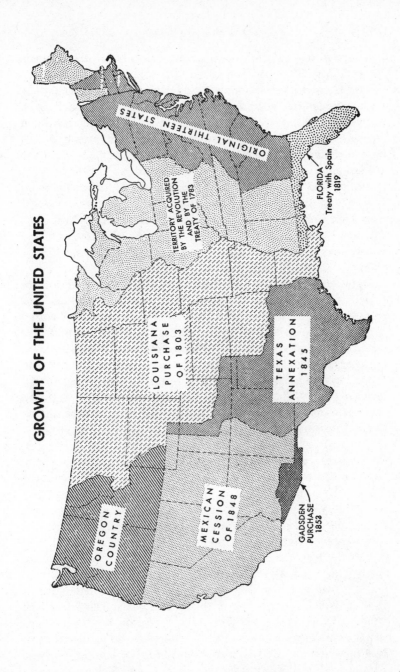

ORIGINAL THIRTEEN STATES

FLORIDA
Treaty with Spain
1819

TERRITORY ACQUIRED
BY THE REVOLUTION
AND BY THE
TREATY OF 1783

LOUISIANA
PURCHASE
OF 1803

TEXAS
ANNEXATION
1845

OREGON
COUNTRY

MEXICAN
CESSION
OF 1848

GADSDEN
PURCHASE
1853

Jefferson told Livingston to begin talks with the French. Livingston was shortly reinforced by James Monroe. Jefferson wished them to buy a suitable place for transshipment on the lower Mississippi, or at least to get a firm commitment to be allowed to use the river and a place of deposit. If they could get New Orleans and West Florida the Congress promised two million dollars, and there were hints that ten million might be available.

But, as has been seen, Napoleon had already abandoned his New World hopes and, to the surprise of the American negotiators, his Foreign Minister offered to sell the whole of Louisiana. The deal was quickly closed at the price of fifteen million dollars; in addition, the United States assumed liability for the claims of American citizens against France.

Many Federalists were startled. Soon they cried, "Unconstitutional!" (Even Jefferson had doubts on this point.) The fact was that the Federalists saw their northeastern commercial corner of the country becoming less influential as the agricultural area was extended westward. They feared, too, an eventual coalition between southern and western agrarian interests. No constitutional lawyers today deny that a sovereignty may acquire territory by treaty. The Federalists and Republicans had reversed themselves on the question of "loose" and "strict" construction of the Constitution. (This reversal set the pattern that, usually, those in office are "loose" and those out of office are "strict.")

The treaty was approved by the Senate with little difficulty. Because the treaty promised the inhabitants equality with the other citizens of the United States, there was grumbling, but no effective opposition, when the present state of Louisiana was admitted to the Union in 1812. Thirteen states were eventually created in whole or in part as a result of this magnificent real-estate deal. Two questions remained to be answered, and the answers affected American history profoundly: Where, exactly, was the western boundary of the nation? And what of West Florida, which Monroe had started out to buy in the first place?

For patriotic and scientific reasons, Jefferson had long hoped to promote the exploration of the territory he had just purchased. In the years 1803–06 he sent Meriwether Lewis and William Clark to the Pacific Ocean via the Missouri and Columbia valleys in a heroic expedition which added luster to the reputations of sponsor and leaders and much new data to geographical science.

Ratification of the Louisiana Purchase Treaty in 1804 intensified the opposition of the Federalists and they planned to have New England secede from the Union in company with New York. This scheme required that the governor of New York be sympathetic to secession; therefore, in the New York gubernatorial campaign of 1804, the Federalists connived with the outcast Vice-President Aaron Burr to be their candidate. Alexander Hamilton frustrated Burr's candidacy, and the plan failed. Hamilton's undoing of Burr climaxed years of rivalry between the two men; Burr challenged him to a duel, in which Hamilton was mortally wounded. Burr fled to the West, with other conspiracies in mind. In 1807 he was tried for treason. Although he was acquitted, his public career, long on the downgrade, was permanently terminated.

Attempts at Neutrality. With the purchase of Louisiana the administration of Thomas Jefferson had begun well, but never again did it achieve an outstanding success in diplomacy. The rivalry of France and Britain, dating back to the seventeenth century, had entered its final phase, with France, led by the brilliant, ambitious Bonaparte, pushing toward world domination and restrained principally by British power. Under the circumstances the rights of small neutrals were fragile.

Britain was supreme upon the sea and France upon the land. It was to Britain's interest to prevent France from drawing strength from seafaring neutrals, and it was to France's interest to prevent a British blockade from strangling her. The French, in peacetime, had severely restricted American trade with the French West Indies but now allowed it as a defensive measure. Great Britain tolerated the movement of French produce, if it was first landed in America and then re-exported, but in 1805 she refused any longer to recognize this "broken voyage" practice, asserting her "rule of 1756"—that trade which was illegal in peacetime was equally illegal in wartime. Seizure of American ships followed, and the British practice of impressing American seamen into the Royal Navy added to the anger already felt by the Americans.

This was just the first stride on a long road to war. A British blockade of the coast of Europe from Brest to the Elbe River in 1806 was promptly answered by Napoleon's "Berlin Decree," declaring the entire British Isles blockaded, which meant that neutral ships touching there, and later apprehended by French officials, would be confiscated. Britain, in a series of "Orders in Council," retaliated with an extension of her blockade and more stringent regulation of neutral shipping. Napoleon's "Milan Decree" announced that any shipmaster who obeyed the British could expect to have his ship seized. It was British blockade versus Napoleon's "Continental System."

The Americans were caught between the hammer and the anvil. Because the British had control of the sea and the French could only molest American shipping which entered Continental ports, American retaliatory measures were directed against British practices. In 1806 the Congress enacted the First Non-importation Act (effective in 1808), which barred the import of those goods from Britain which could be imported from other places. An attempt by James Monroe and William Pinkney to negotiate a treaty in England, 1807, failed. The threat of non-importation being ineffective, Jefferson secured the passage of the Embargo Act which was intended to put a complete stop to all foreign trade. Known as the "Damn-bargo" or the "O-grab-me," it was much resented in American shipping centers. Neither Britain nor France was hurt. Britain developed a South American trade instead, and Napoleon seized American evaders on the ironic ground that they must be Britishers carrying false papers.

The disastrous embargo was replaced in 1809 by the Non-intercourse Act which allowed trade with all nations except France and Britain and permitted the resumption of trade with either if that belligerent ceased to violate neutral rights. An unauthorized British spokesman said his country would revoke its obnoxious orders, but the suspension of the act in Britain's favor was, of course, short-lived. When the act was due to expire another was substituted, Macon's Bill Number Two, which authorized reopening the trade with both nations but also re-quired that it be closed down on one if the other treated the Americans properly. Napoleon, through chicanery, secured its operation in his favor in 1811.

It might be expected that the abuse of neutral rights and shipping would inflame the maritime centers, but, actually, the chief anti-British feeling was on the frontier. There was a time, in 1807, when a war with Britain would have had united support—after the British warship *Leopard* attacked the unsuspecting United States ship *Chesapeake*—but Jefferson allowed the national indignation to be expended in proclamations and international "notes." Western grievances included the knowledge that local British traders and officials had encouraged Indian leaders such as Tecumseh, whose followers were defeated in 1811 at Tippecanoe. Above all, Americans felt nationally threatened by the many small infringements of national honor on the seas, in diplomacy, and the frontier. Congressional leaders, from the New England frontier to the western forests of Georgia, known as the "War Hawks," kept up a constant incitement to fight Great Britain.

The Elections of 1808 and 1812. After 1809 the burden fell on James Madison, who in 1808 easily won out over the Federalist Charles Cotesworth Pinckney, who had also been defeated by Jefferson in 1804. Madison was re-elected in 1812, defeating De Witt Clinton.

THE WAR OF 1812

Early in 1812 Madison became convinced that the British would never yield on the question of neutral rights, and he drafted a message to the Congress asking for a declaration of war. In the Congress the southern and western elements overruled the reluctant northeasterners, and war was declared on June 19. With a diminutive navy and an inefficient army the United States was fortunate in that Britain was caught in a death struggle with Napoleonic France.

In the war the army suffered a number of humiliating defeats which added no glory to its colors. However, the principal frontier aims were achieved by crushing the Indians at the Battle of the Thames in 1813 and at Horseshoe Bend in 1814. On the seas the sixteen-ship navy distinguished itself but, of course, its activity was not decisive. The epoch-making "sea" fights took place on fresh water. By the Battle of Lake Erie, Oliver Perry secured command of the Great Lakes in 1813, and on Lake Champlain in 1814, Thomas McDonough prevented an invasion from Canada. Probably the most spectacular events of the war were two which did not affect its outcome: the burning of

Washington by the British in 1814; and Andrew Jackson's triumph in the Battle of New Orleans, where the victor of Horseshoe Bend annihilated a British army, after peace had been signed (a fact at the moment unknown in America).

American and British commissioners had met at Ghent (in present-day Belgium) in December of 1814. The Treaty of Ghent settled not one of the questions which had provoked the war, but battle had "solved" the Indian problem, east of the Mississippi. Thus, peace without victory was achieved by both parties.

An anticlimax of the war occurred as a result of ill-feeling in New England. Three of the maritime states for whose protection the war was ostensibly fought opposed the conflict in public statements. Connecticut refused to furnish militia, and the Governor of Massachusetts discouraged enlistments. New England and New York contractors supplied provisions to the British forces. Toward the end of the war, delegates from all of the New England states gathered at the Hartford Convention, where it was proposed to amend the Constitution to protect "states' rights." The language of these pessimistic Federalists was practically the same as that used by the Republican statesmen Jefferson and Madison sixteen years before. The decisions of the Hartford Convention reached Washington with the news of the Battle of New Orleans and the Treaty of Ghent and were not taken seriously, except that thereafter popular suspicions killed the Federalist party.

THE NEW NATIONALISM

The years after the War of 1812 were years of great and rapid change for the United States, which was both engendered by and reflected in an increased spirit of national unity.

Western Expansion. The most spectacular change was the steady and large growth of the regions west of the Appalachians; tens of thousands went west to join the pioneers of an earlier generation.

The pressure of western movement encouraged innovations which made travel easier. Even before the drafting of the Constitution there had been a project to join Chesapeake Bay and the Ohio River by a canal up the Potomac Valley. In 1811 construction of the Old National (or Cumberland) Road was begun. This paved wagon toll road eventually reached Vandalia, Illinois, and is now part of "U.S. 40." In 1817 the steamboat, first proved commercially practicable by Robert Fulton in 1809, appeared on the Ohio River and, in its shallow draft, paddle-wheel form, made speedy travel possible on every stream with a few feet of water in it. Its success was copied on the Great Lakes as well. The steamboat served the rapidly growing metropolises of the Lakes and the Ohio and Mississippi rivers. Access to the Great Lakes was made easier by exploitation of New York's "water-level route" from the Hudson River to Lake Erie via the Erie Canal, which was begun in 1817 (and which, in time, made New York City the first city of the New World). Meanwhile, the successes of the National Road and the Erie Canal led to an excess of speculation in attempts elsewhere to imitate these accomplishments.

The growth of the hitherto unsettled region was shown by the rapid admission of new states. From 1790 to 1820 the following were admitted to the Union: Vermont (1791), Kentucky (1792), Tennessee (1796), Ohio (1803), Louisiana (1812), Indiana (1816), Mississippi (1817), Illinois (1818), Alabama (1819), and Maine (1820). In 1820 these ten states had a combined population of 2,662,000, or about as much as the Old Thirteen states had in 1776, and this increase came at a time when the flow of immigration from foreign countries was at a relatively low rate.

The expansion was accompanied by feverish speculation in lands and the overextension of credit in many lines until the Congress, in 1817, required hard money for land payments. Overextended western banks collapsed and brought on the Panic of 1819, which left a permanent animosity in the minds of westerners toward eastern "conservative" banking practices.

Settlement of Boundaries. The postwar years saw the conclusion of two agreements which settled Anglo-American problems. The Rush-Bagot agreement of 1818 demilitarized the Canadian border, and the Convention of 1818 settled the boundary between the United States and Canada along the forty-ninth parallel, from Lake of the Woods to the Rocky Mountains. The Convention also provided for joint occupation of the disputed Oregon area (now the states of Washington and Oregon

WESTWARD EXPANSION OF THE U. S.

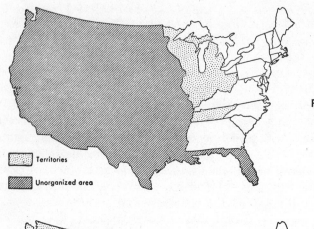

Territories

Unorganized area

1790
Population
4 million

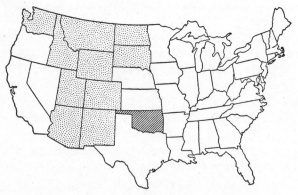

1870
Population
38 million

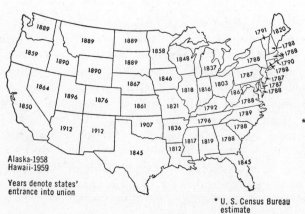

Alaska-1958
Hawaii-1959

Years denote states'
entrance into union

1965
Population
* 195 million

* U. S. Census Bureau
estimate

and the province of British Columbia) for a ten year period.

A more difficult puzzle of diplomacy was the Florida question. West Florida had been Spanish since the War for Independence. American migrants took charge there and proclaimed a republic which was joined to the Mississippi Territory by the Congress. In the War of 1812 American rule was extended as far east as Mobile. East Florida remained under the feeble hand of Spain, an inadequately policed sanctuary for debtors, criminals, runaway slaves, and hostile Indians. Major General Andrew Jackson "policed" it, but was called back after he quelled an Indian uprising so vigorously that it appeared to be a conquest of Florida. Finally, in 1819, Secretary of State John Quincy Adams negotiated a treaty which settled the Spanish-American boundary from coast to coast and included the cession of Florida to the United States.

Internal Affairs and Elections. The decay of the Federalist party left the field to the Republicans. As a result the elections of James Monroe to the Presidency in 1816 and 1820 (Madison had served two terms, 1809–17) gave the deceptive appearance of near unanimity. Because of the lack of electoral-college contests, some historians have called this "the era of good feeling."

In economic matters there truly was substantial agreement. This was nowhere more visible than in the chartering of the second Bank of the United States, which provoked nothing like the contention that accompanied the chartering of the first Bank in 1791. The first Bank of the United States had been allowed to go out of business when its twenty-year charter had expired, but its absence had been felt when the government found it necessary to finance the War of 1812. After a false start in 1814 and 1815, the second Bank was chartered in 1816, the chief motives being to provide a federal depository and to regularize the currency.

The Republicans (who by this time were called the Democratic-Republicans) also forgot their scruples over a protective tariff. During the war, tax rates on imports had been raised as a military necessity. In 1816 the raises were confirmed by a new act which was purposely protectionist, to promote American manufacturing, although it was passed over the protests of the shipping industry. The Tariff of 1818 extended the practice.

Manufacturing was beginning to be important. The twenty-two

years of Anglo-French wars, which ended at Waterloo in 1815, encouraged domestic industries, which were further promoted by the spread of Eli Whitney's principle of "interchangeable parts." Weapons, nails, clocks, and textiles all flourished before 1820, and the ancient iron industry was on the verge of the greatest industrial expansion yet known in world history.

John Marshall, Chief Justice. John Marshall, Federalist Virginia-bred diplomatist and Congressman, was appointed Chief Justice of the United States by John Adams in 1801. A case could be made for the proposition that his appointment was the most important decision ever made by a President of the United States. Marshall, a Revolutionary War veteran whose patriotic nationalism was case-hardened in the miseries of Valley Forge, sat on the supreme bench from 1801 to 1835 and profoundly influenced the interpretation of the Constitution in a series of decisions which are still landmarks, and, which established the superior authority of the national government. He was, of course, not alone on the bench, but his logical clarity carried the other judges with him most of the time.

In *Marbury v. Madison* (1803) the court ruled a section of the Judiciary Act of 1801 unconstitutional, thus establishing what is now settled policy—that the Supreme Court can review the constitutionality of acts of the Congress. When the legislature of Georgia repealed land sales of a preceding legislature because of fraud and corruption in the sales, the court, in *Fletcher v. Peck* (1810), pointed out the constitutional prohibition against any state laws which impaired the obligation of contracts. The legislature of New Hampshire tried to revise the royal charter of Dartmouth College, but in the *Dartmouth College Case* (1819) the court identified a corporation charter as a contract not to be impaired—a decision obviously of vast importance to the conduct of American business. The question of the authority of the Supreme Court to inquire into the constitutionality of the decisions of the state courts was an issue in *Cohens v. Virginia* (1821), but John Marshall successfully asserted it and thereby added another stone to the national fabric. In *Gibbons v. Ogden* (1824) the Court upset the attempt of the State of New York to establish a monopoly of steamboat navigation in the state. Marshall's ground was the Constitution's grant of power to the Congress to regulate interstate and international commerce. The second Bank of the United States figured in *McCulloch v. Maryland* (1819). Marshall ruled that when the end is legitimate and within the scope of the Constitution, and the means are appropriate and not prohibited, an act of Congress cannot be unconstitutional. His position was plainly Hamiltonian in that he defended the reading of "implied powers" of government into the Constitution. He also denied the power of a state to tax a federal agency.

Twice, in 1831 and 1832, in cases involving the Cherokee Indians, Marshall was successfully opposed by the State of Georgia, which made good its defiance only because the President did not support the judiciary. Otherwise, every timber and brick of the judicial edifice erected by John Marshall exalted and strengthened the federal government and protected it from state restraints. The federal government might well have collapsed under the long series of states' rights attacks, from the Whiskey Rebels to the Dixiecrats, except for Marshall's work.

Foreign Policy: The Monroe Doctrine. We have already examined some of Monroe's diplomatic successes—the Rush-Bagot Treaty, the Convention of 1818, and the acquisition of Florida. He and his very capable Secretary of State, John Quincy Adams, went on to take advantage of Spanish difficulties in America to construct a resounding statement of the national interest.

Spain's American provinces had been in rebellion since 1809 and 1810, but when Napoleon was finally defeated it was feared that European nations might combine to reduce the Spanish colonies to obedience. The United States could not calmly accept an armed invasion of the Western Hemisphere in the interest of monarchism. Another interested party was Great Britain which had developed a profitable trade with Central and South America and stood to lose by the rumored attack. The United States had been aloof from the Spanish-colonial struggle, fearing to alienate Spain before the settlement of the Florida question. Meanwhile, the Russians were expanding south from Alaska. With the Florida question no longer an issue, it was time to speak.

Disdaining an invitation to join with Great Britain in a warning to the powers of the Continent, President Monroe enunciated his famous doctrine in a message to the Congress in 1823. In essence, he proclaimed that America was no longer a field for colonialism, and that European intervention in New World affairs would be considered unfriendly. At the moment the effect of Monroe's statement was not great because the Americans were known to be too weak to enforce it. It was not law, but it was a brave warning from a young state and in time was to become one of the weightiest of international pronouncements.

A National Culture. America's political independence long preceded its cultural independence, but in the first half of the nineteenth century its culture began to become distinctively American. In this emerging culture, women became entrapped and glorified by an ideology that proclaimed them unsuited for the outside world, paragons in the home surrounded by children. The law, employment, and education were all influenced by women's image as virginal yet mothers, helpless yet morally superior.

A number of eminent naturalists, inventors, and medical researchers appeared and were at work while Jefferson was President; their numbers were to be augmented by the products of the expanding secondary and professional schools. The book and periodical press, the theater, and the fine arts were being patronized. In literature this was the age of "the flowering of New England." In architecture the classical revival marked American towns with dignified Grecian columns. Writers, musicians, and actors found the American audiences responsive.

Public education expanded tremendously. With the separation of church and state in New England, where the school system was the most advanced in the country, education became the responsibility of the secular state. As a reaction to this, Catholics founded their system of church-affiliated schools.

American Protestantism showed great vigor. The influx of deistic and rationalistic ideas was combatted by a wave of "revivalism" at the beginning of the nineteenth century. Much energy was expended in the promotion of missions at home and abroad. The modern pattern of voluntary religious association was set by the disestablishment of the remaining state churches from 1818 to 1833. The moral scene was accented by reform movements, of which feminism and abolitionism were probably the most influential in the long run.

The same age saw the firm planting of the factory system of mass production. Transportation facilities and cities expanded rapidly, and new waves of immigration flooded the country; a large fraction of the newcomers were Catholics. The Catholic Church, once a small minority, and for the most part southern, began to grow enormously in the North and Northwest; about two-thirds of its adherents swelled the population of the growing cities. There was a rise of feeling that these people were unassimilable, and organizations of "native Americans" were formed to prevent their participation in public life and to place restrictions on further immigration. This "nativist" movement achieved the dignity of a national political party but presently disappeared.

The First Crisis of Sectionalism. The North-South differences revealed so glaringly in the Hamiltonian-Jeffersonian cleavages of the 1790's seemed less apparent for a time after the War of 1812. But the forces were still there, under the surface, and the magic password to open the gate of pandemonium was "slavery." The larger population of the free states dominated the lower house, but in the Senate the division of free and slave states was equal. When Missouri applied for statehood with slavery, the balance of power was threatened. It occurred to antislavery people to ask whether or not slavery was legal west of the Mississippi.

When the Missouri enabling act came before the House of Representatives early in 1819, James Tallmadge of New York moved to bar the further introduction of slaves into Missouri and advocated that slave children born after the admission of the state would be free after age twenty-five. He won in the House but lost in the Senate. Almost simultaneously John W. Taylor, also of New York, had moved to bar slavery from the Territory of Arkansas and from the rest of the Louisiana Purchase but also lost. Arkansas Territory, with its northern boundary at 36°30', was organized without such restrictions. In a running debate through late 1819 and early 1820, the issue was clearly stated. One group contended that the Congress could make the prohibition of slavery a prerequisite to joining the Union. The other side argued (and the courts have since agreed) that states are admitted equally, with identical powers.

Meanwhile, Maine and Alabama were rapping at the door. Alabama was admitted by joint resolution, and Senator Jesse B. Thomas of Illinois proposed to couple the admission of Maine and Missouri, the one free and the other slave. Thomas included the condition that future states created from the Louisiana Purchase north of the line of 36°30' (the southern boundary of Missouri) must be free states. This suited the Senate but failed to pass the House of Representatives, which adopted Taylor's restriction mentioned before. In conference, however, it was agreed to admit Missouri as a slave state and Maine as a free state, and to bar slavery in the future from the rest of the Louisiana Purchase north of 36°30'. This is the famed Missouri Compromise. Maine had existed as a district of Massachusetts since the seventeenth century. Now she became the sixth New England state.

However, the sectional crisis was not wholly resolved. The fire was rekindled by a provision of Missouri's new constitution which excluded free Negroes from the state. Antislavery men were outraged at the creation of two classes of free men, and the tension was not relaxed until Henry Clay—getting his start as the "Great Compromiser"—offered what has been called the "Second Missouri Compromise" (1821), by which the admission of Missouri was held up until the legislature agreed that the clause would not be interpreted as sanctioning any law which restricted the privileges and immunities of citizens of the United States. This was not a wholly satisfactory solution since the legislature could probably not speak in this way for posterity, but Missouri was admitted. (The cloudy notion of American citizenship shown in this episode was to bring the nation to peril until it was clarified fifty years later by the Fourteenth Amendment.)

In the midst of the discussion a presidential election occurred (1820). The Federalist party had disappeared. No Democratic-Republican came forward to oppose the incumbent James Monroe. As a result, of the presidential electors who balloted, all but one voted for Monroe. There is a pleasing legend that the lone dissenter wished to preserve the honor of unanimous election for the solitary glory of George Washington. More likely, he voted for his candidate, John Quincy Adams, because he preferred him to Monroe.

7

The Jacksonians

The second quarter of the nineteenth century saw a democratic upheaval, of which Andrew Jackson was the symbol, and which was a true "Second American Revolution." It was not only political but also social, intellectual, and humanitarian. In its first stages, western farmers, southern planters, and eastern laborers, led by politicians taking advantage of a broadened suffrage, promoted Jackson through two campaigns to the presidency and later supported his chosen successor, Martin Van Buren.

THE RISE OF ANDREW JACKSON

Although the Federalist party, as an institution, was dead, its economic and political ideas have never disappeared. The ideal of rule by the "wise, good, and rich" and the attachment of the commercial leaders to government by their own interests survived. In the 1820's these principles were represented in public life by Henry Clay and his followers.

Another fact of the political scene was that members of Monroe's cabinet were engaged in some deft maneuvering for political power, centering around the conflicting ambitions of Treasury Secretary William H. Crawford and War Secretary John C. Calhoun. But this was merely prologue to the presidential campaign of 1824.

The Election of 1824. Nominating machinery was imperfect. Previously, nominations had been made by congressional caucuses. This method was passing into disuse, and the national convention had not yet been invented. Partly as a **result and** symptom of the disorder, the contest in 1824 saw **five major**

candidates—Calhoun, Jackson, Clay, John Quincy Adams, and Crawford—all at least nominally Democratic-Republicans. They were catapulted into the ring by state legislatures, by state conventions, and, in the case of Crawford, by a poorly attended congressional caucus.

All of these men have left their imprint on the American nation, but none so deeply as Andrew Jackson. Born in South Carolina, he was a frontier lawyer of Tennessee at the time of its admission to the Union and became its first member of the House of Representatives. He also served on his state's supreme bench. But he was best known to the west as a soldier. Starting as Major General in the militia, he received the same grade in the regular army; he severely chastised the Florida Indians, and he was the hero of the Battle of New Orleans. He remained a volatile and controversial figure in public life.

In the campaign of 1824, Crawford was handicapped by a physical collapse. Calhoun withdrew and became a candidate for the vice-presidency. Clay, Adams, and Jackson remained in the race, with Clay and Adams in fairly close agreement on national issues.

Calhoun was elected Vice-President, but the electoral college gave no candidate a majority for President. The votes were: Jackson, ninety-nine; Adams, eighty-four; Crawford, forty-one; Clay, thirty-seven. The Constitution requires that in such cases the election be settled by the House of Representatives, with each state having one vote. No more than the three leading candidates may be considered; hence Clay's name was dropped. He and his supporters switched to Adams, who was elected by thirteen votes to Jackson's and Crawford's combined total of eleven votes. When Clay was appointed by Adams to the office of Secretary of State (a very normal arrangement under the circumstances), the Jackson men cried that there had been a "corrupt bargain."

Party Cleavage. The bitterness after the election results was symptomatic of an Adams-Jackson or conservative-liberal cleavage of the party into two factions: National Republicans (Adams and Clay) and Democratic Republicans (Jackson). This was the age of a broadening democracy. The older restrictions on the privilege of voting were disappearing. More and more offices were being filled by election rather than appointment (a "reform" of debatable value). Nearly all of the presidential electors were chosen by the people. It was natural that Jacksonian leaders would court the newly enfranchised and that conservative minds would be repelled by the popularization or "vulgarization" of politics.

The cleavage was helped along by the revival of the tariff as a national issue. The growing textile industry in the Northeast took the lead in pushing for protective rates while the southerners, dependent on foreign trade, opposed them. At this point, in 1828, the Jacksonians outwitted themselves by supporting a tariff bill with excessive rates. They thought this Tariff of Abominations would surely lose, that they would gain favor with protectionists for "trying," and that the South would be content with the failure of the bill. To their surprise it passed and became law. Protests were adopted by several southern state legislatures, most conspicuously by South Carolina as stated in its *Exposition*, a document issued anonymously by Vice-President Calhoun. It advanced the portentous idea that a federal law could be "nullified" by a single state.

The Election of 1828. Against this stormy backdrop was played the drama of the presidential election of 1828. Jackson had begun his campaign in 1825. It would be fair to say Adams never began his at all, for he took no step toward building an organization bound to him by self-interest. Jackson won the popular majority in a ratio of 13:10 and the electoral college by 178 to 83, a truly decisive sweep for the apostle of the newly enfranchised. Jackson is thought of as a candidate of the West and the South, but analysis of his vote showed that seaboard wage earners had much to do with the national decision.

POLITICS AND POLICIES

Few administrations have had as much internal dissension as afflicted Jackson's during his first term. And no earlier President so aggressively attacked those he regarded as enemies of the best interest of the people. Jackson saw himself as the only man in Washington who was elected by the whole people; therefore, he was their chief representative. This view implied that the President, as a national leader, would exert influence on legislation, and such exertion made this the most exciting

Presidency until Lincoln's day. For advice Jackson leaned on an inner circle of friends whose enemies called them the "Kitchen Cabinet." The true Cabinet became merely a group of administrators, not an executive and political council as it had been before. Unlike his predecessor, John Quincy Adams, Jackson attached his followers by self-interest in that he expanded the already prevalent custom of appointing deserving followers to public office—the so-called "spoils system." The effect of Jackson's policy in this matter has been exaggerated as have the evils of the notion. There are advantages in interesting large numbers of average undedicated souls in the daily practice of politics by the hope of some ponderable gain to themselves.

The Jackson-Calhoun Split. One of the most significant events of Jackson's period was the cabinet split by which Calhoun and his following left the "regular" party ranks. In 1818 Jackson, then a Major General, had invaded Spanish Florida and caused the execution of two British subjects. Calhoun, a Cabinet member, thought he should be disciplined. In 1830 Jackson learned of Calhoun's attitude, and their relations became chilly. The chill became downright arctic when Secretary of War John H. Eaton married Peggy O'Neale, a barmaid in her father's tavern. Mrs. Calhoun and the other Cabinet wives refused to receive her. The widowers concerned, Jackson and Martin Van Buren, sided with the Eatons. Van Buren saw a chance for a coup and resigned from the Cabinet in order to precipitate a minor "cabinet crisis" leading to the Cabinet's disruption. Eaton did the same. Their actions made it possible for Jackson to reorganize his Cabinet, which he did, sending Van Buren as Minister to Great Britain and Eaton to be a territorial governor. The Cabinet was filled with true Jacksonians, among them names destined to be famous, such as Lewis Cass and Roger B. Taney. Vice-President Calhoun, President of the Senate, cast the tie-breaking vote against confirming Van Buren's appointment to Britain. As will be seen, he thereby nullified the designation of a diplomat and created a President. Calhoun, now isolated, resigned his office and was returned to Washington as a senator from his state of South Carolina.

The Webster-Hayne Debate. The Calhoun imbroglio represented more than partisan intrigue or teapot squall. It was part of a realignment which was best illustrated by the Webster-

Hayne debate in which the nature of the Union was examined from conflicting viewpoints of nationalism and localism. It started as an attempt by Senator Samuel A. Foote of Connecticut to curtail public land sales in the West. Senator Thomas Hart Benton of Missouri replied that New England was thereby attempting to limit the prosperity of the West, and he was joined by Senator Robert Y. Hayne of South Carolina, who hoped to continue a southern-western alliance by attacking federal centralization. Senator Daniel Webster of Massachusetts engaged Hayne in the debate. Hayne had argued that states' rights were in danger. Webster assailed sectionalism, replying that the Union, in effect, was a Union of the people. The Foote resolution was forgotten, but sectionalism continued.

Diplomacy. Jackson's first term was also notable for the settlement of two old and vexing diplomatic problems. American shipping was admitted to the British West Indies (mostly because Britain was abandoning the mercantilist system), and a start was made toward collecting claims due from France for spoliations in the Napoleonic era. Jackson's Indian policy was a kind of diplomacy, too, since it was based on "treaties" whereby the Indians, for the most part, were to be moved to a new and perpetual "Indian Territory" west of the Mississippi River. The exodus was a tragic one, but only the Black Hawk War and the longer-lived Second Seminole War resulted from the sorrow and discontent of the tribesmen.

The Nullification Controversy. The most serious crisis of national life between the time of the Revolution and the Civil War occurred in Jackson's first term. Dissatisfied with the Tariff of 1832, John Calhoun repeated his doctrine of nullification and defended it as a correct interpretation of the Constitution. A special session of the state legislature called a convention which met in November and "nullified" the tariffs of 1828 and 1832, declaring them void and prohibiting the collection of duties in the state. Jackson alerted the armed forces, recommended that the Congress cut the tariff, and warned South Carolinians they were on the road of treason. In his proclamation he denied both nullification and the alleged "right" of secession.

South Carolina was not cowed. Her new Governor, the same Hayne of Webster-Hayne fame, called a national convention of states to study the nature of the Union, but he received no encouragement. Jackson now sponsored a force bill in Congress which would permit him to use the army to collect the revenues. At the same time Congress was considering a new compromise tariff bill introduced by Clay. Both the Force Act and the Tariff Act passed. South Carolina, mollified by the tariff cuts, subsided but fired its parting salvo—an act to nullify the force bill.

In personality, it had been Jackson, the national Unionist, against Calhoun, who loved his state more than he did the federal Union. Both were to have successors.

The War on the Bank. Next to the nullification crisis, the affairs of the second Bank of the United States provided the most serious issue of Jackson's administration. The President's war on the Bank at once unified his opponents and solidified his supporters as warriors against financial and commercial monopoly.

The Bank, it will be recalled, had been chartered in 1816. After 1823 it was managed by Nicholas Biddle. Most of the stock was privately owned, yet it acted as fiscal agent for the United States and, by redeeming the notes of state banks, whether they were willing or not, it policed the banking community. Objectors said private men were making a profit from public funds (true) and, by persecuting state banks, the same men were unduly restricting credit (not so true).

The charter was not due to expire until 1836, but in his first year in office Jackson let the world know he disapproved of both the principles and operations of the Bank. In 1831 Senator Thomas Hart Benton, Missouri's famous hard-money leader, attacked the Bank. Clay persuaded Biddle to make the Bank an issue in the presidential campaign of 1832 by applying for rechartering then, instead of later toward the expiration date. When the recharter bill passed the Congress, the irrepressible Jackson accepted the challenge and used his veto, sending along with it a denunciation of special privilege and monopoly. The veto appeared not to have hurt Jackson, for in the election of 1832 (the first in which the national nominating convention was used) Jackson was re-elected over Henry Clay, candidate of the National Republicans (as the dissidents now called themselves). Martin Van Buren, his career apparently assisted by Calhoun's opposition, became Vice-President.

In order to defend his beloved Bank, Biddle began to tighten credit, which he thought would be a way of pressing the administration. Jackson struck back on the assumption that his re-election was a mandate from the people to destroy the Bank. He asked his Cabinet's advice and then proceeded to reorganize his following around the men who seemed to agree with him. William J. Duane, of Pennsylvania, became Secretary of the Treasury. Jackson ordered him to withdraw the government's funds which were on deposit with the Bank, but Duane refused. Jackson then let his Cabinet know formally that he looked upon the Cabinet merely as an agency of the office of President, and Duane was replaced by Roger B. Taney. The federal funds were withdrawn, in 1833, and redeposited in selected state banks which came to be known, jeeringly, as "Pet Banks." Jackson assumed full responsibility and was censured by the Senate, on the motion of his old opponent, Henry Clay, but the House of Representatives passed resolutions supporting him. The Senate declined even to enter on its journal a presidential message on the subject, but by 1837 Benton managed to get the censure resolutions expunged. As for the Bank of the United States, it secured a state charter in 1836, but state banks carried on the fiscal business of the United States thereafter.

Indirectly related to the great banking controversy, because it involved the currencies of the country, was the Specie Circular. The period of the war on the Bank saw a remarkable inflation as state banks expanded their note issue and also used the federal deposits as a credit base. Land sales jumped almost 1,000 per cent from 1832 to 1836, much of the increase being based on credit. The President's cure was to issue the Specie Circular, a proclamation requiring that public lands be paid for in gold and silver. The immediate effect was a double one: land sales were sharply reduced; and state banks were severely strained by banknote-holders who wished to redeem the notes in hard money. Confidence in all banks declined. The Congress passed a bill rescinding the Circular in 1837, but Jackson did not agree. Finally, in 1838, it was repealed by joint resolution of the two houses.

The 1836 Election. In this election, Jackson's favored choice, Martin Van Buren, was opposed by two nominees of the opposition (which now called itself the Whig party), Daniel Webster and Hugh L. White, but his vote was larger than theirs combined. With the accession of Van Buren the party alignment was clear.

Against the Jacksonians were the business community and its allies. For the Jacksonians—everybody else. In departing from public life Jackson left a farewell message which appealed to nationalism over provincialism and condemned all the economic ideas and institutions against which he had battled.

THE VAN BUREN ADMINISTRATION

Martin Van Buren, as President, has probably been underrated in the popular estimation. Following the Calhoun-Jackson split, as we have seen, he succeeded Calhoun in the Vice-Presidency and in Jackson's favor so that his election to the Presidency was that of "heir apparent."

The Panic of 1837. As soon as Van Buren entered office his administration was beset by the Panic of 1837, the worst economic depression which had yet occurred in this country. The rapid liquidation of excessive debt which accompanies such panics was blamed, in part at least, on the banking policy and hard money practices of Van Buren's predecessor and mentor, which did Van Buren's popularity no good.

To combat the depression, Van Buren set up his own fiscal policies. He favored federal control and, a few months after his inauguration, asked for legislation to establish federal depositories or subtreasuries. These institutions would be independent of both state and private banks; hence the scheme was called the "Independent Treasury." The bank-minded Whigs, still Hamiltonian in their economic thought, opposed the idea; but the Calhoun Democrats supported it, hoping for an increase in United States paper money, the issue of which would inflate farm prices. When the paper-money feature was dropped there were difficulties in securing votes for passage, but the scheme became law in 1840. By use of subtreasuries the government became its own fiscal agent. The plan was repealed in 1841 but when it was later re-enacted it lasted into the twentieth century.

Foreign Relations in Distress. The foreign relations of the United States were complicated by the many defaults of states and businesses which owed money to foreign creditors. Many of these defaults were on debts for canal projects which had to be written off during the Panic. They gave strength to the contemptuous opinions about the United States and its citizens already held by Englishmen and widely publicized by English travelers and writers. Against this background the Van Buren administration had to deal with border incidents and boundary controversies which caused grave concern. One such incident was the "*Caroline* Affair."

After an unsuccessful rebellion in Canada, some of the rebels occupied Navy Island in the Niagara River, from which they harassed the Canadian government. They were supplied by means of the American steamship *Caroline* until in 1838 a party of Canadians crossed into United States waters, captured the ship (inflicting one American casualty), and sent it over Niagara Falls. Anti-British Americans were naturally outraged, and there were several clashes along the international boundary despite Van Buren's attempts to prevent them. When a Canadian, Alexander McLeod, was arrested in Buffalo in 1840 for the "murder" of the man killed on board the *Caroline*, international feeling was tense. However, he was acquitted—to the relief of the American State Department.

Another strain on Anglo-American relations was caused by the vagueness of the northern boundary of Maine, resulting from mutual ignorance of geography at the drafting of the Treaty of 1783 at the end of the War for Independence. Massachusetts had made land grants in the Aroostook Valley, but Great Britain claimed the region. Canadian timber cutting there precipitated the so-called (and bloodless) "Aroostook War" in 1838 and 1839, with both sides making ready to shed blood if events turned that way. Van Buren sent General Winfield Scott to the scene. He arranged a "truce" until the matter could be settled by arbitration.

The Election of 1840. The presidential campaign of 1840 was the most "modern" which had yet occurred, making much use of songs, symbols, slogans, and abuse.

After twelve years in power, the Jacksonians had accumulated a good many enmities. Businessmen were alarmed at the death of the Bank and the strength of labor. Snobs feared the rise of the "common man." States' rights men disliked Jackson's nationalism. Farmers deplored the hard money policy. The discontented attached themselves to the Whig party, which was descended from the Democratic-Republican followers of Henry

Clay and John Quincy Adams, first called the National Republicans and then, in 1836, the Whigs. By 1840 this group's two
most active leaders were Henry Clay of Kentucky and Daniel
Webster of Massachusetts, the latter a noted orator who well
represented the industrial and financial interests of the northeastern states. Unlike some of the southern Whigs, he was a firm
nationalist.

The Whig convention rejected Clay's candidacy and nominated
William Henry Harrison, who had commanded American troops
against the Indians at the battle of Tippecanoe. His other
principal advantages were an absence of political enemies and
the fact that his views on major issues were unknown. A states'
rights Democrat, John Tyler of Virginia, was nominated for
Vice-President. The Democratic convention naturally renominated its incumbent President, Van Buren, but did not name a
vice-presidential candidate. Its platform supported the party's
record and opposed any federal legislation on slavery. This was
the first time that slavery had been introduced as a campaign
issue.

Although the Democratic platform was on the side of vagueness, the Whigs restrained themselves from adopting any platform at all, preferring to exalt the personality of their hero-nomi-
nee who, in time, became an almost unrecognizable symbol of all
the rural virtues. When a Democratic editor uncautiously implied that a pension of $2,000 and a barrel of cider would lure
Harrison back to his log cabin, the delighted Whig managers
made it the "Log Cabin and Hard Cider" campaign. Practically
every "modern" political contrivance except, of course, radio or
television, was used to develop this sturdy, rustic theme. Against
Van Buren the business community skilfully reversed the truth,
making him a symbol of monied power (he was actually a self-
made man). The campaign became one of the most abusive and
irrelevant yet, although the Panic of 1837 was a very important
factor. Harrison carried nineteen states while Van Buren carried
only seven.

The Whigs had learned what the Federalists had not. "Aristocracy" (or "plutocracy") could not win elections as long as it announced its superiority. In 1840 it won by proclaiming itself as
"democracy" and the best defender of the people against an
imaginary phalanx of privilege.

THE NONPOLITICAL ASPECTS OF JACKSONIAN DEMOCRACY

The age of Jackson has been described as a time when every man carried in his pocket a plan for utopia, calling for reform of the relations of man to man or of society to man.

The greatest social problem of American history was the question of slavery, an institution thoroughly clarified and firmly established by the second quarter of the nineteenth century. Eighteenth-century scruples were shown in the Constitution which allowed the abolition of the international slave trade by the Congress in 1808, although enforcement of the prohibition had to be continuous thereafter. As population moved west the domestic or interstate slave trade became brisk and, to opponents of slavery, distressing. The constant dread of slave insurrections, and the occasional outbursts or discovery of alleged plots for uprisings, led to increasingly severe state slave laws to prevent assembly, arming, education, or movement of slaves. Sympathetic persons secretly assisted thousands of Negroes to escape from the South to the North or to Canada. The secret, conspiratorial network of assistance was nicknamed the "Underground Railroad." Simultaneously, Abolitionism, the movement to abolish slavery, grew under such leaders as William Lloyd Garrison, Theodore Weld, and James G. Birney.

Free labor, especially in the North, was beginning to sense the possibilities in the power of organization, which began locally and extended nationally in support of the economic hopes of wage-labor. Following the first local unions, some of which were founded in the eighteenth century (and had to resist prosecutions as illegal conspiracies), the next step was the association of local unions in city-wide trade and labor assemblies of which a dozen existed by the date of Van Buren's election. As the privilege of voting became more widely diffused these labor groups plunged into politics to elect their friends, members, and sympathizers to office. They generally favored the "ten-hour day," easing the treatment of debtors, and universal free education. It was but a logical extension of activities to federate nationally. In 1834 the National Trades Union, an association of city labor assemblies, was formed. A number of craft unions.

had national meetings in these years, but the labor movement as a whole suffered serious shrinkage in the Panic of 1837. The "ten-hour day" for federal employees was established by order of President Van Buren in 1840 and was enacted by several states in succeeding years.

Labor dissipated its energies to some extent by promotion of various utopian schemes, including different kinds of non-Marxist socialism and collectivism, but it also supported the more practical and durable consumers' co-operative movement.

Imprisonment for debt was fairly common in the early nineteenth century. Reform occurred in two stages: first, by raising the minimum of debt for which one could be imprisoned, and, finally, by abolishing the practice entirely. Nine states had done so before 1850.

The desirability of widespread education had been an ideal for generations, although, before 1800, it was not even approximately realized outside of New England. Among the earliest programs of social improvement agitated in the 1790's was universal public education. In the next seventy years this idea was reduced to practice throughout the country. It had to combat the invidious attitude that free schools were for paupers, but under the leadership of Horace Mann and Henry Barnard, free elementary education under state auspices became the standard American practice. In the late 1820's the public high school gradually became a standard institution but, for generations to come, secondary education, for the most part, was chiefly the work of private "classical" academies. "Adult education" through the establishment of lecture circuits was instituted in Lyceum courses; the first national organization of Lyceums was formed in 1831. In the age before automobiles, motion pictures, radio, and television, they were very popular.

The notion that women might benefit by more than elementary education, a not especially popular idea between the Middle Ages and the nineteenth century, was popularized by establishing co-education in high schools and colleges (Oberlin College, the first) and by the foundation of a series of excellent colleges for women, of which four founded between 1836 and 1861 still flourish. A feminist movement, to establish the rights and equality of women in political and economic matters, gathered a core of dedicated women after the first women's rights convention at Seneca Falls, New York, in 1848. Before the Civil War, feminists accomplished little except the passage of laws granting married women some property rights and sharing a knowledge that other women also felt wronged.

Higher education, which had been almost wholly a private concern before the Revolution, saw the beginnings of the state university system before 1860, when seventeen state-supported colleges existed.

Prisons, as distinct from temporary detention centers, were also a product of the early nineteenth century. Earlier punishments had been financial or physical, such as flogging and mutilation. Now the use of incarceration for set periods as a punishment for crime became an accepted procedure. The Pennsylvania practice of solitary confinement was succeeded by the more endurable cell-block system, where the inmates worked together in the daytime at hard labor. This was the "Auburn type," copied in a dozen other places before the 1840's.

One outgrowth of the interest in prison inmates was the discovery by reformer Dorothea Dix of the number of mentally ill locked in jails. She began a lifelong crusade which resulted in the creation of separate institutions in most states for the mentally ill.

Other reformers suggested many reshapings of social customs, ranging from the temperance movement (which began a crusade for total abstinence and state prohibition laws) to the communal experiments scattered throughout the states. The communes agreed on only one thing, that society needed changing. They practiced alternatives that varied from total celibacy to group marriage, from pietistic religion to free thinking. Most offered more rights to women than did the outside world.

8

The Sectional Crisis

We have already seen that in the early nineteenth century a silent revolution of ideas and attitudes was taking place. A rivalry of sections was steadily hardening in the mold until, as will be seen, it could be broken only by war. Westward expansion produced great economic and social changes which not only changed the ways of American living but also increased the hostility of proslavery and antislavery people.

ECONOMIC DIFFERENCES BETWEEN THE NORTH AND SOUTH

The regional diversity between the North and the South can be illustrated in an examination of their different economic systems and how they grew. Population groupings partly tell the story. In 1790 almost half of the Americans lived south of Pennsylvania, and the largest city, Philadelphia, had only 42,000 people. In 1860, of the five largest cities, three were northern with 1,800,000 people, while the remaining two had only 380,000. The slave-states' share of national population had declined from 48 per cent to 39 per cent. Almost a third of the southern population consisted of slaves. The South had declined in relative population because the climate did not appeal to people from northern and western Europe, because of a reputation for unhealthful conditions, and—most important—because a region where labor was the mark of servitude repelled poor but free men who hoped to "get ahead" by means of manual labor. Hence the European immigrants congregated in the North.

Transportation provides another illustration. Except in the matter of steamboats, the South was far behind the North in the improvement of transportation. In canals, roads, and railways the South lagged, partly because the river network was of great utility, partly because the scattered population could not support the tolls and freights, and partly because of the nature of the southern economy.

Northern Economy. The center of northern agriculture was shifting steadily westward to the region of the Old Northwest, from which its products could easily be shipped southward by way of the Mississippi River. But there was a steadily growing industrial population in the northeast which required western grain, pork, beef, butter, and cheese. The completion of the Erie Canal in the 1820's and the steady expansion of the northern railway network gradually tied the northwest to the northeast and established an alliance of these two sections that was to be reflected in national politics. Mississippi River traffic continued to grow, but cotton from southern states was the chief commodity floated by the great river.

The diverse economy of the North provided cargoes for merchant ships so that northern seaports bustled. The establishment of regular sailing schedules benefited the North because shipowners could usually count on outgoing cargoes from the North at any time of the year, while southern exports tended to be seasonal.

The story of American foreign trade is inseparable from the story of the tariff. In this matter the southerners fared well, as they needed to, since most of their sales were made abroad and Americans had to allow foreign buyers to sell to the United States if they were to buy from the United States. After the Compromise Tariff of 1832, the general course of the tariff was downward until the Civil War. This trend was another cause for rivalry, because protectionism was becoming a dogma to northern manufacturers.

The marks of American Industrialism were the great increase in the use of steam power, especially in textiles and transportation, and the enormous rise in iron production. The production methods of the ironworkers improved and the market (for example, for engines and railway rails) grew rapidly. These changes were almost wholly in the North. The handweaving of textiles came to be virtually unknown in New England. In the twenty years before 1850 the capacity of the cotton textile industry doubled. Production in these lines was therefore a reciprocal process, inasmuch as steam-powered machines produced goods and themselves required the production of iron and coal. The same process extended into many other lines of production, such as farm machinery and shoes.

The prodigious expansion of northern industry required financing. The use of the corporation, a practically immortal artificial person, enabled producers to draw on the growing banking system with more promise of safety for the investor than could be provided by the partnership form or the unchartered joint-stock company. The point about the corporation was that it had "limited liability," that is, the stock holders were not liable for the debts of the company beyond the actual assets of the company. Their personal resources were not pledged beyond the amount of their investment. The growth of the New York Stock Exchange, which became the nation's largest security-trading center, symbolized the financial leadership of that city at the same time as it became the largest city in the country. Another source of capital was the foreign investor. By the time of the outbreak of the Civil War, three-fourths of American capital was home-supplied (chiefly from the northeastern states) and one-fourth came from abroad. With the expansion of finance-capitalism came great life insurance companies, credit-rating agencies, savings banks, clearing houses, and the other necessary agencies—again, centered in New York City.

Meanwhile the South had changed much less. It preserved its agricultural environment but at the cost of becoming financially tributary to the North in freight rates, brokers' commissions, interest, and insurance premiums. Southern businessmen grumbled, but for the time being their feelings were no stronger than annoyance or irritation.

The Cotton Kingdom. Long-staple sea-island cotton, easily separated from the seed by hand, was grown in South Carolina before the War for Independence. However, it did not become a major American crop in the eighteenth century because of two reasons: (1) it required the humidity of the sea coast and (2) the other varieties which could grow away from the coast were difficult to separate from the seed. The first difficulty was overcome by the introduction of hardy, short-staple Mexican upland cotton, and the second problem was solved in 1793 by

Eli Whitney's invention of the "cotton gin" (from "cotton engine") which separated the seeds and the fibers mechanically.

Thereafter, everywhere south of the "border states," cotton marched west with the population. In 1790 the country exported a little less than ten thousand pounds; in 1800, it was eight million pounds. On the eve of the Civil War, production was in almost astonomical figures and accounted for more than half of American exports. Cotton was worth almost a billion dollars a year in foreign trade. Most of the cotton which was exported went to British cotton mills. The leading cotton-producing states were Mississippi, Alabama, Louisiana, and Georgia, with the cotton acreage of Texas expanding rapidly. The westward advance of cotton to rich, virgin soils caused a relative decline in the value of southeastern lands, particularly in South Carolina, which helps to explain some of the volatility and quick temper of the South Carolina body politic. The tremendous consumption of American cotton by the British textile industry led some Americans to feel that Great Britain was dependent for its continued existence (or at least its prosperity) on an uninterrupted flow of the cotton from America.

It would be improper to leave the impression that the economy of the South rested solely on cotton. Considered as a whole, the South had a diversified agriculture. Everything suitable to the soil and climate was grown there, but no one became rich on subsistence agriculture. The individual fortunes from agriculture came from cotton and from several other "staple" or cash crops, notably rice, sugar, and tobacco. Rice had been introduced into the coastal flats of South Carolina in the Colonial period and continued to flourish there and along the coast of Georgia in the nineteenth century. Cane sugar, introduced from the West Indies in the late eighteenth century, became a profitable crop within a generation. It required conditions of growth that were found in very few places outside of the state of Louisiana. Tobacco, of course, was the great staple of southern Colonial agriculture from the early seventeenth century, when it was the practical monopoly of Maryland and Virginia. In the late eighteenth century, tobacco crossed the mountains with the pioneers of Kentucky and Tennessee, but Virginia was still the prime producer on the eve of the Civil War.

The chief cereal crop of the South was maize, more commonly

corn. The southern farmers of all degrees and with all sizes of acreage planted this native American grain and produced about a third of the nation's crop. Some of it went to feed animals, another part went to the new national tipple, bourbon whiskey, and the rest of it made the southerners a race of corn-bread eaters.

This attention to staple crops produced that unique social unit, the plantation. It will be noticed that each of the crops mentioned—cotton, rice, sugar, and tobacco—can be grown in large tracts with relatively little attention being given to each plant, little attention as compared with orchard crops, for example. This meant that the land did not require the loving care of the owner but could be cultivated by gang labor under hired supervision. Land could be farmed practically (although not most profitably) by a system of reports rather than personal observation. Hence the growth of huge farms devoted mostly to single crops and worked by slave labor. These great plantations did much of their own manufacturing. In spite of fiction and folklore to the contrary, these establishments were not the typical southern farms. Less than one-fifth of southern farms could be properly styled plantations, and a very tiny minority of planters owned fifty or more slaves.

That minority lived in comparative luxury and had a good deal of leisure, but its luxury would not compare well with that of an urban merchant prince who had access to the arts and sciences and to municipal services unknown to most southerners. Only the South Carolina grandees regularly experienced the city life of the local metropolis (in their case, Charleston). The leisure of the southern planter aristocracy was generally used for outdoor sports, such as hunting, fishing, and racing, or for sociability. The planter class was so widely scattered as to make it next to impossible, in their rural isolation, to club together to patronize cultural or charitable efforts in the way, say, that their Bostonian counterparts did in promoting Harvard College.

One positive, historical effect of their leisure was that it freed men such as John Calhoun, Andrew Jackson, and Jefferson Davis for the school of practical politics—which helps to explain the intellectual strength of the South in American politics for a quarter of a century before 1860.

SLAVERY

The gravest social and moral problem of the American story is the race problem, which is rooted in the now defunct system of chattel slavery. Introduced in the Colonial period, slaves, at the time of the first census, in 1790, numbered almost seven hundred thousand, a little less than one-fifth of the population of the United States. Six-sevenths of the slaves lived in Maryland, Virginia, and the Carolinas. A few more than forty thousand lived in northern states.

The Constitution prohibited the importation of slaves after 1808. The export of slaves from the country was banned during Washington's first term. In 1820 the Congress declared the international slave trade to be piracy subject to the death penalty, but enforcement was not immediately very vigorous. The abolition of the international slave trade was frequently protested by southerners, and it is estimated that another quarter of a million slaves were imported illegally before 1860. The westward expansion of the plantation system created a brisk interstate slave trade between the southeastern and southwestern states, which explains the phrase "sold down the river." By 1860 there were almost four million slaves in the country, with Virginia, Georgia, Mississippi, and Alabama leading in that order. The price of a prime field hand had risen from about three hundred dollars in 1790 to an average of about fifteen hundred dollars.

On large plantations the slaves lived in colonies in specially provided small houses, the group of houses being known as "the quarters." Of course the majority of slaveowners were not "great planters," and their two or three or half-a-dozen slaves lived in outbuildings close to the owner's house. Slaves were either house servants, field hands, or artisans, most being of the fieldworker category. The house servants were usually the ones referred to in expostulations that slaves were treated as "members of the family." The skilled workers were blacksmiths, carpenters, coopers, bricklayers, and so on. Many achieved a high level of skill and the masterpieces of southern domestic architecture are monuments to those anonymous artists. The rewards of slave labor—coarse clothing, coarse diet, crude housing, and maintenance when too old to work—provided a kind of primitive social

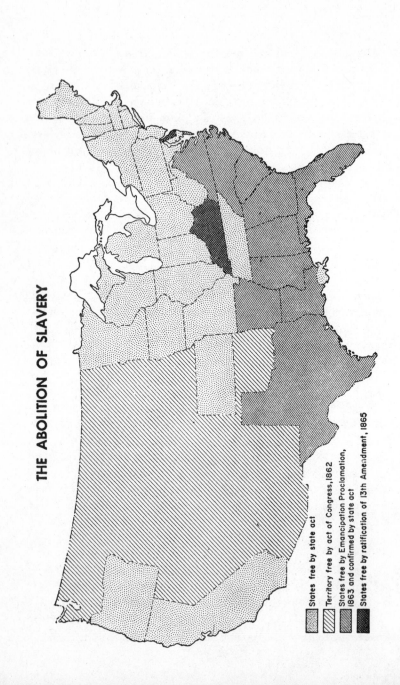

THE ABOLITION OF SLAVERY

Legend:
- States free by state act
- Territory free by act of Congress, 1862
- States free by Emancipation Proclamation, 1863 and confirmed by state act
- States free by ratification of 13th Amendment, 1865

security, but under obligations which free men have almost always spurned.

Education was deliberately restricted to the barest essentials needed to work the land. This did not usually require any ability to read. The movement of slaves was generally circumscribed by regulations which, in many places, were enforced by mounted patrols operating at night. Some owners hired-out their slaves seasonally for agriculture or for skilled work. Some owners allowed their slaves to work for themselves on holidays and keep what they could earn, a means by which a few purchased their freedom. The family status of slaves hardly deserves that description, since either parent could legally be sold away from the place, as could the children. Interracial mixture was not legally tolerated anywhere in the South but, of course, occurred in countless instances. It is thought that more children were born of mixed parentage under slavery than since slavery was abolished. The parentage in such unions was almost invariably white father–black mother. As one black scholar put it, since the abolition of slavery Negro women have had some protection against white men.

From the viewpoint of Western civilization, which has exalted the monogamous family, the slave system seemed destructive by preventing legal marriages and parental responsibility. However, strong family ties did develop among slaves in a different context. A noted feature of emancipation was the number of freedmen traveling to find lost family members. The strength of the black family came outside traditional roles, within a community that often blended African and Western culture. The condemnation by historians rests most heavily not on the forms of black family structure but rather on the hypocrisy of whites who praised monogamy and female chastity among themselves as God's order while creating an institution destructive of these values among blacks.

The Proslavery Arguments. Apologists for slavery and its opponents worked equally hard to justify their positions. Basic to the proslavery argument was the notion that the Negro was of an inferior race. The idea that some peoples were fated by their natures to do servile labor for superior races was justified by references to the fate of the Canaanites and to the obedience-texts of the New Testament. The high proportion of slaves in the Greek and Roman world was cited to show the general acceptance of the institution by mankind. It was asserted that slavery provided a proper means of civilizing the Africans, a kind of bridge between barbarism and civilization. The finest culture of the Western world, whether of Athens, Rome, or Memphis, Tennessee, depended on the presence of slave laborers who allowed a cultivated leisure class to exist. Perhaps more realistic was the argument that slaveowners had acquired their property in good faith and therefore deserved the protection of the law, particularly since the prosperity of the nation depended on agriculture, which in turn depended on slave labor. Finally, the proponents of the South's "peculiar institution" pointed out that the Constitution explicitly noticed slavery, and, therefore, it could hardly be considered alien to the American panorama.

The Antislavery Rebuttal. The opponents of slavery charged that it was a tyrannical institution, the existence of which frustrated the American dream as manifested in the Declaration of Independence, with its flaming words on human equality. The popularization of the democratic ideal which proceeded in the first half of the nineteenth century made the idea of an accidental and permanent condition of slavery increasingly repugnant. Instead of admitting that slavery allowed a cultural improvement, opponents said it was bad for white people because such arbitrary power brutalized the owners, and the existence of slavery made labor appear intrinsically ignoble. As to the Negro being naturally inferior, the examples of outstanding Negroes were held up, the implication being that they were certainly superior in character and ability to many whites. Again, it was observed that in the nineteenth century the culture of the free world was generally accepted as more desirable than that of the parts of the world where slavery existed. The biblical arguments in support of slavery were answered with the New Testament charity-texts and the historical fact that slavery withered in a Christian atmosphere. Before its revival in the late Middle Ages slavery had almost entirely disappeared from the Western world, and in those few places in Europe where it existed they were not Christians but Moslems who were held as slaves. As for an economic dependence, enemies of slavery cited figures to prove that driven labor was unproductive and wasteful when compared with voluntary labor.

The debate over the merits and demerits of slavery was not an academic discussion of abstract rights and wrongs. Some of the people involved were academic people, but they were also people of action dealing with a concrete, immediate problem. The earliest movers against slavery promoted voluntary emancipation, or else mass-transfer of Negroes into separate communities, the movement called "colonization." The permanent fruit of the work of the American Colonization Society, founded in 1817, was the creation in 1822 of the Republic of Liberia in Africa. It has been said that the Society was not so much opposed to slavery as to the presence of free Negroes in the South because they might, by their very presence, encourage those still in bondage to dream of freedom.

The Legislative Battles. From the time of the First Congress, petitions to abolish slavery or ameliorate it were submitted. In the earliest instances they met with forceful opposition only from the representatives of South Carolina and Georgia. The thoughtful eighteenth-century southern leader generally regarded slavery as an evil, but a dying one, which might safely be left to wither in silence. As has been remarked, Eli Whitney changed that.

As early as the 1780's there seem to have been loosely co-ordinated attempts to pass runaway slaves from place to place, ever farther north. By the 1830's probably several hundred runaways annually made good their escape with this help—the method referred to above as "The Underground Railroad." By the 1840's, although it had no formal organization, "the underground railroad" had many permanent "stations" and its workings were well understood by sympathizers. To make the recovery of runaways more difficult, several northern states enacted "personal liberty" laws which threw procedural difficulties in the way of the pursuers.

The turning point in the southern attitude toward slavery came in the Virginia State Constitutional Convention of 1831–32 when several provisions for freeing slaves failed by narrow margins. Never again was the South so nearly equally divided on the question.

The Congress and state legislatures found the slavery question a perennial source of vexation. For example, the governments of the southern states warmly objected to the use of the mails to spread arguments among them for the abolition of slavery and tried to prevent such circulation by legal or illegal means. President Jackson in 1835 recommended enactment of a federal law to bar antislavery matter from the mails. In the Senate a bill to require local postmasters to obey state laws on the subject received nineteen of forty-four votes.

The House of Representatives had a stormier and more lengthy battle on a similar question: whether or not to receive antislavery petitions. Taking advantage of the right of petition as established in the Bill of Rights, antislavery leaders sent many petitions to the House, a large number of which prayed for the abolition of slavery or of the slave trade in the national capital. When angry southerners observed that to give each petition the usual parliamentary processing would mean seriously impeding the work of the House, they roused the former President and now Representative John Quincy Adams to insist repeatedly on the sanctity of the right of petition. Despite Adams's vigorous defense of the petitioners, the House adopted the "Gag Rule" in 1837, which provided for automatic tabling of all such petitions; it was not repealed until 1844. The position of the friends of the petitioners, who were mostly Whigs, constrained Henry Clay to say on the Senate floor that he condemned abolitionist agitators and did not think the Congress could overthrow slavery in any place where it already existed. (This was the "rather-be-right-than-President" speech.)

The abolitionists were widely organized in groups varying in their beliefs as to the best methods to pursue. The American Antislavery Society, led by fiery William Lloyd Garrison and his friends, regarded a "moderate" approach as a compromise with evil. The American and Foreign Antislavery Society broke with them and advocated passive resistance. Frederick Douglass, an escaped slave, traveled and lectured for the abolitionist groups. Abolitionism was inextricably political by the time of the founding of the Liberty party in 1839, an avowedly antislavery party which proposed the abolition of slavery by constitutional means.

THE FEVER OF EXPANSION

The westward flow of pioneers which had continued throughout the history of the nation, reached a foreign border, that of

Mexico, in the 1820's. Spilling into the Mexican province of Texas, the Americans eventually created their own republic there. Moses and Stephen Austin, formerly lead manufacturers in Virginia, later colonists of the Spanish province of Missouri, in 1821 made arrangements with the Mexican government for land grants in proportion to the number of settlers brought in. Their success was copied by other *empresarios*. When Mexico forbade slavery in Texas, friction began which led to violence in 1835 and, finally, to Revolution.

The Lone Star Republic. A punitive force of six thousand Mexicans besieged 188 Texans in the Alamo at San Antonio early in 1836 and annihilated them. Sweeping on toward the Gulf of Mexico, the Mexicans met a Texan army under Sam Houston, at San Jacinto, near Galveston Bay, and were defeated. Their commander, Santa Anna, was captured. Although the Mexican government refused to honor Santa Anna's promise to recognize Texan independence, Sam Houston was inaugurated President of the Lone Star Republic in the fall of 1836. The question of relations with the somewhat embarrassed "mother country" was uppermost in the minds of Texans; their request for admission to the United States was refused in 1837.

The Oregon Question. In another corner of the continent, Americans were moving into a region where boundaries were significant. This was Oregon. Since 1818 the Oregon country (present-day Oregon, Washington, and British Columbia) had been jointly occupied by Britain and the United States. The bone contended for was the present area of Washington. The claim of the United States was based on four types of activity: exploration, fur-trading, missionary work, and actual farming of occupied land. The British founded their claim on the first two types of activity. Since the time of President John Quincy Adams, the United States had offered to compromise on the line of 49° north latitude, but the British would not agree. In the early 1840's American migration had increased so much that the Oregon settlers set up a provisional government, and, elsewhere, Americans began to insist on the northernmost possible boundary, 54° 40'. But the British still hoped to fix the dividing line at the Columbia River.

The Election of 1844 and the Annexation of Texas. The Oregon and Texas questions, occurring simultaneously, became linked in the popular mind. Southerners urged the annexation of Texas. Northerners foresaw Texas as a great new area of slavery and suspected that annexation was a slaveowners' plot. Texas leaders began to court Great Britain, which favored the independence of Texas as a source of cotton and a buffer against the expansion of the United States. As for Mexico, it was immovable. President Santa Anna said that United States annexation of Texas would be an act of war.

The principal block to annexation, however, was not Britain, not Mexico, but the antislavery leaders of the United States who still saw the movement as a conspiracy of slaveholders.

The issue was finally settled in the presidential campaign of 1844. William Henry Harrison, old Tippecanoe, had died shortly after his inauguration in 1841 and had been succeeded by Vice-President John Tyler. An habitual Democrat, he was not on good terms with the Whigs who had elected him. As a man elected by Whigs, he had no standing in the Democratic party. Hence, he was not renominated.

The newly-formed Liberty party nominated James G. Birney, a former slaveholder, and condemned the expansion of the area of slavery, which was, of course, an anti-Texas position. The Whigs named Henry Clay for his third try at the Presidency. Their platform deliberately omitted any reference to Texas. The Democratic party chose James K. Polk of Tennessee (supported by Jackson). It cynically linked the "reannexation of Texas and the reoccupation of Oregon" to capture voters both in the North and in the South. The Oregon half of the equation was emphasized for the benefit of northern voters by the Democratic slogan, "54–40 or fight!"

The popular vote was close. Birney received enough votes in New York to cause Clay to lose the state and, without New York, he lost the nation, and Polk was elected.

When the election returns were studied by outgoing President Tyler, he interpreted them as a mandate to annex Texas. Although it might be difficult to secure a two-thirds vote in the Senate to approve a treaty of annexation, it was possible to get a majority in each House. Therefore, the annexation was made as a simple declaration, a joint resolution of both houses.

The Mexican War. Mexico, outraged, broke off diplomatic relations with the United States and began to build up her armed forces. She also stopped payments owed to American citizens and ordered Americans to leave California. The most explosive question was a boundary question: Which nation had jurisdiction over the land between the Nueces River and the Rio Grande? It was in this disputed area that the detonation occurred. President Polk, now in office, ordered General Zachary Taylor into the disputed region. He had half of the United States Army with him—a colossal total of thirty-five hundred men. (During these threatening maneuvers the Oregon question was settled by an Anglo-American agreement, in 1846, to draw the boundary from the Rocky Mountains to the Pacific at its present place, 49°.)

Negotiations between the United States and Mexico having come to nothing, President Polk, on May 11, 1846, asked the Congress to declare war and gave the members the news that Taylor's force near the Rio Grande had been attacked. Even before the Congress voted war, further engagements were fought and won by American troops in the disputed territory, the victories being chiefly due to the excellent American artillery.

In time the United States Army outnumbered the Mexicans about three to one and had superior equipment. These advantages outweighed whatever spirit the Mexicans might have gained from fighting most of the battles on their own soil. The American plans (rather sketchy) included a blockade of Mexico's Pacific coast from California south and early strikes at Mexico's weak northern provinces, particularly California and New Mexico (which had been eyed by American expansionists along with Texas).

Assisted by Captain John Charles Frémont, of the United States Army, American settlers in California proclaimed the "Bear Flag Republic" in 1846. United States naval and army forces promptly made good the claim. Meanwhile, General Taylor pressed into Mexico proper and captured the city of Monterey in September. In the following month Colonel Alexander Doniphan began a three-thousand-mile march which ended with his successful entrance into Chihuahua on March 1, 1847. General Winfield Scott was sent to follow Cortez's route by landing at Vera Cruz and driving inland. The landings and the Battles of Cerro Gordo and Churubusco were successful operations, and the Americans were within five miles of Mexico City by late August, 1847.

Negotiations for peace, with Nicholas P. Trist representing the United States, occupied several weeks. These failing, General Scott took the national capital and "the halls of Montezuma" in an eight-day campaign. Trist, this time without authority, resumed negotiations and worked out the Treaty of Guadalupe Hidalgo which ended the war. The United States received the area from which New Mexico, California, and parts of Utah, Nevada, Arizona, and Colorado have been carved. Mexican claims to Texas were given up. The United States paid in cash to Mexico and to Mexican claimants eighteen and a quarter million dollars.

THE QUESTION OF SLAVERY IN THE MEXICAN CESSION

The Mexican War brought no display of national unanimity such as has been produced by American wars since 1898. There were quarrels on the subject from the declaration of the war to the peace treaty and on into the postwar organization of the conquered empire acquired from Mexico in the southwest. In the end the war brought the eviction of the Democrats from the seats of the mighty and—in the persons of Whigs—exalted the proud.

The House of Representatives was a sensitive indicator of the popular feeling. To begin with, fourteen members, all northerners, voted against the declaration of war. A special resolution obliquely censuring President Polk's conduct on the eve of war was easily beaten, but it rallied twenty-seven supporters. And sixty-seven Whigs voted against the bill to raise troops and money, one of them categorically blaming the President for the war. Political tension was symptomatic in the mistrust of Whig Generals Winfield Scott and Zachary Taylor by Democratic President Polk and his administrators. Some ill will was generated when enthusiasm for the war was whipped up in the South for fighting the war as an anti-Catholic crusade. Among those who were sceptical of the alleged self-defensive character of the war was a promising thirty-seven-year-old Whig Congressman from Illinois, Abraham Lincoln.

The Wilmot Proviso. Into the broth of political tension at this time Representative David Wilmot, of Pennsylvania, added an

ingredient that made it a pepper pot. A Democrat on bad terms
with the Democratic presidential administration, Wilmot may
have been seeking personal revenge by way of embarrassment.
Or he may—and this seems more reasonable—have been express-
ing his personal conviction. What he did was to move an
amendment to the bill to finance negotiations with Mexico in
1846. His proposed amendment became the famous "Wilmot
Proviso." Its substance was to prohibit slavery in any territory
acquired from Mexico. Polk-men tried to manipulate a compromise by rewording the Proviso so that it only applied to land
north of the old Missouri Compromise line—36° 30'. This amendment to an amendment lost; the House adopted the Wilmot
Proviso by twenty-three votes, but the bill to which it was attached as an amendment was defeated in the Senate. In the
recrimination which followed, the war was re-debated. Democrats defended the war as justified. Whigs called it a plot to
expand the area of slavery by conquest, an unconstitutional
presidential aggression.

The position of the southern Democrats and their northern
allies was championed in February, 1847, by John C. Calhoun,
who set up the standard southern defense in the great slavery
controversy. Calhoun argued that the territories were the common property of the United States; that congressional legislation for the territories could not discriminate for or against
some states; that the Congress could not constitutionally interfere
with slavery nor impose unequal conditions on the admission of
states to the Union.

The Election of 1848. With the Wilmot Proviso on one side
and Calhoun's statement on the other, the lines were now
drawn. The election of 1848 was strongly influenced by the war
and the ensuing controversy over the proper government of the
newly acquired lands. The off-year congressional election of
1846 had been a portent. Whig candidates for the Congress
attacked the war as well as Polk's opposition to "internal improvements" and to a protective tariff. They were heard with sympathy,
and the result was a Whig majority in the House of Representatives.

The Democratic party entered the campaign with serious
strains showing. The Jacksonian tradition inclined northern,
urban Democrats to favor the Wilmot Proviso. In New York

the party split into "Barnburners" (Jacksonian) and "Hunkers" (nonideological). (The Barnburners were so named after the legendary farmer who burned his barn to rid it of rats.) Each group sent a delegation to the national convention of 1848. Neither would compromise, so their seats remained vacant. The split was reflected to a lesser degree in other delegations. The convention ended by nominating Lewis Cass of Michigan, who believed in "popular sovereignty" by which was meant letting the inhabitants of a territory decide for themselves on the question of slavery. However, this view was not written into the platform, which said nothing of importance.

The Whigs had three contenders—Clay and the two hero-generals, Scott and Taylor. Taylor was chosen, and the Whigs studiously avoided any commitments on policy beyond a statement praising Taylor.

The New York Barnburners, the Liberty party, and some anti-slavery Whigs united as the Free Soil party and nominated Van Buren. The Free Soilers opposed the extension of slavery in the territories. The slogan of their party well expressed its character: "Free soil, free speech, free labor, and free men."

In the voting, Van Buren destroyed Cass's strength in New York. Taylor carried the state and with it carried the Whigs back into power.

The Compromise of 1850. The Union had passed through severe crises before, but the difference of opinion and clash of emotions on the question of extending slavery westward brought on the worst crisis of the nation's history.

The quarrel over the Wilmot Proviso was still warmly remembered when the question of the proper organization of Oregon came up for settlement. The people of Oregon had themselves ruled out slavery, but the problem was not solved that easily. In the House of Representatives it was moved to extend the line of the Missouri Compromise all the way to the Pacific. If adopted this proposal would have admitted slavery to southern California and New Mexico, contrary to earlier Mexican enactments. It also would have acknowledged the power of Congress to chart the westward march of slavery—something that Calhoun and like-believers could not admit. A reluctant Senate finally concurred in a House bill which organized the Territory of Oregon (1848) without slavery. Calhoun said it was unconstitutional, but it nevertheless became law. Looking to the next probable fights, forty-eight Congressmen signed an "Address" condemning northern interference with the return of fugitive slaves and censuring the exclusion of slavery from the territories. The lines of division were stiffening.

Before President Polk had left office he had hoped to see California and New Mexico organized as territories, but the slavery controversy prevented this from happening. The discovery of gold in California in 1848 brought a rapid increase in population and made the need for local government even more urgent. President Taylor's hope was that the two regions would organize themselves and apply to the Congress for recognition, thus localizing the problem. California drafted a constitution prohibiting slavery and applied for admission as a free state in 1850. At the time of this application there were fifteen slave and fifteen free states.

The stage was set for clash or compromise. As it worked out, a compromise was arrived at which postponed the clash for ten years. This was the "Compromise of 1850." Henry Clay, from the Kentucky area in and adjoining the Ohio Valley, the region from which most intersectional compromises sprang, began the work by offering a series of resolutions. He proposed to admit California as a free state, to organize the remainder of the new lands without mentioning slavery, to settle the disputed boundary between Texas and New Mexico (which had even caused military operations), to take over the debt of the old Republic of Texas, to take a position tolerating slavery in the District of Columbia while prohibiting the slave trade there, to facilitate the return of fugitive slaves, and to assert that the Congress could not interfere in the interstate slave trade.

The debate on this series of resolutions was one of the longest and most significant of American history. Calhoun, near death, opposed Clay, insisting (on constitutional grounds) that the South could take slavery into the territories. Daniel Webster of Massachusetts (in his famous "Seventh of March" speech) said legislation on slavery in the territories was unnecessary because slavery was barred by geography. He pitched his appeal to nationalism as above sectionalism. William H. Seward of New York spoke for the Free Soil group, supporting the Wilmot Proviso, and defined a "higher law" which took priority over any man-made law supporting slavery. Clay supported his resolutions on the ground that mutual concessions were necessary to preserve the Union, that secession was not a proper remedy for sectional grievances.

More congressional luminaries opposed the resolutions than supported them, but a select committee, headed by Clay, reported favorably on bills to put the resolutions into law.

First, California was admitted as a state, directly, without passing through the territorial phases. This would probably have been done if there had been no controversy because of its rapid increase in population. The Texas-New Mexico boundary was settled. Texas was compensated with ten million dollars, and New Mexico and Utah territories were organized according to "squatter sovereignty," or their own choice as to slavery. The slave trade was abolished in the District of Columbia. The Fugitive Slave Act was strengthened to penalize its obstruction and—especially offensive to many—United States Commissioners were specially rewarded for determining that an accused person was actually a fugitive slave.

Most persons assumed that these settlements ended the slavery controversy with "finality." But abolitionists and southern extremists, called "fire-eaters," were both dissatisfied, as shown by a split in the New York State Whig party and by statements of southern groups dissenting from their "moderate" brethren who accepted the Compromise of 1850. In the North, stronger "personal liberty" laws were the answer of some state legislatures to the strengthening of the Fugitive Slave Act, and slaveowners seeking to recover runaways were harassed and even prosecuted for false arrest.

In the midst of the excitement President Taylor, "Old Rough and Ready," died (1850), probably from the effects of typhoid fever contracted in Mexico. He was succeeded by the colorless Millard Fillmore of New York.

FOREIGN RELATIONS, 1849–50

Although pretty well occupied with their own internal affairs, the American people made some important decisions relating to foreign policy in the years between the Mexican War and the Civil War.

Almost since its discovery there had been hopes of piercing the Isthmus of Panama by digging a canal. In Polk's administration it seemed that British influence in appropriate canalizing areas was becoming too strong. Polk sent an envoy to make an agreement with the Nicaraguans, favorable to the United States. This envoy and another after him arrived at an understanding with Nicaragua for an isthmian canal route, although the British seized an island at the western terminus in 1849. While Taylor was President the Clayton-Bulwer Treaty (1850) was negotiated with Great Britain; it provided (in effect, although not in so many words) that any future canal would be under joint auspices of Britain and America.

This period saw a new type of foreign activity by Americans, the privately organized attempts to conquer foreign soil by expeditionary forces illegally operating from bases on United States territory—the operations called "filibusters." American citizens were led to Cuba (in 1851) by a Spanish adventurer. The sally failed. About fifty Americans were executed and about eighty others taken to Spain. Anti-Spanish demonstrations occurred in the United States. Release of the prisoners was secured with difficulty. William Walker led expeditions into Nicaragua and became its dictator in 1855; there he established slavery, but was evicted by neighboring powers in 1857. He was executed when his Honduran invasion failed in 1859. Such filibusters were usually attempts by southerners to expand the South into a slave-based tropical empire.

In 1853 the lands acquired from Mexico were rounded out by the "Gadsden Purchase" from Mexico of the southern part of present Arizona and New Mexico, land thought necessary for the right of way of a future transcontinental railroad.

The self-isolation of Japan was brought to an end by Commodore Matthew C. Perry in 1854, when he compelled the Japanese to open their ports.

The same year, 1854, saw another manifestation of the southern tropical dream of empire when three American Ministers in the foreign service issued the "Ostend Manifesto" which said the United States must acquire Cuba, by purchase if possible, by force if necessary.

9

The Civil War

In regarding the Compromise of 1850 as "final," the political leaders were probably lagging behind the people. There were too many in both the North and the South who felt that the Compromise was a compromise with evil. Actually, after several years the controversy was renewed and intensified and gained greater momentum until in 1861 it could no longer be contained. The sparks of dissension burst into the holocaust of civil war.

THE COLLAPSE OF COMPROMISE

The presidential campaign of 1852 was one of relative calm, reflecting the spirit of the Compromise. But under the surface lay the embers of the old sectional hatred; it was but two years later that these were again rekindled, with the passage of a controversial bill, the Kansas-Nebraska Act. The events which followed this legislation were fuel to the fire.

The Election of 1852. In 1852 it was again time to elect a President. The Democrats nominated Franklin Pierce of New Hampshire, after prolonged balloting. The Whigs passed over their incumbent President Fillmore and named General Winfield Scott (after equally prolonged balloting). Both parties adopted platforms accepting the Compromise of 1850 and opposing further generation of excitement over the slavery issue. The Free Soil party entered the battle again, with John P. Hale of New Hampshire, and opposed the Compromise and slavery. It favored free land grants and free immigration. Pierce was elected by a decisive margin, carrying twenty-seven of the thirty-one states. The Whigs showed a special weakness in the South.

The Kansas-Nebraska Imbroglio. In 1854 a bill was introduced by Senator Stephen A. Douglas of Illinois and, as amended, provided for the erection of the territories of Kansas and Nebraska with the question of slavery to be decided by vote of the settlers, that is by "popular" or "squatter sovereignty." It passed after more than a hundred days in the Congress. The effect was to repeal the Missouri Compromise, because both territories were north of 36° 30'. Independent Democrats of the Congress published a furious protest at what they regarded as a proslavery violation of a solemn promise to the people.

Writers have speculated on Douglas's motives ever since. He could have been moved by honest belief in popular sovereignty, enhancement of the value of his Chicago real estate (if this area could be organized, a transcontinental railway could be built, terminating in Chicago, thus making that city prosper), a conviction that slavery could not exist in Kansas or Nebraska, secret proslavery views derived from the influence of southern relatives or a hope of securing southern support for his presidential aspirations.

Few events of the American past have called forth such a passionate reaction as did the passage of this act. Democrats became Douglas Democrats or Anti-Nebraska Democrats. Whigs became Cotton Whigs or Conscience Whigs. Free Soilers were able to enjoy the satisfaction of saying, "I told you so." Men who hoped, like the self-deluding ostrich, to avoid trouble by refusing to see it, formed an anti-immigrant, anti-Catholic party—the Native American or "Know Nothing" party. Those outraged by the Kansas-Nebraska Act's permission to extend slavery into the territories and, worse, north of 36° 30', formed a truly political party, the Republican party. Before the Kansas-Nebraska Act there were Democrats, Whigs, and Free Soilers. After the law was passed, there were Democrats (Douglas Democrats and Cotton Whigs), Republicans (Anti-Nebraska Democrats, Conscience Whigs, Free Soilers), and "Know Nothings" (human ostriches). Thus occurred the greatest partisan realignment in American history, so great that no party now in existence can validly trace its succession back beyond the year 1854.

On the basis of climate and location, it seemed certain that Nebraska would be a free-soil area, but Kansas, it appeared, might go either way. And it would take numbers to make any "popular sovereignty" decision. The New England Emigrant Aid Company assisted about two thousand settlers to move into Kansas by 1857. Almost no slaveowners cared to risk their valuable property in the wild West, so the only reply to abolitionist emigrant-aid was the organization of "border ruffians" in Missouri, to ride en masse into Kansas to vote on election days or to terrorize at any other time. The violence that naturally followed showed that Kansas sadly needed effective government. In its first stage that would be the traditional territorial government.

The first territorial governor was A. H. Reeder of Pennsylvania, appointed in 1854. The first territorial delegate was a proslavery man who was chosen by the fraudulent votes of visiting Missourians. A similar invasion elected a proslavery legislature which promptly penalized abolitionist propagandizing. The reply of the antislavery people was to draft the Topeka Constitution, prohibiting slavery. They set up a government, a military organization, and a Free State party. (They were not moved by love of their fellow man who happened to be of African descent, as shown by a clause in their constitution prohibiting *all* Negroes from entering Kansas.) Thus, Kansas had two legislatures. A proslavery governor replaced Reeder who was quickly "elected" delegate to the Congress by the Free State party. By the end of 1855 the territory had been the scene of acrimony and violence which were leading the people of Kansas to the verge of civil war.

Throughout the country Kansas gained the name of "Bleeding Kansas." Early in 1856 President Pierce made it clear that he regarded the proslavery territorial government as the legal government. In the spring actual war broke out in Kansas. The Free State group had been armed with the most advanced small arms, by eastern help. Proslave men raided Lawrence, the Free State center; they killed two, wrecked newspaper offices, and burned and pillaged in the so-called "sack of Lawrence." John Brown, his sons, and two others made a reprisal by seizing five proslavery men and killing them in cold blood. He was not acting for or with the approval of the Free Staters. Feeling had now reached the boiling point. When the new governor warned armed bodies to disperse, the antislavery men seized a town and the slavery men did the same. From summer, 1856, partisan warfare flamed throughout the territory. Including the opening skirmishes, about two hundred people had been killed in the thirteen months before

January, 1857. A new governor, the third in two years, proclaimed Kansas to be in "insurrection." A fourth governor, John W. Geary, used federal troops to impose temporary quiet.

Early in 1856 Senator Douglas had introduced an "enabling" bill which provided for a state constitutional convention in Kansas. At the same time he denounced the Free State element and their out-of-territory friends as lawless. Antiadministration men, on the other hand, favored the Free State group which had already elected two "Senators" to Congress (the "Senators" of course had no legal right to sit in the Senate). The Senate voted for a free election of delegates to a constitutional convention, but the House of Representatives ignored the Senate's act and sent an investigating committee to study the voting practices of Kansas. The committee's report confirmed the tales of fraud, and the House voted to accept the Free State (or Topeka) Constitution as the Constitution of Kansas. The Senate did not concur. Republicans in the Congress then attached an amendment (called a "rider") to the army appropriation bill, providing that no troops would be used to support the proslavery "government" of Kansas Territory. It took a special session of the Congress to get the bill passed without the rider. The emotional climax of the session was the brutal assault, in the Senate chamber, upon Senator Charles Sumner of Massachusetts by Representative Preston S. Brooks of South Carolina, because of Sumner's vituperative speech against the South and against Brooks's uncle, Senator Butler of South Carolina.

In 1857 a proslavery constitution, the Lecompton Constitution, was drafted. Its supporters proposed only the slavery clause for popular ratification. If slavery were rejected, present slaves would remain slaves anyway. The Lecompton Constitution was denounced throughout the North, but President Buchanan supported it. Senator Douglas (considering events a travesty on popular sovereignty) felt compelled to oppose the administration openly. In the voting in Kansas, Free State men abstained, and more than a third of the votes favoring the Lecompton instrument were fraudulent. But the Free State men were a majority in the legislature. They held another election, allowing votes for or against the document. In January, 1858, it was rejected by a ratio of about sixty-three to one.

In 1858 an attempt was made by the administration to bring

Kansas into the Union as a slave state. This was acceptable to the Senate, but in the House it was necessary to compromise by requiring a popular vote on the Lecompton Constitution as a whole and making certain adjustments in the division of the public lands between Kansas and the federal government. The Kansans rejected the Lecompton Constitution in the summer of 1858; Kansas had to wait until 1861 to join the Union as a free state.

The Election of 1856. The nativists of the "Know Nothing" party (so called because its members professed to know nothing of its principles) nominated former President Fillmore. He was also named by the remnant of the dying Whig party. Neither group ventured into the slavery controversy. The Democrats nominated James Buchanan of Pennsylvania. He had not been involved in the Kansas quarrel but was acceptable to the South because he was one of the authors of the Ostend Manifesto, written while he was Minister to Great Britain. The Republicans chose a popular hero, John Charles Frémont, who had been active in western exploration and in the conquest of California. They urged congressional limitation of slavery in the territories and the admission of Kansas as a free state.

The chief specific issues were "bleeding Kansas" and alleged defects in the character of Frémont who had once faced an army court-martial. Democrats also charged the Republicans with being a sectional party, dangerous to national unity. On election day Buchanan did not receive a majority of the popular vote but carried all of the slave states except Maryland (which went to Fillmore) and five free states. His majority in the electoral college was decisive. Frémont polled an impressive vote, and the Republicans looked confidently to 1860.

The Dred Scott Case. At the same time as the change-over from Pierce to Buchanan took place, the Supreme Court was deciding what may well have been the most momentous lawsuit in our history—the case of *Scott v. Sandford,* usually called the Dred Scott case. Scott, as a slave, had been taken from Missouri into territory made free by the Missouri Compromise and then had been returned to Missouri. He sued in state courts for his freedom but lost. He next sued his new master, a New Yorker, in federal court and the case eventually reached the Supreme Court. The case posed several questions: Was Scott a citizen of Missouri (and therefore entitled to sue a citizen of another state in a federal court)? Did his stay in free territory make him free? Another question followed from that one: Had the Missouri Compromise been constitutional?

The court, through Chief Justice Roger B. Taney, ruled that Scott was not a citizen and could not sue. That was enough to dispose of the case, but Taney went on, gratuitously, to declare the Missouri Compromise unconstitutional. Each justice wrote an opinion, but the majority agreed that Negroes had not been intended to be citizens when the nation was founded. Scott was a slave because Missouri law, where he lived, said he was.

The effect of the ruling was that the Congress could not prohibit slavery in the territories because the prohibition would deprive citizens of their property without due process of law as required by the Fifth Amendment. The central plank of the Republican party seemed to be canceled. Antislavery opinion was outraged.

Literary Combustibles. Two authors of the late 1850's poured oil on the flames. Hinton R. Helper's *Impending Crisis of the South* tried to demonstrate that slavery brutalized the South. Frederick Law Olmsted, in a series of works now collectively known as *The Cotton Kingdom*, gave the intellectual history of a traveler in the South, who inclined at first toward slavery, but who later disapproved of that institution and its effects. However, the one book that many people believe supplied the emotional cleavage necessary for civil war was Harriet Beecher Stowe's novel, *Uncle Tom's Cabin.* Published in 1852, this work established stereotypes of oppressed slaves, cruel overseers, and white people living on wealth earned by slaves. It was an instantaneous and colossal success and was soon adapted to the stage as a melodrama. Wandering companies toured in it as late as the 1920's.

The Lincoln-Douglas Debates. In Illinois Abraham Lincoln, a political leader of growing reputation, was nominated for United States Senator by the Republican party's state convention. In his speech on the occasion he said "a house divided against itself cannot stand," and he predicted the country would become all "slave" or all "free." Lincoln debated his Democratic opponent, Douglas, in each Illinois congressional district. Douglas was impaled on the dilemma of "popular sovereignty." If the Dred Scott rulings were correct, then a territory could not prohibit slavery by exercising "popular sovereignty"—and popular sovereignty was Douglas's central plank. He had to repudiate it or the Supreme Court decision in the Dred Scott case. Either way he would have been ruined politically. In his "Freeport Doctrine," Douglas attempted to reconcile the two contradictory views. He stated that theoretically he supported the Dred Scott decision, but in actuality slavery could exist only when supported by police regulations enacted by the local legislatures. Douglas was elected by the legislature, but Lincoln seems to have won the debate.

John Brown's Raid. The controversy was jerked sharply out of the talking stage in 1859 when John Brown horrified the South by committing armed insurrection against Virginia, with a view to abolishing slavery by force. He was hanged for treason, but the atmosphere of debate was permanently changed. Southern "fire-eaters" now moved into the forefront of leadership. Some demanded revival of the African slave trade; others wished for federal statutes to protect slavery in the territories. Senator Jefferson Davis, early in 1860, tried to swing the Senate to formal endorsement of southern views on slavery in the territories. The resulting debate revealed the desperate cleavage of the sections, and serious threats of secession began to be heard in the land.

In this black mood the country approached the presidential election of 1860.

The Election of 1860. As the presidential election approached, the somber mood of the country deepened. An omen was the difficulty of the Democrats in trying to smooth intersectional hostility. When southerners insisted that the party promise to protect slavery in the territories, northerners balked and southerners walked out. The remaining delegates nominated Douglas on a "popular sovereignty" plank. The seceders named John C. Breckinridge of Kentucky and wrote a plank supporting slavery in the territories.

The fragments of the Whigs and Know Nothings formed the Constitutional Union party and nominated John Bell of Tennessee. They obviously intended to preserve the Union by some compromise to be worked out later.

The Republican party rejected the abolitionist William H. Seward, who led in early ballots, and chose Abraham Lincoln. The old Wilmot Proviso became their central plank.

The campaign was odd in that it seemed to be two campaigns.

The Breckinridge and Bell supporters fought hotly in the South, while in the North it was Douglas versus Lincoln. Actually, the appearance of both Breckinridge and Douglas as serious candidates meant grave weakness in the Democratic party and practically guaranteed Lincoln's election. (The brief but destructive Panic of 1857 also helped to unseat the Democrats.) The popular vote was in the ratio of three to two for his opponents, but it was so scattered that Lincoln's electoral vote was decisive—180 of 303 possible votes.

"THE IRREPRESSIBLE CONFLICT"

The election of Lincoln ignited the fuse which set off the explosion. The initial detonation occurred in South Carolina, which, within weeks of the election results, declared itself out of the Union, justifying the act primarily by reference to Lincoln's hostility to slavery. South Carolina's action was followed by other southern states, not because they felt as fiercely about the situation, but because South Carolina had put the constitutional principle of secession in the balance. If secession did not succeed now, it could never succeed in the future. Mississippi, Florida, Alabama, Georgia, Louisiana, and Texas had followed suit by February, 1861. Of course, secession was not suddenly caused by one national election. It was the act of an angry group of southern leaders who felt that their way of life was despised by their northern partners, who saw their political weight in the Union threatened by the probable increase in the number of "free states" in the Far West, and who were convinced that they were the economic thralls of a vulgar, money-grubbing, northern business power. Many of them had idealized the South as the seat of a great civilization and the place of the last stand of the Western world against middle-class materialism and crassness. This was a rather sentimental view, but it had power to move the southerners' hearts and to stiffen their resistance to the fighting point.

President Buchanan mourned secession but said the United States could do nothing about it. Compromisers urged revival of the Missouri Compromise line of 36° 30′ to the western limits of the territories, but this was at once contrary to the Dred Scott opinion and to the platform of the victorious Republican party; hence, an impossible project.

The Confederacy. In February, 1861 the Confederate States of America was founded by a convention at Montgomery, Alabama, with a Constitution similar to that of the United States, but which emphasized states' rights. Jefferson Davis of Mississippi and Alexander H. Stephens of Georgia became President and Vice-President, respectively, of the Confederate States. Davis was a West Point alumnus and had been a military officer, Secretary of War, and a Senator; he appeared "on paper" to be much superior to Lincoln if it came to directing a war.

From December, 1860 to February, 1861 state officials within the Confederacy busied themselves with the seizure of United States military installations, none of which was defended by President Buchanan. These seizures were carried out by state troops at various places from Charleston, South Carolina, to the United States' posts in Texas. The chief and most significant omission was Fort Sumter, at Charleston. When the President tried to supply the fort from the sea, in January, the supply ship was fired upon and withdrew.

Meanwhile, the time for the inauguration of the new President was approaching. On report of a plot to assassinate Lincoln when he arrived at Baltimore, the President-elect was hurried into Washington by special train, at night. In his inaugural address he assured the South that he did not intend to interfere with slavery in the states, but he denied the legality of secession.

His immediate problem was Fort Sumter, which had supplies for only a few weeks. Hearing that provisions were en route, South Carolina forces bombarded the Fort and compelled its surrender. The war was on. It has been said that Lincoln thus maneuvered the South into firing the first shot. Witnesses recorded that the South Carolinians cheered when the United States flag went down. Americans in that mood hardly needed to be "maneuvered." Northerners had felt the crisis less intensely than had southerners, but the fall of Fort Sumter made them welcome Lincoln's call for 75,000 ninety-day volunteers.

Now the border states on the edge of freedom had difficult choices to make. Virginia, Arkansas, Tennessee, and North Carolina overcome their unionist feelings and seceded. Virginia was such a welcome addition to the Confederate States that she was rewarded by having Richmond designated as the national capital. She brought a greater gift to the Confederacy—Robert E. Lee, of the United States Army. The western counties of Virginia balked and in 1863 were permitted by the unionist "government" of Virginia (which sat at Alexandria behind the lines of the army of the United States) to separate and become a new state, West Virginia.

Although a slave state, Delaware was isolated from the Confederate States. Indeed, Delaware showed no inclination in its legislature to secede. Maryland might have seceded but, to guarantee the safety of Washington, military rule was imposed by the federal government along the rail line between Baltimore and Washington, and any incipient secessionism was thereby throttled.

Kentucky hovered in indecision and "neutrality" until an invading Confederate force treated it as an enemy land, whereupon indignant Kentuckians held the state in the Union.

Missouri had a pro-southern government, but the zeal and energy of Captain Nathaniel Lyons of the United States Army raised up a "federal" militia which tore power from the governor's grasp.

The Advantages of the North. In this epic contest, the most deeply etched national experience in the American past, the North had such obvious advantages that the Confederate leaders now seem to have undertaken a forlorn and irresponsible adventure. In white population the ratio was four to one. In industrial development, communications and transportation, financial resources, and naval power the North was far superior. The South was basically agricultural, lacked technology, had a railroad "system" that was almost a self-set trap, and was so situated geographically that its coasts and borders invited invasion from every quarter. The North had a secret weapon of unexpected power in the character of Lincoln and the grandeur of his political theory.

The South could win, but only if the North lacked the will to fight or if substantial assistance—moral, political, and logistic— came from Great Britain and France, who were thought to be dependent on King Cotton.

The War in the Field. The strategy of the Union was to blockade the South, making her dependent on her unbalanced economic system, and to defeat the Confederacy in the field by cutting it into digestible portions. The Confederate strategy was to hang on until the North tired or until European assistance became decisive.

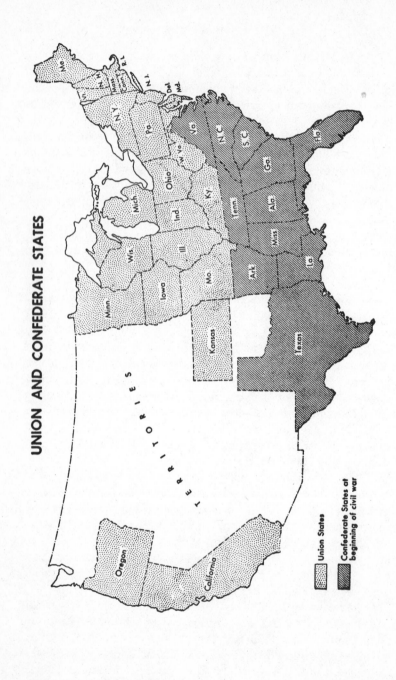

UNION AND CONFEDERATE STATES

Union States

Confederate States at
beginning of civil war

The earliest encounter was premature. Southern troops crushed a Union force at Bull Run, Virginia, in June, 1861, but were too disorganized by their victory to exploit the advantage. The South discovered a great soldier in this battle, "Stonewall" Jackson. This early humiliation gave a new determination to the North, and the Congress voted half a million men for three years. Henceforth, neither side was guilty of overconfidence.

The United States Navy, relatively weak at the moment, was put into effective "condition" and increased in size by the efficient Secretary Gideon Welles. Its primary mission was to blockade. Although never perfectly effective (no great blockades have been perfect), it was only occasionally evaded by "blockade runners." Eighteen Confederate commerce raiders made maritime life hazardous for the merchant marine on the high seas in the early years of the war.

At the beginning, Great Britain recognized the "belligerency" of the Confederacy, and this action meant that world opinion compelled the Union to behave toward the enemy as toward soldiers and sailors, not traitors and pirates. When the British steamship *Trent* was stopped by a United States ship and two Confederate diplomats were removed, the British spoke so heatedly that the two men had to be released to avoid a risk of war with Britain. However, British public opinion seemed generally to be on the side of the United States; the growing British urban population saw the struggle simply as one of freedom versus slavery.

After Bull Run, military affairs moved slowly. The impatient Congress appointed a Committee on the Conduct of the War, dominated by extremely anti-southern members. (This action expressed a very real jealousy of the President, who had gone ahead without consulting them.) The chief military results of the year 1861 were the securing of Kentucky and the preparation of an attack into western Tennessee. The Union forces in the West were led by a significant General, Ulysses S. Grant, heretofore a failure because of drink, but now, unknown even to himself, on the road to fame and glory. Meanwhile, the best-known Union soldier was General George B. McClellan, the thirty-four-year-old commander of the Army of the Potomac, who was jealously attached to all the power and privilege of his lofty office. The ablest soldier of the Confederacy (and some have agreed, the ablest soldier of the war, although such debate is fruitless) was Robert E. Lee, who could have had command of the Union forces but put his state above his nation.

Lee and McClellan opposed each other in the Peninsula Campaign (the York peninsula of Virginia) in 1862. McClellan once reached a point within a day's march of Richmond, but the desperate Confederates drove him off. It has been thought that had his audacity matched his thoroughness he would have won. Lacking the confidence of his government, he was relieved of command, but his successor, General John Pope, did no better and was defeated at Second Bull Run, in August.

Naval designers were showing great ingenuity. They developed underwater rams, contact mines and electrically activated mines, and experimented with submarines. The most successful new development was the armored vessel. When the U.S.S. *Monitor* and the C.S.S. *Merrimac* fought the first marine duel between ironclads in March, 1862 (technically a draw), the wooden-walled navy was made obsolete.

While the war on land seemed deadlocked in the East, great deeds were done in the West. Grant took western Tennessee early in 1862, and naval forces opened the Mississippi as far south as Vicksburg, whereupon Flag Officer David Farragut pushed his squadron up from the Gulf of Mexico and took New Orleans (April, 1862). By the end of the year, eastern Tennessee was overrun, and the Confederates there had dropped back to Chattanooga, the sole railway link between the eastern and western sectors of the Confederacy. But, still in the East—deadlock, despite the fighting of the war's bloodiest battle, Antietam, in September; at Antietam, McClellan, newly restored to command, held the field but was unable or unwilling to pursue Lee's retreating army.

Wars, of course, are fought with words and ideas as well as with small arms and artillery. President Lincoln was steadily urged to make this a war to free the slaves. He, as steadily, resisted, saying it was a war to preserve the Union. In 1862 the Congress took steps of its own, freeing slaves who had been armed against the United States, or who were the property of men warring on the United States. Next it abolished slavery in the District of Columbia and in the territories.

Toward the end of 1862 the President decided to act. He did

so as a military measure and timed his publication to come after the partial victory at Antietam so as not to appear desperate and struggling. In September he announced that all slaves in rebel territory as of January 1, 1863 would be free. Actually these slaves were all within the Confederate lines at the moment. Their freedom now depended on the conquest of their neighborhoods by the United States Army.

Although the Emancipation Proclamation helped to create a favorable public opinion for the United States, it was followed by two grisly defeats for the Union: "the horror of Fredericksburg" in December, 1862, and Chancellorsville in May, 1863.

A further crisis was precipitated by northern resistance to the draft law which was passed to meet shortages of manpower. The law aided those with money and for this and other reasons grave rioting occurred in New York City in July, 1863, which required the use of troops to restore order. The Confederacy also had conscription, and it was almost equally unpopular.

However, the war was at its turning point. Lee reached into Pennsylvania in 1863 but was thrown back in the climactic battle of Gettysburg, July 1 to 4, and his strength declined steadily thereafter. This great victory for the United States was bolstered by the simultaneous collapse of the defense of Vicksburg in the West, whereby General Grant gained control of the entire Mississippi River. The Confederacy lay in two parts. In the same summer the eastern sector was further divided by the taking of Chattanooga, which broke rail connections between points east and west of that strategically located city. It was clear that Grant, the western commander, was now the most successful of the generals.

A crisis with Britain was avoided that same summer when the British ceased to produce cruisers for the Confederate States Navy, those commerce raiders which had so severely hurt the United States merchant marine. A diplomatic affair which defied handling during the war (but was successfully concluded thereafter) was the establishment of a puppet emperor in Mexico, supported by the French army, to make Mexico a satellite of France contrary to the Monroe Doctrine.

From the summer of 1863 the Confederate cause was failing. The United States bested the Confederate States both psychologically and militarily. The psychological weapons were chiefly the stirring words of Abraham Lincoln in the Emancipation Proclamation, the Gettysburg Address (November, 1863), the Proclamation of Amnesty (December, 1863), and his Second Inaugural (March, 1864). At Gettysburg he stated the aim of the war to be the preservation of the greatest experiment in human freedom. In the two later documents he explained a fair plan for reconstructing the nation and called for an end to malice and hate. Thus, he put the cause of the United States on an unshakable moral foundation, beside which "nullification," "states' rights," and "secession" had a dry and abstract appearance.

Union military successes flowed from the successes of 1863. Throughout 1864 the defenses of northern Virginia and the resources of the South were cramped and choked as in a closing vise in the hands of a new master military mechanic, U. S. Grant. The capital of the Confederacy, Richmond, was besieged in trench warfare. The Shenandoah Valley was made useless as an invasion route to the North. Unlike McClellan, Grant knew that war meant killing, and he fought it so.

Election of 1864 and End of War. During this bitter war of attrition, the Republicans and "War Democrats," those Democrats who approved of national policy, merged as the Union party. They nominated Lincoln and chose a Tennessee War Democrat, Andrew Johnson, for his running partner. The Democrats put up the once-more-relieved general, George B. McClellan. Lincoln expected to lose but was decisively re-elected.

Throughout the summer and fall of 1864 General William Tecumseh Sherman, "Uncle Billy" to his troops and Satan to southerners, marched across Georgia to the sea at Savannah. Civilians in a hitherto sheltered place learned that Sir Walter Scott's chivalric tales were poor war correspondence.

The end was near. Confederate desertions increased. At Richmond, Lee foresaw the fall of his capital and tried to break away to the West. At Appomattox Court House, Virginia, in April, 1865, his wonderful Army of Northern Virginia could go no farther; Lee surrendered to an old acquaintance. The war, for practical purposes, was over. Arms had done what laws and debates had not. Slavery and secession were dead. But dead also, in a matter of days, was the great captain-commander of the reunited Union. Abraham Lincoln was assassinated on Good Friday, April 14, 1865, by a conceited and vindictive actor whom he never had injured. The War Democrat from Tennessee, Johnson, took the oath as President.

The Home Front. Why and how the victory went the way it did is not a purely military problem. In this war the entire strength of each antagonist was used, and the fighting men were only the cutting edges of massive weapons. We need also to look to the organization of society for war.

The inspiration of the northern ideal was probably stronger than the southern ideal—the one being concrete and dynamic while the other was abstract, even metaphysical: National patiotism to preserve the Union as a democratic experiment versus localism or sectionalism or state pride. The failure of early military efforts, the lack of foreign intervention, the fact that northern wheat was as valuable to English bellies as southern cotton was to England's trade—these disappointments inevitably lowered the southern spirit. It appears that all through 1864 the South was fighting on nerve, not zeal and high spirits. Nor was the South as solid as the magnolia-scented legend has it. Southern volunteers of every rank fought in the United States forces, and Union sympathizers secretly organized in several southern states. Actually, as we can see now, when the war entered its second year the Confederacy was doomed. Its only real chance had been the possibility of quick victory. The blockade against the South was ruinous. Unable to export its cash crops to its regular customers, the South could not establish the credit necessary to win a war. The cost of the war is not calculable. More than six hundred thousand men lost their lives; the governments spent over eight billion dollars. If this was a war to preserve republican government, no cost could be too high. If Lincoln was wrong, the reader may make his own calculation.

In the economic order the Civil War had the impact of a tremendous revolution. After initial fumbling and groping, a grand expansion occurred in the North. The absence of farm boys made machinery a genuine necessity, and acreage and production jumped high. Every manufacture which an army, navy, and prosperous civilian population could use was now thriving. The industries of woolens, shoes, meat packing, iron, and oil were particular beneficiaries. With the southerners out of the Congress, the industrial community secured the adoption of an almost permanent protectionist tariff policy on the argument that it paid the cost of the war (or at least loaned it) and its prosperity should be thus guaranteed.

The war could not be (or, at least, was not) financed by taxation. (Although a federal income tax was levied for the first time, it was a meager source of revenue for the government.) Hence, more attention had to be given to the banking system than it had yet received. To create a reservoir of credit the government chartered special banks under the National Bank Act of 1863. The act provided that United States bonds could be used to capitalize such banks. State banks were deliberately handicapped by taxing their issues of bank notes. The promoters of the National Banks profited doubly; they drew interest on the bonds which were their reserves and on the loans they made. Government bonds were also sold to the public and to institutional investors (trustees, savings banks, and so on). The principal salesman was Jay Cooke, of Ohio, "financier of the Civil War." Another device was the issue of paper money (greenbacks) supported only by the government's indefinite promise to pay. This was the quickest and most effective method, although it was inflationary and thus raised the cost of the war in dollars. The value of greenbacks fluctuated with the fortunes of the United States armed forces. This rise and fall attracted the interest and sharp intelligence of speculators. Speculation in currency, and, even more, in stocks and bonds reached new levels of excitement and participation. Dividends occasionally ran as high as 40 per cent. For the first time the United States was accumulating capital rapidly.

But in the South, with small credit and less cash available, everything invested in defeat was lost. For day-to-day expenses the Confederacy printed about a billion dollars in unbacked paper money, all worthless at the end of the war.

In addition to the abolition of slavery (which was the greatest social result of the Civil War), the great conflict brought about other sweeping social changes.

Free labor, except for temporary full employment, made no gain during the war. Organization did not proceed. Wages rose more slowly than did farm prices, farm prices more slowly than manufacturers' prices. But the Republican Congress pushed through what had long been a hired-man's and tenant's dream, the Homestead Act of 1862, by which 160 acres of public land was given to anyone who cultivated it for five years. Although tens of thousands of farm families benefited by the Homestead Act, its effects did not measure up to the hopes of its sponsors. In fact, only one-sixth of the public land which was given away by the government went to *bona fide* farmers. Every kind of fraud was practiced by land speculators, and vast tracts were given to railroads (sometimes in dubious circumstances) to encourage their construction. In the same year great tracts of land were reserved for the endowment of state colleges of agriculture and mechanics by the Morrill Act. Sixty-nine land-grant colleges have since been founded. Partly to secure uniformity of operational practices, railroads tended to merge into fewer systems. Most of them made money during the war, but the southern roads were severely damaged. Talk of a transcontinental line was revived, and, in 1862, a great land grant was passed through the Congress. By 1869 the continent was linked by the completion of the Union Pacific line.

Women took a larger part in this war than in any previous one: organizing military nursing, and recreational facilities; replacing the schoolmaster with the schoolma'am; promoting public loans and raising private charitable funds. Church groups supported the recruiting chaplains (who had been commissioned beginning with the Mexican War). The good will of the civilian community was made effective through new organizations, including the United States Sanitary Commission, the United States Christian Commission, and numerous local groups which helped former slaves, transient service men, and military dependents. This charity and benevolence was in luminous contrast to profiteering, corruption, and the ostentatious vulgarity of the public lives of the newly rich.

To the American people at large the most valuable—and to some, unexpected—legacy was the United States Constitution, which, although its provisions may have been dented, remained intact. Abraham Lincoln fought a civil war against fellow citizens without destroying the basic instrument of government. Whether any but Lincoln could have done it is debatable. Other than the Thirteenth Amendment which freed the slaves, the constitutional effect of the Civil War was to establish as a truth that the Union was a Union of the people of the United States.

10

Reconstruction

After the bloody Civil War the victorious North faced the problems of repairing the Union. From the attempts, and from the quarrels which divided the victors, came a harsh struggle that has left a bitterness which still infects the relations between the two sections.

THE POSTWAR SOUTH

The society of the South was in upheaval. Its natural leaders, the planters and professional men, were being deposed by the victors in retaliation for their attempt to dissolve the Union. At the bottom of the southern social pyramid were several million slaves who had been set free with little or no preparation for life in liberty. (It is a tenet of Western civilization that all men are fit to be free, but assistance out of a servile status into freedom was certainly necessary at the time.) The economy of the South had been disorganized. Much of its productive property—farm buildings, gins, warehouses, and the like—had been destroyed. Its railway network and rolling stock were greatly damaged. Its financial structure had been undermined by deliberate inflation. Most of the men who might be best suited to revive the economy and revise the society were suspect because they had been leaders of the Confederacy. Northerners were unable to believe, for example, that men who had owned slaves could be trusted to advance the interest of newly freed Negroes.

The blacks had come from a high culture in Africa but had been forcibly deprived of their arts and crafts. A few had learned new skills, but most were now practiced only in the rougher work of agriculture. They were not fitted for a world where material plenty depended on a mastery of figures, contracts, and "how-to-do-it" directions because most were illiterate. Left to themselves they would be the prey of sharpers and exploiters. Left to their old masters—it was believed in the North—they would soon be tricked into a slavery under some other name.

THE BATTLE OVER RECONSTRUCTION

The problem of the treatment of the conquered South had been long on President Lincoln's mind. It was his conviction that there was no such thing as true secession, hence that the states had never left the Union. Since it was the President's job to execute the laws, Lincoln believed it was his job to do what was necessary in the southern states to enable the federal government to function there. Late in 1863 he announced his plan (the "10 per cent plan"): amnesty for all but a few specified groups of southerners, and state self-government for any southern state in which 10 per cent of the voters of 1860 swear loyalty and accept the abolition of slavery. This was too lenient for many congressmen. They refused to seat men elected from states so "reconstructed," and they set about formulating a policy known now as "radical" reconstruction.

Johnson's Policies. When Johnson became President, on Lincoln's death, some of the so-called "radicals" thought he might be more inclined to their way of thinking, but Johnson continued Lincoln's program. While Congress was out of Washington, in recess, he recognized four southern governments which had been set up by Lincoln. In personality Johnson was a keen contrast to Lincoln. Earthy where Lincoln was spiritual, stubborn where Lincoln, in politics, was somewhat conciliatory, truculent where Lincoln was humane, Democrat-Unionist where Lincoln was Whig-Republican, Johnson was living proof that no man should try to wear a predecessor's mantle, especially in politics where the ability to be oneself, and not "act like" a politician, is all too rare.

Johnson moved quickly. He organized governments in the remaining, former Confederate states; he issued pardons generously, and, when the Congress met in December, 1865, he announced that the United States was whole again.

Congressional Reaction. Johnson's measures were not acceptable to the Congress, which refused to seat the newly elected southern representatives. The reaction of the Congress could have been predicted by anyone who recalled the 1864 Wade-Davis Bill, which Lincoln had disposed of by a much-criticized pocket veto. Now Congress was worried by the increased congressional representation for the South, since former slaves would now be counted in full in apportioning representatives, but former Confederates were not inclined to include blacks within the electorate. The victorious North, with a Republican majority, was faced with the ironic possibility of a Congress controlled by former Confederates and northern opponents of the war. Johnson's intention to follow Lincoln's reconstruction plans would, they believed, hurry such a day. Congress set up a joint House-Senate committee of fifteen to inquire into southern voting and participation in legislation. The committee was led by congressmen who argued that the southern states were either "conquered provinces" or had committed "suicide." Either interpretation supported the committee's contention that there were no southern state governments and that the Congress was the sole agency of reconstruction.

The President versus the Congress. The contest between President Andrew Johnson and the congressional "radicals" grew into an open battle for control of the reconstruction program. It was to erupt beyond the limits of normal administrative processes and became an issue of the off-year election of 1866. The results of that election were to be interpreted as a mandate by the victorious congressmen, and the next few years witnessed the strongest attack on executive authority and power since the days of King George III.

The first skirmish of this phase of the political war was the passage of "Black Codes" in southern states, which were codes of racial law that appeared to enact second-class status for the Negro. The Congress responded by strengthening an emergency agency, the Freedmen's Bureau, to enforce the Negro's civil rights. Johnson vetoed the bill, but it passed over his veto (July, 1866).

Next was the Civil Rights Act, giving citizenship to all (except Indians) and guaranteeing civil rights. The Supreme Court found this act unconstitutional, saying that these matters had been reserved to the states. To give the federal government power in this field the Fourteenth Amendment was drafted, defining national citizenship and protecting its privileges and rights. Never again could a Dred Scott be turned out of court on the claim that he was not a citizen. The Dred Scott case was permanently undone.

In the congressional campaign of 1866 Johnson tried to win popular support by means of a speaking tour which did him little good. He also tried to preserve the Unionist coalition which had won the election of 1864, but he failed. Republicans identified their party with the preservation of the United States and carried the Congress, two to one.

"Radical" Reconstruction. The morally strengthened Congress began its full-scale offensive against "presidential reconstruction" by passing the First Reconstruction Act (over Johnson's veto) which divided the South into five military districts. No state was to be readmitted unless it allowed Negroes to vote and unless it ratified the Fourteenth Amendment. When southern states failed to call the necessary constitutional conventions, other reconstruction acts were passed, putting the political machinery under the Major Generals of the occupying forces. Under this system the state governments established according to Johnson's plan were discarded, and voters acceptable to the Congress were organized and put in control. Names applied by resentful southerners to those who met the standards and who co-operated with the United States have entered our daily language and have, in a way, convinced posterity that the South was abused: "carpetbagger" for a northern civilian who worked in the South; "scalawag" for a southerner who co-operated with congressional reconstruction.

The Congress continued its work. New state constitutions were written which disqualified former rebels and which guaranteed for all men their civil rights and the privilege of voting. Seven states were ruled to have met the standards for readmission to the Union by the end of 1868. The Fifteenth Amendment, which denied race as a standard for the privilege of voting, was initiated in 1869 and was proclaimed as ratified in 1870. By the middle of 1870 all the southern states were held to be duly qualified, although Georgia had been briefly resubjugated owing to the expulsion of Negroes from the state legislature in 1869.

The Impeachment of Johnson. At the same time as the Congress "reconstructed" the states, it was devising a series of laws which, if they had been permanent, would have more effectively "reconstructed" the Presidency. In fact if the trend had persisted for a generation, the President might have been reduced to a patriotic symbol.

Bitter at their frustration by Johnson, the "radicals" in Congress plotted to unseat him from office by passing legislation which they hoped he would violate. The Army Act prohibited the President from giving orders to the army except through the General of the Army, who, at the time, was General Grant. This law was flagrantly unconstitutional. The Tenure of Office Act denied the President the authority to dismiss any official who had been appointed with the confirmation of the Senate, unless the Senate approved the dismissal. (This notion had been argued at the very inception of the republic and had been discarded.)

Johnson dismissed Secretary of War Edwin Stanton. Within weeks the House of Representatives impeached Johnson on eleven charges, one of them being the violation of the Tenure of Office Act. The trial, by the Senate (as provided in the Constitution), ran from March, 1868, to the middle of May. It is now plain that the prosecution was a political, not a criminal, case. In order to be convicted, an impeached person must be voted guilty of a "high crime or misdemeanor" (the word "high" modifies both) by a two-thirds vote of the Senate. Because several Republicans put conscience above party, the prosecutors failed of a conviction by one single solitary vote.

THE GRANT ADMINISTRATION

The Republicans, mindful of the glory of a successful commanding general, named Grant as their presidential candidate for 1868. He was opposed by Governor Horatio Seymour of New York. Grant's supporters "waved the bloody shirt" (reviving bitter Civil War memories). The Democratic platform was inflationary, but their candidate was a "hard money" man. The popular vote was close; the deciding factor in Grant's election was the Negro vote.

Grant would be remembered less frequently but with greater admiration if he had failed to be elected. As it was, his terms as President tarnished the memory of his judgment and prudence, although his presidential record certainly established him as a man loyal to his friends, even if they were unworthy. Perhaps his main weakness was a too great respect for material achievement. He seemed to think that business cleverness proved the possession of other qualities desirable in the leadership of a republic. In the end the administration of a simple man was corrupted by his harpy friends and managers.

Attempts at Legislation. The currency program, the Civil Service gesture, and the Amnesty Act, whether one approves of them or not, were constructive public measures. As such they are the only really memorable measures of Grant's first term which were not part of the congressional reconstruction program or part of the squalid tale of corruption.

Grant's first term was marked by a currency dispute. Representative George H. Pendleton of Ohio had proposed the "Ohio Idea," which was to pay off the increased national debt by printing more paper money—the "greenbacks" of the war years. The Congress, instead, in 1869, decreed that government bonds be paid in gold. Meanwhile, over a third of a million dollars in greenbacks continued to circulate.

There was current a hope, which still exists, that the standards of government performance would be raised by choosing public employees by merit only. The Congress authorized a Civil Service Commission but made no appropriation for it. The Commission accomplished nothing and its first head resigned, after which the Commission ceased to be.

In 1872 the Congress passed the Amnesty Act which removed the legally imposed political disabilities on nearly all veterans of the Confederate Army. Only about five hundred men were thereafter excluded from public life.

Political Corruption. In the growing industrial centers the war-begotten wealth made Americans appear a vulgar, gluttonous, avaricious people. Misbehavior and corruption were by no means confined to public life, but they were more noticeable there, since Americans have declined to admit an important political truth: that their system is not intended to staff the government with an elite but with a cross section of the voting population. An example of the tone of the time was the conduct of William Marcy Tweed and his fellows who looted the treasury of New York City of not less than seventy-five million dollars. In a more respectable part of the city, Jay Gould and James Fisk tried to "corner" the gold market by spreading false rumors of the government's gold policy. When the falsity of the rumors was shown, the price of gold fell sharply, and many people were ruined on a day of 1869 remembered as "Black Friday."

The worst scandal to be revealed in Grant's administration was the episode of the Crédit Mobilier which reached high enough to dirty the name of Vice-President Schuyler Colfax. The Crédit Mobilier was a construction company formed to build the Union Pacific Railroad. Shares of the company were given to certain members of the Congress in return for political favors. By charging the Union Pacific exorbitantly for its services, the company intended to make exorbitant profits from the construction. After a congressional investigation two Representatives were formally censured.

The Reconstruction Cases. Of greater permanent importance than the scandals of the Grant administration were several vastly important rulings of the Supreme Court in cases arising out of the Civil War. (Cynics have noticed that all these cases were decided long after the war was over.) In *Ex Parte Milligan* (1866) the court said that civilians were not to be tried by courts-martial where the civil courts were open. In another case Congress removed jurisdiction (which was Congress's constitutional right) before the Court ruled. But a year later the Supreme Court made its most significant reconstruction ruling. In *Texas v. White* (1869) the Court finally, once and for all, ruled that secession was impossible. (The Articles of Confederation provided for "perpetual" union; the Constitution said the new Union was even "more perfect.") Then the Court went on to give Congress the unquestioned right to reconstruct politically states that had been in rebellion. In *Ex Parte Garland* and *Cummings v. Missouri* (both 1867) the Court heard cases in which former Confederates had proved they were barred from their professions by inability to swear they had not been rebels. The court nullified such loyalty oaths because the Constitution forbids "test oaths."

The Liberal Republican Uprising. In the Republican party there was an element which looked upon Grant's intimates with distaste, as on a group which put its own interest before the common good. It also had reservations about the "radical"

Republican program of congressional reconstruction. Some of the leaders were Carl Schurz, Gideon Welles, Charles Francis Adams, and Horace Greeley. Schurz was a German liberal who rose to high rank in the war. Welles had been Secretary of the Navy. Adams (son and grandson of Presidents) had been Minister to Great Britain. Greeley edited the *New York Tribune*. As a group they and their followers were known as the Liberal Republicans.

In 1872 they met in convention and nominated Horace Greeley for President, in the hope of unseating Grant. The Democrats hopefully did the same. The regular Republican organization, of course, renamed the hero Grant. In the popular vote Grant ran ahead of his 1868 record, and in electoral votes won in a ratio of about nine to two. Poor Greeley found politics so cruel that he said he was not sure whether he had been running for the Presidency or the penitentiary; he died a few weeks later.

The Panic of 1873. The Panic of 1873 was probably precipitated by reckless speculation in railroads and by an expansion greater than could be managed with the skills then possessed by the responsible business leaders. Banks were weakened by the country's internal strains, and agriculture was depressed by a falling off in exports. The first symptom was the failure of Jay Cooke and Company, and the panic was on. It left a permanent scar in the national history.

The Second-term Scandals. Apparently the Grant-men felt they had been given a full endorsement by the electorate. It is evident that they were not intimidated by the Liberal Republican movement because new scandals, equal to the old, were found.

The first shocker was not illegal, but one could say it was in exceedingly bad taste. The Congressmen voted themselves a retroactive 50 per cent pay increase. Public clamor at this "salary grab" caused them to lose their nerve and repeal it. In 1875, an investigation ordered by the Secretary of the Treasury resulted in the indictment of 238 members of a swindling group—the "whiskey ring"—for defrauding the government. Among them was O. E. Babcock, Grant's private secretary. When the President offered himself as a character witness, the prosecutors could not bring themselves to push the case. A congressional investigation in 1876 revealed that Secretary of War William W. Belknap took bribes in return for awarding jobs in the Indian country. He resigned, to avoid trial, after impeachment, and was acquitted on the technical ground that the Senators agreed his resignation put him out of their reach.

The Election of 1876 and End of Reconstruction. Grant's second term saw the rise of active hostility, both northern and southern, to the process of congressional reconstruction. The Liberal Republican movement was a northern manifestation. In the South the activities of secret terrorist societies brought passage of the Civil Rights Act in 1875. This act was aimed at the Ku Klux Klan and similar secret organizations of night riders who aimed to restore white supremacy by frightening the Negroes. Federal laws to counter them had been found partly unconstitutional. In 1875 the Civil Rights Act attempted to guarantee equal rights in public places and in jury service, regardless of race. Some years later the Supreme Court ruled this an attempt to prevent the infringement of rights by private individuals, an attempt not warranted by the Fourteenth Amendment which only operated on public officials in their public capacity.

It was the direct effect of the tangled election of 1876 which ended formal, congressional, or "radical" reconstruction. The Republicans nominated Rutherford B. Hayes of Ohio after the elimination of James G. Blaine of Maine who, like so many others, suffered from the endemic railroad-poisoning of the times. The Democrats put up Samuel J. Tilden of New York. In the popular voting Tilden had a plurality of a quarter of a million, but the returns in Oregon, South Carolina, Florida, and Louisiana were disputed. If Tilden were to lose all of the disputed electoral college votes he would lose the Presidency by one vote.

In practically all election disputes in the United States the decisions are made on straight party lines. Career politicians, their bread at stake, fight for their livelihood as fiercely as men in any other business. There is little in the Constitution to guide the mechanics of elections. Therefore, in the disputed election of 1876 the Congress had to originate a technique for dealing with what could become a very unpleasant situation. Its answer was the Compromise of 1877, which created the Electoral Commission composed of five persons each from the House, the Senate, and the Supreme Court. The Commission, as finally selected, had eight Republicans and seven Democrats. Every dispute in the contest was settled by an eight to seven vote, along party lines. Southern Democrats agreed to accept the election of Hayes to the presidency in return for demilitarizing the South, for putting a southerner in the cabinet, and, it must be added, for aiding in the construction of the Texas and Pacific Railroad. The greatest long-range effect probably was that the Negro was returned to the political leadership of men committed to "white supremacy."

Reconstruction was ended. As Southerners forced the Negro out of political importance, they labeled the age of black participation as one of inefficiency and corruption, resulting in higher state expenditures and tax rates. On the other side, historians point out that "Negro legislatures" built the first schools, hospitals, and asylums for the dependent in many parts of the South. Ironically, the white South "redeemed" itself from "black rule" by election fraud and terrorism.

Foreign Relations. The distractions of a civil war and its turbulent aftermath did not allow much time for concentrating on international relations, but some problems pressed hard for settlement.

Relations with Great Britain had been cool through the war years, with British upper-class sympathies appearing to be on the Confederate side and British assistance to blockade-runners a source of ill-feeling in America. Britain was soon given a grievance from this side of the water by the activities of an Irish revolutionary society, the Fenian Brotherhood, which launched unsuccessful invasions of Canada from New York and Vermont, in 1866 and 1870, with the idea of conquering Canada and ransoming it in exchange for Irish independence.

Another source of ill will was the claim of the United States for damages inflicted by British-built Confederate warships, the *Alabama* and others. Some Senators proposed to add to the "*Alabama* claims" the "indirect damage" of prolonging the war (over two billion dollars) and suggested taking Canada as compensation. Eventually the direct damage claims were settled by arbitration as provided in the Treaty of Washington of 1871, and fifteen and a half million dollars was awarded to the United States.

The French intervention in Mexico required attention if the Monroe Doctrine were to be preserved (see page 119). An American ultimatum in 1866 backed by a veteran army in Texas soon brought the withdrawal of French troops and the prompt collapse of the puppet Emperor Maximilian, who was executed by the Mexicans.

In 1867–68 Secretary of State William H. Seward persuaded the Congress to accept Russia's offer of Alaska for a little over seven million dollars. Scoffed at as "Seward's folly" or "ice-box," it has since shown the purchase price to have been trivial.

Islands occupied a good deal of American attention. Midway Island was taken over for the United States by a naval officer, in 1867, by right of earlier discovery. Seward tried to buy the Virgin Islands from Denmark, but the Senate showed no interest in ratifying the treaty he had negotiated. President Grant conceived a fondness for the idea of annexing Santo Domingo and in 1870 engaged in a power struggle in his Cabinet and in the Senate, but his proposal was defeated. In 1873 Americans in the service of Cuban rebels were executed by the Spanish government after capture in the gunrunning ship *Virginius*. Secretary of State Hamilton Fish secured an indemnity for their families. Finally, the first legal step toward the Americanization of Hawaii was the signing of a commercial treaty with its royal government in 1875.

11

The Age of Transformation

In a brief thirty-five-year period, from the end of the Civil War to the advent of the twentieth century, were laid the foundations of modern America. The country changed in all aspects, from its physical proportions to its foreign policy. Population swelled, and the land stretched itself to full size with the closing of the frontier. The economic revolution wrought by the Civil War ushered in a remarkable period of industrialization which changed America from an agricultural economy to an industrial power. The impact of this transition was felt by every American businessman, farmer, and worker. Although America was primarily concerned with internal development at this time, it was not long before her growing industrial and commercial might made her aware of the possibilities that lay beyond her natural borders.

THE LAST WEST

The end of the nineteenth century saw an end to "the wild West" which has since become the most glamorous chapter of American history in the minds of millions of Americans. The West is also a technical term of the historical profession, meaning the relatively unoccupied region immediately ahead of the advance of population which moved across America generally from east to west. Hence, there was a time when Massachusetts was West. But, ordinarily, the phrase "the West" is used to identify the high plains and mountain region between the longitude of the Missouri River and the eastern boundary of California, from Mexico to Canada. This was the last West to be settled and organized.

Subjugation of the Indians. The last West was also the last home of the nomadic Indian who had been driven in that direction since 1607 and who had "finally" been guaranteed the high plains as his own, forever, when statutorily dispossessed of everything east of 100° (except for scattered eastern Indian "reservations"). During the Civil War, Indians of the plains twice rose against the unremitting pressure of white settlement. Each time they lost much and gained nothing. The last great Indian success was the slaughter of General George A. Custer's command on the Little Big Horn River in 1876.

The Indian business of the government consisted of quietly sanctioning the slaughter of the buffalo—the Indian's main source of food — conferences with Indians, "treaties" (as though the tribes were sovereign nations), presents and rations given annually in exchange for the surrender of Indian rights by "treaty," weak protection of Indians and whites from each other, war, defeat of the Indians, conference, "treaty" again, and so on around the cycle. The detailed administration of Indian business arising from these contacts was in the hands of the Indian Bureau of the Department of the Interior. Until the time of President Hayes and Interior Secretary Carl Schurz, the Bureau had a poor reputation for honesty and efficiency.

In 1887 Congress tried to create a humane policy towards these "wards of the nation" by passing the Dawes Act, aimed at integrating the Indian into American life through ownership of land for farming. The Indian had no choice. He was protected from speculators and frauds (or moving) by being prohibited from selling the land for twenty-five years. The final reward was to be set apart from the tribe and gain U.S. citizenship. The actual effect was to release additional land to whites, undermine tribal government, and leave the Indians on marginal land. It was not until 1924 that citizenship was conferred on all Indians in America.

Settlers of the West. Four types of men developed the last West: the explorer (who was usually a soldier, a missionary, or a trapper), the miner, the cowboy, and the farmer, in that order. Excluding the farmer, these were the heroes of the American saga. They shared in common—poverty and a hard life.

The miners sought gold and silver. Nevada, Colorado, Idaho, Montana, Wyoming, and the Dakotas all had mining rushes in the years after the Civil War. The surest way to wealth, although not very frequent, was to find a rich deposit and sell one's claim to a company with sufficient capital to develop the site. The miners made a lot of history, precipitating Indian wars, causing territorial governments to be established, emphasizing the need for communications, and contributing precious metal to the national supply of currency, thus helping to solve a perennial problem of that age.

The cowboy of fact was a herder of semidomesticated beef animals. The rich "buffalo grass" of the open plains provided free food for the taking. The industry of grazing private cattle on public grass began in Texas and spread northward into Canada when it was seen that the animals could survive the winters. With the development of railroad refrigeration, western cities were able to pack this relatively inexpensive beef and compete successfully with older packing centers. The great day of the open range cattle industry lasted from the end of the Civil War to the middle of the 1880's. The cattle ran wild. Their calves were rounded up annually and branded with the owner's mark. There was also an annual roundup of animals to be sold, followed by a long drive of the herd to the nearest railroad, sometimes hundreds of miles. On restless nights the cowboys rode around the herd, crooning soothingly, a practice which developed into the "cowboy song" of the music business.

The coming of the farmer meant the end of the open range and the domestication of the wilderness. The invention of barbed wire in 1874 made it possible to fence the treeless plains, and the open range cattle industry became another kind of farming, although there were local wars when unyielding cattle barons tried to bar the would-be farmer from the land or cut the fences he erected. The farmer, or the "nester" as he was called, devised means of insuring his other needs. He used the windmill to pump small quantities of water regularly, and on the barren plains he built houses of sod, cut like bricks, to provide his family's shelter. The army kept the Indians away most of the time. Railroads which had acquired vast tracts of government land pushed steadily westward and conducted vigorous campaigns to sell farm lands along their tracks in order to finance construction and to assure freight for the future.

Today the West is much like the rest of the country, except

that, like the former Confederate states, it is somewhat more sentimental about its past than are most regions.

INDUSTRIALIZATION

The region that is now the United States was generously endowed with natural resources which could be exploited in order to develop heavy industry. Most of the raw materials which are valuable in the manufacture of machinery, transportation facilities, and consumers' goods lay ready to be worked into wealth. Iron, coal, and oil—the basic ingredients of industrialism—were plentiful, and needed only the application of technical genius, organizational skill, and labor.

Machine tools, the tools that make goods, were steadily improved in the latter part of the nineteenth century, always with an eye to speedier production and lower unit costs. The railway network expanded rapidly until the railroad map of the United States looked like a spider's web, with the steel filaments connecting all important sources of raw materials, their places of manufacture, and their centers of distribution. The railroads contributed to the industrial growth not only by connecting these major centers of materials, manufacture, and distribution, but also by themselves consuming enormous amounts of fuel, iron, and coal.

The products of the factories were rapidly absorbed by the growing cities which sheltered the workmen and the distributors. The increased urban population was nourished by the increased farm production which, in turn, was made more productive by the use of the new farm machinery. American agricultural production kept up with the urban demand and still had surpluses for sale to the industrial centers of Europe.

The labor which manned the factories and built the railways was recruited in part from American farm areas where men were being displaced by farm machinery and in part from Europe which now began to send tides of immigrants from eastern and southern Europe—Poles, Hungarians, and Italians, especially—most of whom were originally peasants but who settled in American industrial cities.

The money to finance this tremendous expansion of the American economy still came from Europe for the most part, but the

Americans were approaching the day when their expansion could be financed in their own "money market."

The Industrial Giants. The economic revolution caused by the Civil War had the effect of making industrial control easier by means of modern communications and flexible financing. It also created conditions in which competition seemed, at least to the managers, to be destructive. Although the United States has never had a wholly free-enterprise system, competition has been rather less since 1865 than before. When the investment in a business becomes very large, competition becomes to that degree more distasteful to the investors, as risking greater loss. And investments were becoming very large.

The vast growth of the steel industry is a good example. As railroads found their ways everywhere, the demand for steel, for rails, engines, cars and equipment, grew at the same rate or faster. The iron ore of Michigan and of the Mesabi Range in Minnesota provided most of the material. Having the necessary ability and knowledge of production, steelmakers turned out wire, tubes, sheets, and structural parts. Blast furnaces were larger and fewer. Iron production in 1880 was more than four million tons, steel a million tons. Greatest of the early titans of steel was Andrew Carnegie, the Scottish-born industrialist and philanthropist, who came to America with his impoverished parents in 1848 when he was a child of twelve. After a successful career in the telegraph and railroad businesses, he went into the steel industry in 1868. In thirty-two years (the period in which American steel production came to surpass that of England) he created a colossal steel empire which controlled the major part of American steel-making. Having achieved this pinnacle he sold his interest in the industry to a group which made it a part of the new and greatest steel company, United States Steel, and spent the rest of his life giving his money away to build libraries and to found several great benevolent trusts and research institutions.

Another industrial giant born in this age was the petroleum industry, which killed the use of whale oil in the 1860's. John D Rockefeller built the great Standard Oil Company by combining refineries, manipulating railroad rates, and controlling pipe lines. In less than ten years from its founding, the company controlled nine-tenths of refined oils.

Monopolistic Practices. Several monopolistic practices were used by these colossal industries. In "pools," a number of industrial concerns controlled prices by agreeing to divide the market among them. Thus none would destroy another by price-cutting. This feature of price-maintenance is the certain mark of monopoly. "Trusts" were arrangements by which stockholders of competing companies deposited their shares with trustees who thereafter, by controlling the votes, were able to fix a uniform management policy for the industry, including, of course, a uniform price policy. Success of the Standard Oil Trust paved the way for the consolidation of other businesses, and America saw her economy being controlled by a small number of huge combines: the Beef, the Sugar, and the Copper Trusts, etc.

The industrialists built the great American industries. Now the financiers began to manage those industries, for the credit requirements of these behemoths of business were so large that bankers began, quite naturally, to insist on membership in the boards of directors, in order to safeguard the loans made to the companies. The outstanding example was John Pierpont Morgan, who exerted a decisive influence in almost every major industry of the time.

A good many people began to fear the great companies because of their ability to fix the prices of necessities. However, the defenders of the system found a philosophy to justify their practices. Popularizers of the work of Charles Darwin interpreted evolution as the survival of the fittest. This idea was borrowed from the field of biological science to be applied to society. Actually, it should have justified the most rigorous enforcement of free competition, but it served to protect any practice which was successful (except the old, more conventional crimes) on the ground that the complainers had shown themselves unfit to compete in a world of fierce struggle for survival. This doctrine of Social Darwinism has thoroughly permeated our society.

The courts reluctantly created new laws to support the corporations, first by including corporations within the meaning of the word "person" and using the due process clause of the Fourteenth Amendment. Due process, which had meant the procedures of law, thus broadened to a general concept of justice (substantial due process) that protected property from confiscation. By 1900 the courts claimed close supervision over any government regulation of business.

AGRARIAN DISCONTENT

Between the end of the Civil War and the beginning of the twentieth century, American farmers found that the national economy worked to their satisfaction in about one year of seven; that is, in this period of thirty-five years, there was one five-year stretch (1879–84) in which farmers' compaints diminished rather than increased. (Of course, what was "unsatisfactory" to an American farmer would have seemed the wealth of Rockefeller to a peasant of eastern Europe in the same years.) What irked the American farmer was not an absolute level of destitution and pauperism but the fact that his dividend from the national wealth seemed smaller than it ought to be and, also, seemed to diminish in inverse ratio to his productivity, or more simply— the nation was getting richer but the farmer was getting poorer, even though he produced more and more.

The easiest illustration is the farm price trend. From 1866 to 1886 (which was not a depression year) wheat declined from $1.45 to 68 cents a bushel, corn from 75 cents to 30 cents, cotton from 31 cents a pound to 9 cents. To hold his income level the farmer tried to produce more, which resulted in periodic gluts and still lower prices.

Naturally, the sturdy yeoman looked for someone to blame. It was clear that prices to the consumer had not declined equally. Two visible groups seemed to be getting fat by farming the farmer—the bankers and the railroads. The bankers had loaned money when it was cheap and were now being repaid, or asking to be repaid, when it was dear. They could be defeated by deliberate, governmental inflation of the currency to make money cheaper. The railroads, by manipulating their rates and rebates, were discriminating against persons or regions; they had "pools" to split the business and hold up rates; they competed furiously where necessary and made up the losses by overcharging where they had no competition; they bought individual officials or whole legislatures.

The Granger Movement. In moving to fall on these foes, the farmer had an association at hand. The Patrons of Husbandry, known for short as the Grange or the Grangers, was founded in 1867 as a social organization, but it soon became a co-operative association, which was willing to act politically against monopolies.

The Grange and other concerned groups won railway regulation in Illinois in 1871. The railroads went to court with the claim that state regulation deprived them of their property without due process of law, but the Supreme Court, in *Munn v. Illinois* (1877), said that property devoted to public use was property in which the public had an interest. The right to regulate such public utilities was not unlimited. As various states passed legislation like the Illinois laws, other cases came to the Court. In 1886 the Supreme Court reversed itself in the Wabash decision, by limiting state control to intrastate business. A federal law was needed to regulate interstate commerce (see pages 68–69).

The Greenback Movement. In addition to fighting the railroads, the farmers advocated inflation. The notion of raising prices by deliberate inflation has always captivated debtors and those whose incomes are easily adjustable to rising price levels. It is a great blessing of the American system that all deeply felt wishes can be tested in politics. Currency reform, no exception, had its own party, the Greenback party, which entered a presidential candidate, the New York philanthropist Peter Cooper, in the campaign of 1876. He was unsuccessful, of course, but the party was enlarged in 1878 with delegates from a much wider area, who attempted to weld the unjoinable interests of labor and inflation and polled over a million votes in the congressional off-year election. They sent fourteen members to the national House of Representatives. Although they broadened their platform thereafter, they never did better in votes. In 1884 they had a presidential candidate in General Benjamin F. Butler, notable as the most warmly disliked of all occupation-force commanders in the South during the Civil War.

The decline of inflation as a political ideal reflected the improvement of the national economy when the Panic of 1873 had blown itself out. After the middle 1880's, however, the clouds gathered again in the free-silver controversy.

Two positive, permanent advantages were gained for agriculture by legislation in this period. Scientific agriculture was promoted by federal subsidies under the Hatch Act of 1887, and the Department of Agriculture was given Cabinet standing in 1889.

THE RISE OF LABOR ORGANIZATIONS

The unrestrained growth of industry after the Civil War produced problems in the relations between workmen and their employers which caused labor to intensify efforts to establish national organizations through which it could bargain more effectively for better working conditions. Today's current of labor events may sometimes seem hard to follow, but it is a miracle of clarity compared with the turbulence of the two decades after the Civil War. However, the story can be followed easily if one but remembers that it flows in three streams: (1) social reform movements, (2) political action, and (3) "pure and simple trade unionism." In 1873 these streams plunged together over a fall and into the whirlpool of panic and depression. After 1878 they separated and ran clearly again.

Early Labor Movement. The effect of the Civil War on labor organization was generally harsh. Many of the ablest leaders went off to fight, and national unions lost their southern dues payers. Attempts to expand were successfully opposed by newly formed employers' associations. "Real wages" declined.

Labor then turned to a reform of distribution methods by founding consumers' co-operatives. A few producers' co-operatives were established, but the producers soon became as capitalistic as other corporate shareholders.

In 1872 labor attempted to become active politically with the formation of the National Labor Reform party, which nominated an unwilling candidate for the Presidency. When he declined the nomination, the party collapsed, together with labor's enthusiasm for direct political participation.

Labor had much more success by following the program one author has called "pure and simple trade unionism"—a program of working for improved wages, hours, and working conditions. From the late years of the Civil War more than two dozen national unions were added to the half-dozen founded before. The expansion of the iron industry was reflected by the growth of the Molders Union. Railway extension was paralleled by the founding of three great "Brotherhoods." The shoeworkers organized as the Knights of St. Crispin but were sent into a decline by the Panic of 1873. An association of national unions, the

National Labor Union, existed from 1866 to 1872; it was principally interested in securing legislative enactment of the "Eight-Hour Day." In 1868 Congress legislated the "Eight-Hour Day" for hourly-rated workers in government employment.

The uneven progress of labor achievement was brought to an abrupt halt by the Panic of 1873 and the years of depression which followed. Two-thirds of the national unions disappeared, and five-sixths of the members were forced to leave the rolls.

The Knights of Labor. Although founded in 1869, the Knights of Labor made little progress until its leadership was assumed by Terence V. Powderly in 1878. It was an industrial union as opposed to a union of skilled craftsmen, and it hoped to include all workmen, whether skilled or unskilled. It promoted the eight-hour day, the graduated income tax, arbitration of labor disputes, and consumers' co-operatives. In the 1880's its membership total reached almost three-quarters of a million. It began to decline in the mid-1880's, owing to the failure of several strikes and the public's unjustified assumption that the Knights had participated in the infamous "Haymarket riot." On May 1, 1886, the Knights sponsored a general strike for an eight-hour day. Several days later, an anarchist demonstration was held in Chicago's Haymarket Square. As the authorities were dispersing the crowd a bomb was exploded, killing seven policemen. Seven anarchists were sentenced to death, although the identity of the bomber has never been established. A later governor of Illinois, John Peter Altgeld, insisted that the trials were unfair. The effect of the episode was to blacken the reputation of the Knights and of organized labor in general.

The American Federation of Labor. The 1880's saw the emergence of a great new association, the American Federation of Labor, which was an association of national unions of skilled workers. It left each member union free to govern its own affairs and was chiefly interested in "pure and simple trade unionism." It was to become, in the next half-century, the central agency through which organized labor spoke. Its first president was Samuel Gompers, from the relatively literate Cigar Makers Union, who was elected in 1886. The craft unions, with greater earning power and indispensable skills, often proved more durable than the more generous-minded industrial unions, which carried the "weight" of a large proportion of unskilled workmen.

Radical Unionism. Every great economic depression has provided an opportunity for otherwise unacceptable social theories to catch on. The depression of the 1870's saw the importation of European socialist doctrines, among them Marxism (which supplied Communism with its few and antiquated ideas), anarchism, and milder theories. None became very popular, but they had a genius for attracting attention.

Industrial Warfare. Industrial relations, within the lifetime of many now living, often resembled actual civil war. Worst was the great Railway Strike of 1877 which flashed like an electric shock from the Atlantic to the Mississippi, resulting in the loss of dozens of lives and millions of dollars, with no gain to the railroad men. President Hayes called out federal troops to quell the disorder. In addition to this strike, countless examples of inordinate violence could be cited. Two great strike-episodes of this sort are especially memorable. One was the "Homestead Massacre" at Homestead, Pennsylvania, in 1892, where three hundred private detectives employed by the Carnegie Steel Company were engaged in a pitched battle with striking workers which ended only after seven were dead. The other was the Pullman Strike of 1894. The strike tied up the midwestern railroads, and a force of 3,400 specially deputized federal officers were unable to keep the trains rolling. After violence showed the apparent futility of the use of force by or for the management, President Grover Cleveland intervened with the United States Army, ostensibly to keep the mails moving. The governor of Illinois, John Peter Altgeld, unsuccessfully protested this federal intervention, and the strike leader, Eugene V. Debs, was jailed for violating a court order (injunction) prohibiting the strikers from interfering with the mails or with interstate commerce.

This use of the injunction was significant, for it soon came to be the standard weapon for use against strikers. The ill-feeling typified by the Homestead episode was a principal reason for the fact that the steel industry remained "unorganized" by labor for almost fifty years thereafter.

PRESIDENTIAL POLITICS

To some students, the history of the national political scene from Reconstruction to the 1890's is a story of curious irrelevancy to the dynamic forces which were shaping the country. Certainly the national administrations rarely led any of these significant movements. Whether they should have is, perhaps, debatable.

The Hayes Administration. Once in the White House after his disputed election, President Hayes left a record in his administration best remembered for quarrels with his own party leaders and with the Congress. In his own party he was blocked in the establishment of an honest, efficient customs service in New York Port until he was aided by the Democrats. In the Congress he fought a Democratic majority by vetoing bills because of "riders" (amendments unrelated to the subject) which were tacked onto bills (of which he otherwise approved) as a device to get him to accept legislation he did not wish.

The Hayes administration was involved in the continuing currency controversy, which began with the ending of the coinage of silver dollars in 1873, an omission known to its opponents as the "Crime of '73." Silver men argued, for a generation, that this was a conspiratorial act of "the gold interests."

Government payment of its obligations in gold was guaranteed, not later than 1879, in the Specie Resumption Act of 1875. Inflationists who hoped to cure the effects of the Panic of 1873 by increasing the amount of paper money (greenbacks) in circulation were disappointed that a clause of the Act provided instead for a reduction of paper money. The discovery of new deposits of silver in the West led to further insistence on coining silver dollars. Unfortunately for the silverites, the international trend was toward the single-metal, gold standard. The silver sponsors found inflationary allies among the farmers and managed to secure passage of the Bland-Allison Act in 1878. This law required the Secretary of the Treasury to buy from two million dollars' to four million dollars' worth of silver at the market price, to be coined into silver dollars. But the Secretary did as little as possible to carry out this mandate.

To understand what these people were trying to do, imagine that all there is for sale in the world is one potato and all the money in the world is a million dollars. Price of the potato: one million dollars. Double the amount of money but do not increase the supply of goods for sale. New price of the potato: two million dollars. This is what they hoped would happen to farm prices. If the owner of the potato owed a mortgage loan of two million dollars, the easiest way to pay the debt would be to increase the supply of money, but no one else would benefit.

Specie payments were resumed on schedule in 1879. There was no attempt to reduce the supply of paper money any further, and the Congress enacted a provision that about 347 million dollars in greenbacks should stay in circulation. The paper money reached an equality with gold, in price, for the first time since early in the Civil War.

The Election of 1880. When elected President Hayes said he would serve but one term; consequently, in 1880 the race was "wide open." Leading rivals at the Republican convention were James G. Blaine of Maine and former President Grant who would have accepted the nomination. On the thirty-sixth ballot a compromise gave the nomination to James A. Garfield of Ohio. The Democrats put up Winfield Scott Hancock of Pennsylvania. The only real difference in party programs was that the Republicans favored a protective tariff. The Greenback Labor party nominated James B. Weaver of Iowa, and the Prohibition party, in its second presidential campaign, also presented a slate. The campaign was not very exciting. The Republican tactic of identifying the Democratic party as the party of treason (ignoring the War Democrats) and claiming full credit for preserving the United States was losing its sting. In the popular vote Garfield led by the narrow margin of seven thousand, but his electoral vote was decisive, 214 to 155.

The Garfield-Arthur Administrations. President Garfield was not President long enough to allow a historical judgment of his work. The most interesting aspect of his brief tenure was the quarrel in the Republican party between the progressives, called the "Halfbreeds," and the conservatives, called the "Stalwarts." In a showdown over New York patronage, Senators Thomas Platt and Roscoe Conkling resigned to dramatize their position. Unhappily for their demonstration, the New York legislature refused to re-elect them—a smashing victory for Garfield and the Halfbreeds. After only four months in office, Garfield was shot by a frustrated job-seeker who claimed to be a Stalwart. The President died two and a half months later.

Vice-President Chester A. Arthur, thought to be a New York Stalwart, succeeded. Little was hoped from a dapper "machine politician," which was his reputation. To the surprise of many the new President became a vigorous supporter of the merit system and saw to it that the Pendleton Act of 1883 had the most effective beginning possible in its attempt to establish a career civil service. His administration also saw the founding of the Tariff Commission, a study and advisory group concerned with the most durable political question of American history—the tariff—of which more later.

The Election of 1884. The Republican leaders had not seriously considered Arthur presidential material, nor did they make a real attempt to offer him as their candidate in 1884. James G. Blaine of Maine was nominated, to the disgust of progressive Republicans (at the moment called "Mugwumps") who then supported the Democratic nominee, Governor Grover Cleveland of New York. The campaign was tawdry and scandalous. The public life of Blaine and the private life of Cleveland were vulnerable (in early manhood Cleveland had sired an acknowledged illegitimate child), and much was made of both facts, to the exclusion of graver issues. New York state voted for Cleveland by a narrow margin, a result usually attributed to Irish resentment of anti-Catholicism among Blaine's followers. However, the Irish precincts had been turning toward the Democrats at a regular rate for a number of years, so that explanation is probably too simple. Whatever the reason, Cleveland won the election by winning New York.

Cleveland's First Administration. President Cleveland, a professional career politician who rose to the White House from the office of Sheriff of Buffalo, is generally accounted a superior President. On entering office he "inherited" a treasury surplus which encouraged an extravagant veterans' pension policy. His cure for the surplus was to cut the tariff, but this was contrary to the fixed opinion of Republican leaders. In his years as President he vetoed more special (or "private") pension bills than any predecessor, and he also vetoed a bill which would have granted pensions witnout regard to service disabilities. This lost him favor with "professional veterans" but, apparently, not with the public at large.

During Cleveland's first term the Navy Department was reorganized under Secretary William C. Whitney who began the program of modern, steel ship construction which led to the country's later naval excellence.

This era also saw the passage of the Interstate Commerce Act of 1887 to apply the constitutional, federal remedy for the abuses of the public interest which the Granger laws had earlier fought. The act regulated railroads in interstate commerce; it prohibited pooling, discriminatory rates and rebates, and fluctuating rates. The Interstate Commerce Commission was to invoke the courts to enforce its regulations. Unhappily, the defending roads were able to tie up the commission in long and fruitless litigation, a weakness that waited for a later generation's remedy.

The most dramatic theme of Cleveland's Presidency was the tariff struggle. The tariffs of 1870 and 1872 lowered rates. That of 1875 restored the cuts. In 1883 the rates were reduced slightly. Cleveland and the Democrats, at least the southern ones, thought they should be cut sharply. To emphasize his position the President devoted his annual message of 1887 solely to the tariff and thus made it a major issue in the presidential campaign of 1888.

The Election of 1888. The nominees of 1888 were Cleveland for the Democrats and Benjamin Harrison of Indiana for the Republicans. The campaign was an education in economics for those who followed it closely, as the tariff argument was predominant. A tragicomic touch was the indiscreet letter of the British Minister, Sackville-West, endorsing Cleveland. This was a clever entrapment of the Englishman by a Republican letter-writer, which cost Cleveland votes and the Minister his post. In the election Cleveland received ninety-six thousand more popular votes than did his opponent, but Harrison won the electoral vote, 233 to 168.

The Harrison Administration. Harrison was a solid, conscientious man but lacked color. His term is probably best remembered for a continuation of the antimonopoly battle, which ensued from the passage of the Sherman Antitrust Act of 1890 that made restraint of competition in interstate commerce ("conspiracy in restraint of trade") illegal. It was aimed at the new industrial giants, among them combinations in sugar, beef, and oil. The law as drafted lacked clarity. Inclusion, by the courts, of organized labor as a group subject to its penalties probably went beyond the intention of the framers of the law.

An attempt to satisfy the silver-inflationists (by the enactment of the Sherman Silver Purchase Act in 1890) required the Secretary of the Treasury to purchase four and a half million ounces of silver per month and issue paper money against it. This action, inflationary in effect, frightened the gold-standard adherents but did not satisfy the "silverites."

A tariff increase of almost 50 per cent was written into the McKinley Tariff of 1890. The effect was a rise in retail prices which, it was said, was responsible for a Democratic landslide in the congressional elections of 1890.

THE FARM REVOLT

The generation from 1865 to 1900 was a generation of agricultural revolution. The federal government was ever more active in promoting agriculture. The number of farms and the acreage farmed doubled. More and more the several economic provinces of the country concentrated on the kind of farming they could do most profitably. Mechanical and chemical aids to increase production were developed and utilized to a marvelous extent.

But still the farm population was the least contented segment of the people, and the primary reason was the decline of farm prices in a time when farmers' costs mounted. The price level in the late 1880's was about two-thirds as high as that of the early 1870's. Credit was no cheaper. Indeed, credit, once in use, was a rigid cost. Prices might decline. If so, seed, fencing, and so on, might also decline. But the interest rate on an earlier mortgage stayed at the same figure. In fact, it became a larger fraction of the farmer's income. The harder the times, the greater the proportion of the farmer's income that went to his creditors. As one bitter westerner said, "We raise two crops: corn and interest. The farmer farms the soil and the banker farms the farmer." This explains the frequent excursions of farmers into the wilderness of inflationary finance. A man borrowed a thousand dollars, with wheat at one dollar; he needed a thousand bushels to pay the debt. If wheat dropped to fifty cents, he needed two thousand bushels to pay the debt.

It was becoming considerably harder to own a farm. During Harrison's term there were more than ten thousand farm mortgage foreclosures in Kansas alone. The proportion of tenants was in transition from about one-fourth of all farmers to about one-third.

It came to this—as the country entered the 1890's, agriculture was in depression and no other economic group of the people seemed to be getting so small a slice of the pie.

The farmers turned again to politics. Leaders hoped to unite the farmers and organized labor although the factory worker stood to gain nothing from inflation). Organizations, in the late 1880's and early 1890's, multiplied: the People's party of Kansas, the Southern Alliance, and similar associations. Tactics were disputed: there could be another "Third party"; the farmers could set out to capture an existing party; or, like the American Federation of Labor, they could endorse friendly candidates on a bipartisan (or even polypartisan) basis. All three alternatives were occasionally adopted by one group or another. But it was not long before these groups gathered and founded their own party.

The Populists and the Election of 1892. At a national convention in 1891 the "People's party of the United States of America" was formed, although southern sympathizers held back because they hoped to dominate the Democratic party in their section. The new party, "Populist" for short, nominated General James B. Weaver for President. The platform was concentrated on the cure-all of inflation, although many reform measures were supported, most of which became law in the next generation (for example, the income tax). It remained now to be seen what effect this party, the most auspiciously founded "Third party" since the Republicans of 1856, could have in an election.

The Republicans renominated their incumbent, President Harrison. The Democrats put up the man who twice in a row had received a majority of the popular vote, Grover Cleveland (with the senior Adlai E. Stevenson for Vice-President). The Democrats made a strong declaration against the protective tariff, whereas the Republicans announced their support of it. Cleveland's speeches on the tariff, however, were not nearly so strong as his party's position.

The currency issue had been injected by the Populists, whose platform favored the free coinage of silver at a ratio of sixteen to one. This deserves a bit of explanation. If such a policy were enacted as law, any person would have the right to take silver to the mint and have any amount coined into silver dollars at no charge for the process. The possibilities for increasing the amount of money in circulation were obvious. The ratio of sixteen to one meant that sixteen units—ounces, pounds, tons—of silver would have the value of one of the same units of gold. This is usually expressed in the formula, sixteen ounces of silver equal one ounce of gold. This value would be fixed by law. The desired ratio probably overvalued silver in relation to gold. If true, and if the ratio became law, gold would be hoarded by its lucky owners and silver would become the currency of the land. Cleveland's answer to the proposition was pointed: He supported a single, gold standard.

In the election, bimetallism (the doctrine that two metals should form the currency) earned only twenty-two electoral votes for Weaver. Cleveland received 277 electoral votes; Harrison, 145. Cleveland failed of a popular majority but was elected. The Democrats took both Houses of the Congress but found some Populists there, too.

Cleveland's Second Administration. Cleveland's second term was characterized by a devastating depression and the continuing controversy over the money question. The Panic of 1893 was precipitated by a decline in the government's gold reserve which alarmed traders on the New York Stock Exchange. The collapse was the first crack in a trembling economy. From the point of view of the silverites and farmers, Cleveland's medicine was an aggravation of the disease. Cleveland engineered a repeal of the Sherman Silver Purchase Act and in so doing drove a wedge into the Democratic party.

Discontent became articulate as the press was used to disseminate the accusations and counteraccusations of the people who, in every crisis, seem more interested in fixing the "blame" than in attending to necessary remedies. The most theatrical "remedy" (although a tragicomic affair) was the march of "Coxey's Army"—four hundred unemployed workmen—on Washington to ask relief. Instead of succeeding, Coxey was arrested on the Capitol grounds for walking on the grass. The cause of free silver was popularized by the publication of widely circulated pamphlets and books, among them *Coin's Financial School* by William H. Harvey. Several periodicals devoted much space to the promotion of the bimetallist doctrine. An augury of the immediate future of the Democratic party was the rise of a silver bloc in the House of Representatives, led by youthful William Jennings Bryan of Nebraska and "Silver Dick" Bland of Missouri, in 1895.

The gold policy of the federal government was blamed for the Panic of '93 and, of course, every ramification of current monetary policy was closely and critically watched by the silverites. In 1893, when banking troubles in London caused British investors to sell their American securities, there had been a drain of gold from the United States. At the same time the McKinley Tariff of 1890 had raised duties so high that imports were cut and federal revenue declined. The Harrison administration had, it was believed, depleted the treasury by excessive spending. All this helped to bring on the stock-market crash of 1893. Cleveland's first remedy, as mentioned, had been to drop the silver purchase program. But still the gold reserve declined. With government income down, the reserve had to be used for running expenses. Four times the government borrowed gold, the first three times from private bankers who realized millions of dollars in commissions. This caused great anguish to the silverites, who claimed that free coinage of silver was the true remedy. The fourth loan was from the general public, which easily provided the money. However, the bonds of all four loans were "cashed" by the holders (for gold) so that the treasury continued to be in difficult straits.

It can be easily understood that money, in the sense of currency policy, was the theme of the presidential campaign of 1896.

The Election of 1896. The Republican nominee was Senator William McKinley of Ohio, protégé of the astute, able, and affluent Mark Hanna, who persuaded eastern Republicans to accept McKinley in exchange for a platform pledge to maintain the gold standard. The only consolation offered to silverite Republicans (mostly from the mining states) was a promise to work for international acceptance of silver as a currency basis—on the ground that no one country could take such a step by itself. Disgruntled "Silver Republicans" bolted their party, led by Senator Henry M. Teller of Colorado, and later agreed to support the Democratic candidate.

The choice of the Democrats, Bryan, surprised millions. Bryan electrified the convention with a stirring (and carefully planned) speech which compared the imposition of the gold standard with the act of crucifixion, a speech since known as the "cross of gold" speech. Bryan was nominated for President with Arthur Sewall of Maine for Vice-President. The platform supported "free silver" and the income tax; it opposed the protective tariff and monopolies. Just as Silver Republicans quit their party, now Gold Democrats appeared with their own organization and candidates. Although their cause was hopeless, they were supported by Grover Cleveland.

The Populist party (their main issue of free silver annexed by the Democrats) nominated Bryan but named a different Vice-Presidential candidate, Thomas E. Watson of Georgia. However, people do not vote for presidential candidates but for slates of electors in each state. If Populists and Democrats had their separate slates, Bryan could theoretically get 66 per cent of the popular vote of a state and still fail to carry the state (Populist 33%, Democrat 33%, Republican 34%). Hence, Populists' and Democrats' "fused" identical electoral slates were possible.

Bryan conducted the most energetic campaign yet seen, while McKinley addressed small groups from his front porch. But Bryan sank under the weight of Republican campaign expenditures and hard names. McKinley and the gold standard won a decisive victory over Bryan, debtors, and inflation. The electoral count was 271 to 176.

PRELUDE TO WORLD POWER

It is habitual in some American circles to think that American participation in world affairs as an equal sovereign state is a fairly recent development, but the record clearly shows that the United States was an active and responsible member of the community of nations long ago. In the late nineteenth century there had been a number of influences at work to break down the provincialism and isolationism of American life. These were cultural experiences, economic opportunities, and a romanticism associated with the example of the grandeur of the British Empire.

The newly wealthy American industrial group found European travel intellectually and culturally satisfying and extended the experience by making collections of European art and works of scholarship which, in time, filled monumental museums and libraries. At the same time, American scholars and professional men studied in Europe and brought back with them a familiarity with the most advanced methods of study and techniques of practice in their fields. Thus the American intellectual life partook more and more of the intellectual life of the Western world.

The American industrial revolution made the United States the productive equal of any other nation. American business leaders were soon aware of the opportunities to sell their manufactures to foreign markets and, to some extent, to invest their capital in foreign fields of exploitation. The investment of American capital abroad naturally gave the business community an interest in the stability of international relations. Successive national administrations saw that American investment gave the American people a "leverage" in international affairs and encouraged the practice, sometimes almost coercing American capitalists into the foreign field. This practice of government urging of foreign investment was what was called, in its day, "dollar diplomacy," but today the phrase is used by America's enemies to refer to almost any American economic activity abroad.

The example of the British Empire seems almost to have intoxicated some American leaders, particularly in the northeastern quarter of the country. They were captivated by the notion of "the white man's burden," that is, the responsibility (self-assumed) to extend white men's law, order, and civilization to far parts of the globe. This somewhat unrealistic attitude was encouraged by the racist and imperialist writing of the English poet and storyteller, Rudyard Kipling, and was given a tougher intellectual content by the theorizing of the American naval officer, Alfred Thayer Mahan, whose many books of naval history rationalized the profitable results of age-old British naval policy.

Samoan Islands. A small but continuously disturbing problem dating back to the Grant administration was that of the Samoan Islands. Americans had an interest in the region before the Civil War, but in the 1870's, partly as a check to German ambitions and partly because of the commercial value there, the United States acquired the right to build a naval base and supply station at Pago Pago. British, German, and American officials exercised municipal jurisdiction jointly, but German aggressiveness brought continual tension throughout the 1880's. Each nation had warships there in 1889, but a hurricane destroyed all but one (the British *Calliope*) and negotiators at Berlin thereafter established a three-power protectorate. In 1899 the islands were divided, by partition, between the Germans and Americans. Britain, for her part, was compensated by recognition of rights elsewhere.

Relations with the Far East were marked by treaties with China and Korea. Americans in the western states objected to unrestricted Chinese immigration. In 1880 a Chinese-American treaty acknowledged the right of the United States to regulate such immigration. Later, suspension of Chinese immigration became permanent. In 1882 the United States, by treaty, recognized the independence of Korea, the "hermit kingdom."

Early Interest in Latin America. In this period Garfield's Secretary of State, James G. Blaine, poured the footings for our modern Latin American policy. In solving specific problems he was not markedly successful, but it was his plan of 1881 which finally led to the calling of the first Pan-American conference in 1889. Out of this came the Pan-American Union, a common forum for the governments of the New World.

Hawaii. In 1875 the United States and Hawaii had made a treaty providing that no third power would acquire any Hawaiian territory. This treaty was amended in 1887 to give the United States the right to fortify a naval base at Pearl Harbor. American sugar planters disliked the native royal family and secured, by force, a "liberal" consitution in that same year. Queen Liliuokalani revoked it in 1891 and, by the illegal use of United States Marines, was overthrown. The United States flag was raised over the new "protectorate" by the United States Minister, acting for the sugar growers. President Cleveland refused to accept the action, and Hawaii continued as a republic, which was established in 1894. When McKinley entered the White House, naval strategy outweighed any moral considerations, and the islands were annexed in 1898.

Anglo-American Disputes. As always, relations with Great Britain made up a major thread of the diplomatic story. The two nations had differed on the question of fishing rights ever since the eighteenth century. In 1888 a precarious working agreement for the use of Canadian ports by American fishers temporarily solved the problem. Another controversy, over sealing in the Bering Sea, arose in 1892 when Canadian and other seal hunters began to operate in Alaskan waters and were seized by United States revenue cutters (now the Coast Guard). The United States proposed to close the Bering Sea to all foreign sealers but yielded to arbitration and the adoption of satisfactory rules governing the industry, plus the payment of damages to Britain.

Much more serious Anglo-American tension arose in 1895 from a dispute between Britain and Venezuela over the boundary between British Guiana and Venezuela. The dispute was of long standing but reached a crisis stage with the discovery of gold in the disputed area. The British refused an American offer to arbitrate. Secretary of State Richard Olney, relying on the Monroe Doctrine, sent a very sharp note of insistence to the British government. After a long delay Britain again refused. President Cleveland recommended that the United States make its own survey and then enforce its findings.

America's threat of war came as a surprise to the British who had not thought the Venezuelan affair that important. Taking a thoughtful second look at Great Britain's world position, Britain's leaders saw that a rising German Empire might soon challenge the British Empire; they saw too, that American friendship might therefore be a prize worth having. Thereafter, the United States found Britain very co-operative. A boundary commission, in 1899, awarded Britain most of what she had claimed, and gave to Venezuela the mouth of the Orinoco River. Both were satisfied.

Strained Relations with Italy and Chile. In 1891 the relations between Italy and the United States were upset by the lynching of eleven persons of Italian extraction (three of them Italian subjects) in New Orleans as the outgrowth of suspected Mafia (Black Hand) activities. Amity returned when the United States paid a substantial indemnity.

In the same year two American sailors from the U.S.S. *Baltimore* were killed in Valparaiso, Chile, and seventeen injured. The attack was in retaliation for the American minister's unwarranted interference in a Chilean civil war. The United States took a firm, almost warlike, position, and the Chilean government apologized and paid a large indemnity. Pan-Americanism suffered greatly because of this imbroglio.

The Spanish-American War. All of these events, serious as they were, diminish to mere incidents when seen in relation to the chronic "Cuban Question." Like a semiquiescent political volcano, Cuba had been erupting into rebellions for a generation. Shortsighted Spanish officials used cruel repression as a countermeasure. Spanish policy seemed unnecessarily harsh to the American public, and the Hearst and Pulitzer press found a ready readership for "atrocity stories." William Randolph Hearst's New

York *Journal* published a stolen letter written by the Spanish Minister to the United States, Dupuy de Lôme, in February, 1898, which was scornful of President McKinley. De Lôme had to resign, and relations were worsened.

An emotional crisis was reached when an explosion sank the U.S.S. *Maine,* moored in Havana harbor, on February 15, 1898. The cause of the explosion is still a mystery, but the popular imagination blamed it on Spain. By this time American opinion had been stirred to great excitement. Yielding to this atmosphere, the President asked the Congress for authority to intervene to pacify Cuba. The Congress answered with an ultimatum. Spain did make the necessary concessions at the last moment, but the intensity of American feeling had been pitched too high; war was formally declared on April 25, 1898.

In comparison, the United States Navy was good; the United States Army poor. The Spanish troops in Cuba were good but apathetically led. The Spanish Navy was obsolete.

Oddly enough, a war to liberate the Cubans saw its first operations in the Philippines, where Admiral George Dewey annihilated the Spanish squadron defending Manila Bay at a cost of only eight wounded (May 1, 1898) in seven hours of fighting. American land forces occupied the islands in August.

In Cuba the Spanish naval force was bottled up in Santiago harbor. American troops under General William Shafter, which were so badly organized as to be almost a tragicomic troupe, luckily were unopposed in their landing on Cuba late in June. Acclimated, properly clad, well-armed Spanish troops, but commanded by defeatists, were promptly routed by the individualistic Americans at El Caney and San Juan Hill, on July 1. Two days later the Spanish ships sallied to total destruction outside Santiago; in four hours they lost four cruisers and three destroyers and suffered 474 killed and wounded. Prisoners totaled 1,750. The United States squadron lost one killed and one wounded. By the end of the month Puerto Rico was occupied, almost bloodlessly. The war was soon over.

By the Treaty of Paris, December 10, 1898, the United States received Puerto Rico and Guam outright and assumed control of the Philippines. Cuba was made a protectorate. (During the war Hawaii had been annexed.) The treaty was ratified by the narrow margin of two votes, over the moral protests of "anti-imperialists."

12

The Progressives

The struggles of the 1890's centered around the reform of the currency and the tariff but represented a far larger interest in reform, which is called the "Progressive movement." The movement made itself felt in national life until 1917. The years 1890 to 1917 were merely the climax of a trend which had been gaining force in the nineteenth century. Basically, it was caused by a feeling that the political and economic direction of American life had been given into the hands of a few or had been seized by a few. "Democracy," the progressives thought, "is ill." The remedy they then prescribed was a series of stronger doses of democracy. In every case the purpose was to check the growth of privilege and monopoly.

THE REFORM UPRISING

The ordinances, statutes, and amendments of this period fall generally into two groups. One group, in which women reformers took much interest, consisted of laws we call social legislation, designed to compel society to deal justly with the individual, especially the poor, the ignorant, and the defenseless. The other group was composed of something rather different, laws which tried to prevent accumulations of power in despised hands by changing the rules of the political game. Cities and western states became laboratories of political experiment which produced new legislative controls, new plans for organizing government, and new techniques for exerting popular pressure, and even, on the federal scene, rewrote the national Constitution in an experimental mood.

Social Reform. Social legislation attributable to the Progressive movement included attempts to remedy certain social evils which had become noticeable as accompaniments of the industrial revolution. Only beginnings were made before 1914. A series of laws were enacted by the Congress to regulate the relations between railroad workers and the rail corporations. New York State revised its building codes and labor laws in the interest of the health and safety of factory workers, and Massachusetts passed a minimum wage law applicable to women and minors. Congress also regulated the conditions under which sailors worked. State legislation to compensate workmen for on-the-job injuries (workmen's compensation) began with Maryland in 1902, but it took forty-six years to get coverage in the other forty-seven states, a delay which explains why people so often look to the federal government instead of to the states for remedial legislation. Sporadic interest in the shabby tenement areas where crime and vice so often breed led to attempts at slum clearance, but the problem still faces the country. A permanent trend set in toward the further emancipation of women by extending the privilege of voting. After a number of states had established female suffrage (Wyoming first) the Nineteenth Amendment to the United States Constitution made it national policy (1920). Special courts for young offenders, the "Juvenile Courts," began to be created at the turn of the century.

Municipal and State Reform. Numerous municipal scandals, of which the Tweed Ring was but an example, led people to support changes in the organization of city government. Disastrous floods at Galveston, Texas, and Dayton, Ohio, produced the Commission and City Manager forms of government. Under the "commission" method, the heads of the executive departments are elected and form, also, the legislature. The "city manager" is a hired business manager of city affairs.

In state governments, reforms were intended to make the legislature and officials more responsive to the popular will. The "initiative" allowed the people, by petition, to compel the legislature to give consideration to a desired measure. The "referendum" allowed reference of measures, by petition or act of the legislature, to the direct vote of the people, sometimes with binding force, sometimes only as an expression of popular opinion.

By means of the "recall," public officials (by petition) can be required to submit to a special balloting on their conduct. (When it is applied to judges, competent critics have been opposed to the recall, as tending to make judges seek popularity, not justice.) State income taxes were introduced. The methods of economics research were applied to rate regulation by state utilities commissions. The older, and perhaps more humane, caucus system of choosing party nominees was upset by the impersonal, preferential "primary election." Although expensive to the public and to the candidates, the primary election is cherished today principally because it holds out the possibility that outraged party members can use it to repudiate bad leadership if such feeling is sufficiently intense.

Federal Reform. The Progressive movement made many changes in the federal government, also. Unlimited power to tax personal and corporate incomes was given to the Congress by the Sixteenth, or Income Tax, Amendment. The "direct election of senators" was approved by the people in passing the Seventeenth Amendment. (See page 42.)

"The Muckrakers." Many of the reforms of this period had been espoused by the Populists, but their actual enactment was due greatly to a group of authors of the early twentieth century, nicknamed "the muckrakers," who ferreted out the scandalous conditions in business and politics and brought them to public attention, primarily through the popular magazine. Among these crusaders were Ida M. Tarbell, Lincoln Steffens, and Upton Sinclair.

Some of the progressive reforms of government, after decades of trial, are seen to have achieved much less than their sponsors expected. Such reforms as the primary election, the all-inclusive merit system in the civil service, the initiative, the referendum, and the recall would—it was hoped—make personality less important in public life and make people less dependent on party leaders. It now seems clear that the venality of late nineteenth-century politics (and the venality at other times as well) was permitted not because the popular will was frustrated but because the populace was apathetic. Party leaders have retained their control despite the changes in the mechanics of government (although at an added expenditure of their money and energy), and they will no doubt continue to direct public life as long as they work at it full time and their critics work part time or not at all.

THEODORE ROOSEVELT

The election of 1900 saw a very strong Republican party re-enter the testing ground. The Gold Standard Act of 1900 seemed to have settled the currency issue, and the administration had handily won a short and popular war. McKinley was the obvious nominee for the Presidency and, with him, there was nominated a not-so-obvious running partner, Theodore Roosevelt. The Democrats were still under the spell of Bryan's magic and renominated him despite his decisive defeat in 1896. The Republicans praised their gold standard and their foreign policy and urged the building of a canal in Central America. The Democrats accused the Republicans of imperialist leanings and stood by their doctrine of free silver. What was left of the Populists endorsed Bryan again. None of the Democratic attacks drew blood. In the popular voting Bryan ran about a hundred thousand votes below his 1896 total, while McKinley had about two hundred thousand more. The electoral vote was almost two to one for McKinley, and his party held both houses of the Congress.

Six months after his inauguration, McKinley was shot by an anarchist at an exposition in Buffalo, New York—the third President to be assassinated. He lingered for eight days and died on September 14, 1901. Theodore Roosevelt was sworn in as President.

Political Background. Roosevelt came from an old, well-to-do New York Dutch family. He was educated at Harvard and overcame the handicap of an under-par physique by leading what he liked to call "the strenuous life," including athletics and blood sports. On leaving college he resolved to enter politics and to come up through the ranks; this slow climb afforded him a valuable experience and education in politics. He served as Police Commissioner of New York City, where he made an impression as one who tried to reward merit and to ease the unnecessary material hardships of the men on the police force. His rise was steady; and he entered upon the national scene, first as United States Civil Service Commissioner and then as Assistant Secretary of the Navy and is credited with having the navy up to the mark at the outbreak of the Spanish-American War in 1898. He promptly resigned to accept a commission as Lieutenant Colonel of Cavalry in the army for the purpose of organizing his famous "Rough Riders" Regiment, drawn from college athletes, cowboys, polo players, and mounted policemen and containing, it was remarked, 998 Republicans and 2 Democrats.

After the war he became governor of New York (1898), where he showed the ability to co-operate with Thomas Platt, leader of the state Republican party, and thus confirmed his belief that the practice of politics requires practical politicians. But some of the older leaders resented his rise, his manners, and his theories. Now, in 1900, he was elected Vice-President. The Vice-Presidency has been the junk yard of many political careers. Men who hoped that it was the end of Roosevelt's had double reason to regret the anarchist's bullet when Roosevelt soon became President (1901) and instituted his "square deal" for labor, capital, and the public.

The First Administration. President Roosevelt immediately showed his intention of being a "doing" President by attacking the abuses of monopolies. His particular target was the Northern Securities Company, a combination which practically monopolized railway operation in the northwestern quarter of the country. Prosecution by the attorney general led to the breaking-up of the monopoly. Further action against the railroads came with passage of the Elkins Act of 1903, which strengthened the Interstate Commerce Commission by clarifying the transport laws and providing penalties against agents and officials of offending corporations, as well as the corporations themselves. As a device to handle monopolies and their practices in general, President Roosevelt established the Department of Commerce and Labor with Cabinet rank in 1903.

His interest in the armed forces was continued. In 1901 the Army War College was founded for the advanced study of warfare by officers, and two years later the Congress established the General Staff Corps, which was to be responsible for military planning and for improved administration.

Election of 1904. In 1904 Roosevelt was renominated by his party. The Democrats named the colorless Alton B. Parker, who was a supporter of the gold standard. Both platforms can be described as conservative. The voting proved the truth of the adage that the voters much prefer a Republican conservatism to a Democratic conservatism. Roosevelt polled 336 electoral votes to 140 for Parker. When assured of election, Roosevelt announced that he would not run again.

The Second Administration. In his second term he continued to attract much attention. It has been said that he restored the Presidency to the exalted plane on which Lincoln left it, but his effect was probably owing to his dramatic temperament rather than any deed as great as the Emancipation Proclamation or the preservation of the Union.

The gradual disappearance of the frontier in the late nineteenth century made people conscious that there were limits to the country's natural resources. In the 1880's and 1890's the Congress authorized the setting aside of forest preserves and legislated a program of assistance in the reclamation of otherwise useless lands. Roosevelt took up this program and gave it his support. A White House Conservation Conference in 1908 publicized the need. In 1907 the Inland Waterways Commission had been appointed, and the National Conservation Commission with Gifford Pinchot as chairman followed in 1908.

Roosevelt's practice of federal regulation of "bad trusts" continued with the passage of the Pure Food and Drug Act and the Meat Inspection Act, both in 1906, which attempted to correct the incredibly unsanitary conditions in the manufacture of processed foods, drugs, and patent medicines.

The Panic of 1907—the so-called "Bankers' Panic"—was an economic landmark of the Roosevelt administration. It was followed by the Aldrich-Vreeland Act of 1908 which provided more flexibility for the monetary system. The National Monetary Commission, appointed under the act, pioneered in studies which led ultimately to the Federal Reserve System.

Rooselvelt was probably the President most sympathetic to labor of all those from Lincoln's to his own time. In an age when poverty was felt to be the mark of social unfitness to survive, the labor organizer's lot was not a happy one. Under Roosevelt the labor situation was somewhat softened by the use of the Erdman Act (1898) which provided (but did not require) mediation. A positive result was the mediation of the Coal Strike of 1902, against the will of the operators. Roosevelt's term also saw the birth of the only really revolutionary labor organization which has had any wide appeal in this country, the Industrial Workers of the World ("I.W.W." or "Wobblies"), with a radical socialist program to be achieved by sabotage and "slowdown." Its power was chiefly in the Northwest.

It is a singular mark of the Roosevelt regime that—after the furor of the 1880's and 1890's—not a single important piece of tariff legislation was enacted while he was President.

The Election of 1908. Roosevelt had announced his intention of quitting public life after his elective term. However, he had every intention of influencing the choice of his successor so as to continue the dominance of progressivism in the Republican party. His choice for the Republican nominee was his Secretary of War, William Howard Taft of Ohio, whose nomination was arranged with no great difficulty. The Democrats returned again to William Jennings Bryan. The Republicans promised some undefined tariff reform, antitrust prosecutions, and a continuance of Roosevelt's conservation program. The Democrats condemned monopoly and promised to cut the tariff. In the voting Bryan fell in defeat a third time, trailing Taft by a million votes (although he received approximately the same number as in 1896 and 1900). Taft's electoral vote ratio was an overwhelming two to one.

WILLIAM HOWARD TAFT

Taft is not popularly remembered as a dashing crusader, but in his four years in office he brought more than twice as many antitrust prosecutions as Roosevelt did in seven years. He even advanced the "radical" view that all companies in interstate commerce should be required to secure federal charters of incorporation. The oil, tobacco, and steel monopolies were all attacked by his attorney general.

Legislative Achievements. Taft also tried to regularize government spending by the preparation of a single federal budget. Although the Congress of his day rejected the notion, the country has since come around to the policy. He was more successful in promoting other statutory reforms, including some pertaining to elections, public vice, and small private savings. The Publicity Act of 1910 required candidates for election to the Congress to place on record statements of the contributions they received—a

The Progressives

step toward the solution of an as yet unsolved problem of financing public elections. The Mann Act of 1910 brought the federal commerce power to bear on the problem of public vice by prohibiting the interstate transportation of prostitutes. Small savings accounts were afforded a safe haven from the uncertainties of banking, as then practiced, by the opening of Post Offices to savings depositors, who were paid an interest rate of 2 per cent. The Mann-Elkins Act of 1910 put communications under the Interstate Commerce Commission, and gave the Commission new enforcement powers and authority to fix rates while court review was pending.

Party Dissension. Taft's administration also saw the worst split in the Republican party since Grant and his friends survived the Liberal Republican movement of 1872. First off, there was the tariff question, a serious question which had been suppressed in recent years, rather than solved. The Taft promise of downward tariff revision was not fulfilled with the passage of the Payne-Aldrich Tariff of 1909 which raised the rates. When Taft accepted and signed the act, he created a knot of hostility in his own party, centered in the Middle West and led by Senator Robert M. La Follette of Wisconsin.

Speaker Joseph G. Cannon of Illinois was also a center of controversy. By the peculiar rules of the House of Representatives, he governed its procedures with a grip of steel. Being an extremely conservative man, he prevented the onward flow of progressivism. As a critic said, "If Cannon had been in the caucus on creation, he would have voted for chaos." A revolt in the House, in 1911, deprived the Speaker of his control of the Rules Committee, easing the problems of the progressives but inflaming tensions within the party.

Theodore Roosevelt, with little basis except Taft's tariff record, found it expedient to make a speech in Kansas in the summer of 1911 which was interpreted as an attack on the Taft administration for its love of the status quo. Progressives, irked by the tariff law of 1909 and by the spirit which "Cannonism" represented, rejoiced.

Conservation-minded Rooseveltians saw a basis for suspicion in the eruption of a controversy in 1910 between Interior Secretary Richard A. Ballinger and Gifford Pinchot, chief of the Forest Service. The charge was that Ballinger improperly favored coal interests in the administration of public lands. Pinchot was discharged, but the anti-Taft Republicans harassed Ballinger into resigning.

An ill omen for the Republican party was the capture of the House of Representatives by the Democrats in the off-year election of 1910. The Republican majority in the Senate was nominal because Roosevelt Republicans joined with Democrats to exert actual control.

The growing discord in the Republican party spurred on the founding of the National Progressive Republican League in 1911, led by Senator La Follette of Wisconsin. The League endorsed La Follette for the party's presidential nomination, to be awarded, of course, in 1912. However, La Follette's health gave some concern, and when Roosevelt (by arrangement) received a plea from seven Republican state governors that he allow himself to be nominated in 1912, the Progressives looked to their old leader with enthusiasm. In February, 1912, Roosevelt said he would accept the nomination, if offered, and the Republican party exploded.

The Progressive Party and the Election of 1912. As the election of 1912 approached, it was evident that it was to be the fiercest contest since 1896. Theodore Roosevelt's supporters set to work in state conventions and primary elections to secure the choice of delegates sympathetic to their leader. When the Republican convention opened, they had practically solid delegations from ten states. But there were a good many contested delegations and, with Taft-men in control of the convention and its Credentials Committee, most Rooseveltians whose seats were contested found themselves barred from the convention. The angry supporters of Roosevelt bolted the convention and met to lay plans to carry their battle against the "fraudulent" practices to the people. Taft, under the circumstances, was easily renominated by the "Regulars." The Roosevelt-men met in the first week of August, cheered their hero, sang "Onward Christian Soldiers," and founded the Progressive party, nicknamed the "Bull Moose" party (after Roosevelt applied the term to his own state of euphoria) with Roosevelt as nominee.

The Democratic party had fireworks, too. The principal rivals were Champ Clark of Missouri, Speaker of the House, and Governor Woodrow Wilson of New Jersey. Clark at one time had an actual majority of the delegates but not the two-thirds required by the convention's eighty-year-old rule. Bryan's influence was probably decisive. Suspicious of Clark's eastern supporters, who smelled to him of "Wall Street," Bryan gave his support to Wilson, who was nominated on the forty-sixth ballot.

Virginia-born Wilson, a scholar in political science, had been President of Princeton University, then reform-Governor of New Jersey. Not a man of great personal magnetism, he owed his successes chiefly to the fact that his views so often coincided with the popular will.

The party platforms agreed on conservation, on banking, and on currency. They differed in the degree of their opposition to monopoly, the Democrats taking a stronger position. The Democrats also promised sharp cuts in the tariff. Wilson described his program as the "New Freedom." Roosevelt's platform endorsed all "progressive" measures and proposals.

Wilson did not receive a popular majority, but he had the largest electoral vote thus far in history. Roosevelt ran second and Taft, a poor third. The Socialist candidate, Eugene V. Debs, received a surprisingly high share of the vote—nine hundred thousand, or 6 per cent.

WOODROW WILSON

Persons who call themselves "liberals" claim President Woodrow Wilson as one of them. If true, the proper definition of a "liberal" must be one who works strenuously at the repair and maintenance of America's essentially conservative economic and political system. That was the peacetime mission of Wilson, and he pursued it through a program of wide legislative reform, which he tagged the "New Freedom."

Regulation of the Trusts. Before Wilson took office, the theme of his administration was chorded by a committee of the Democratically controlled House of Representatives when it set its Pujo Committee to investigating the "Money Trust." Its conclusion that the economy was increasingly controlled by a steady concentration of financial power supported the Wilsonians in their projected reforms. Three days before the inauguration of the new President, the Congress passed the Physical Valuations Act whereby the Interstate Commerce Commission could evaluate railroad property in order to determine what rail rates would return a fair profit to the roads.

The Federal Trade Commission (FTC) was founded in 1914 to police interstate commerce so as to prevent "unfair competition." It concerns itself with many aspects of the problem but is best known for its proceedings against false or misleading advertising, whether on labels or otherwise.

The antitrust laws were revised by the Clayton Antitrust Act of 1914. Notable changes exempted unions from the operation of the antitrust laws and forbade the use of court orders (injunctions) in labor disputes except to prevent "irreparable" damage to property. It also, with little success, attempted to apply various legal devices as brakes to stop the seemingly inexorable concentration of economic power in fewer and fewer hands, and to preserve a competition which is more supported by the people in theory than in practice.

Banking Reform. The principal domestic monument to Wilson's administration is the Federal Reserve System. This is a privately-owned, federally-directed system of banking intended to assure a flexible currency. Accepted as part of the economic landscape today, it was opposed fiercely by bankers in the beginning. The Federal Reserve Act, sponsored by Senator Carter Glass of Virginia, established "bank's banks" in nine areas, in which cash could be deposited and businessmen's and farmers' notes used as collateral or discounted for cash. Theoretically, credit could be kept from expanding beyond reasonable limits, by manipulation of interest, currency notes, and discount rates, thus preventing wild booms or deep depression.

Tariff Revision. Democratic views on the tariff were put into practice by the Underwood Tariff of 1913 which made the first great downward revision of tariff rates since before the Civil War, although it did not realize the old Democratic slogan, "a tariff for revenue only."

Aid to Agriculture. Several pieces of agricultural legislation were enacted, as though to echo the Populist battles of an earlier decade. The Smith-Lever Act of 1914, through county extension programs, extended the training given by federally aided state colleges of agriculture to adults remote from the campuses. The Farm Loan Act of 1916 did for farm financing what the Federal Reserve Act did for businessmen. Co-operative farm loan organizations were enabled to help their members secure long-term mortgage loans at lower rates than could be secured from commercial banks. The Warehouse Act of the same year allowed farmers to store their crops and use the warehouse receipts as security for loans. This provided a safer way to finance crops than could be done through a strictly cash-sale program. The Smith-Hughes Act of 1916 provided federal aid to agricultural education by matching the grants made by the states for the same purpose. The result has been the addition of agriculture to the curriculum of many a small high school.

Other Aspects of Reform. The Constitution was twice amended in 1913, although both amendments were proposed before Wilson was elected. The Sixteenth Amendment allowed the Congress to tax incomes without reservation. This provided revenue to meet the growing expense of government beyond the capacity of the excises and tariff. The Seventeenth Amendment required that Senators be elected by the people rather than by the state legislatures and represented an essential alteration of the nature of the Union. It would be rash to assert that the quality of the Senate has been improved, although it is certain that the cost of running for the Senate has been tremendously increased by an amendment aimed to extend democracy. If seats in state legislatures were justly apportioned, it would be hard to praise this amendment.

Three days before Wilson's inauguration the Congress passed (over Taft's veto) the Webb-Kenyon Act to prohibit interstate commerce of alcoholic liquors into "dry" states. This dubious experiment set a trend toward federal regulation of the human diet which steadily strengthened while Wilson was President.

13

America Becomes a World Power

America emerged from the Spanish-American War as a colonial power. Partly because of this new status and partly because of the men at her helm, she became increasingly involved in Latin American, Asian, and European affairs. Having thus entered into world politics America, unknowingly, assumed an important place in the precarious European balance-of-power system, the disruption of which in 1914 cast a good part of the world—America notwithstanding—into the turmoil of war.

A COLONIAL EMPIRE

The conquest of Cuba, Puerto Rico, and the Philippines—the major fruits of victory in the war with Spain—posed serious problems for the United States in the field of colonial administration.

The "Insular Cases." The possession of newly acquired overseas territories immediately presented the question of whether or not their inhabitants had the benefits of the United States Constitution. In the "Insular Cases" the Supreme Court held that they did not unless the Congress explicitly extended the Constitution to them.

Cuba. Cuba itself offered a series of problems which were not settled to the satisfaction of the Cubans until a generation had passed. In 1898 the Congress had adopted the "Teller Amendment" which promised that Cuba would be self-governing when its turmoils had been quieted. After the war, however, the freedom of the Cubans was limited by the United States. Having reorganized the island's finances and sanitation, the United States

THE UNITED STATES AS A COLONIAL POWER, 1900

prepared to withdraw amid some fears that sudden independence might bring with it the evils of political instability and financial irresponsibility. The Cuban Constitution of 1901 made no arrangement for a continuing relationship with the United States. Before accepting the Cuban Constitution, the United States adopted the Platt Amendment to provide such a relationship. In essence it placed the foreign affairs of Cuba under the "protection" of the United States. The Cuban public debt was limited, the United States could police the island in case of disorder (under this provision, American marines were landed in Cuba several times to quell election disorders and race riots), and the United States might acquire a site for a naval base. America abrogated the Platt Amendment in 1934. Although Cuba is now free, American economic influence is considerable.

Puerto Rico. Puerto Rico, acquired in 1898 from Spain as an indemnity after the Spanish-American War, posed a "colonial problem" for the United States. The first step in the solution of the problem was the passage of the Foraker Act (1900) which gave the island a Governor General and Council, appointed by the President. The Council served as the upper legislative chamber and was paired with an elective lower house. This system was practically identical with the old royal government of the "royal colonies" of British North America and the British West Indies, with the President standing in the place of the Kings of England. In 1917 the Jones Act made Puerto Rico an organized Territory of the United States, made the Puerto Ricans citizens of the United States, gave them most of the civil rights provided in the United States Constitution, made the upper chamber elective, and allowed the territory to keep the federal internal revenues collected in the island.

Puerto Rico depended upon the sugar industry for its prosperity, almost to the exclusion of other kinds of enterprise, and when the price of that commodity plunged during the great depression of the 1930's, the island suffered acute distress. Agitation for statehood was heard at the time, but the coming of World War II pushed local problems into the background. In 1948 the Puerto Ricans were given the right to elect their own governor and in 1952 were given "Commonwealth" status, similar to that of the members of the British Commonwealth of Nations except that Puerto Rico does not direct its own foreign affairs. A tiny minority of the people have insisted upon complete independence, and they punctuated their demand with an attempt to assassinate President Harry S. Truman in November, 1950.

The Philippines. When the Americans fought the Spanish, they allied themselves with a going local Philippine revolution led by Emilio Aguinaldo. Aguinaldo gained the impression that the United States had come to establish Philippine independence. When he and his men learned otherwise, they fought as well against the Americans as they had against the Spanish. This Philippine Insurrection, almost unknown to Americans today, was a larger war than the Spanish-American War. Guerilla fighting lasted until 1902. An American Commission, in 1901, recommended independence for the islands, to take effect at some indefinite time in the future. William Howard Taft, as Governor General, began the process of establishing Filipino self-government. This trend continued to 1934 when the Tydings-McDuffie Act granted Filipino independence after a ten-year probationary period, which was interrupted by World War II. In 1946 the Philippines achieved an independent Commonwealth status.

THE UNITED STATES AND THE WESTERN HEMISPHERE

With new territorial interests to be maintained and protected, the United States embarked upon an aggressive foreign policy, reaffirming and extending the principles of the Monroe Doctrine.

The Panama Canal. The Spanish-American War and America's new two-ocean empire emphasized the strategic and tactical need for a canal through the Central American Isthmus. In 1901 the Anglo-American Clayton-Bulwer Treaty of 1850 was modified by the Hay-Pauncefote Treaty which gave the United States sole authority over any isthmian canal, and provided that it be open to all nations. The next question was where to build it. Panama and Nicaragua seemed the most logical sites. In 1902 the United States acquired rights to the Panama route from a French corporation. Panama was then a province of Colombia, so the Hay-Herran Treaty of 1903, with Colombia, arranged rental and other financial terms. Things came to a stop in 1903 when the Colombian government rejected the terms. Four days later the Panamanian Revolution began, led by men who knew President Roosevelt would approve. The United States Navy passively assisted the rebels, and they received legal recognition from the State Department almost immediately. Philippe Bunau-Varilla was soon received by the United States as Minister from the Republic of Panama and negotiated a treaty setting aside the Canal Zone and guaranteeing the independence of the Republic. Construction of the canal began quickly, and after modern medical science and sanitary engineering combined to conquer the local tropical diseases (the work of Colonel William C. Gorgas), Colonel George W. Goethals and his fellow engineers completed the canal by 1914. Before its opening, the Panama Tolls Act of 1912, which discriminated in favor of American ships, brought charges of bad faith from the British. At Wilson's request it was repealed in 1914.

The Roosevelt Corollary. Many Caribbean republics had defaulted in their debts to European countries; it was not unusual for the creditors to sail into the republics' ports and harass the governments into payment. Fearing the possible consequence of such European intervention, President Roosevelt announced in 1904 that, since the Monroe Doctrine forbade European intervention in the Western Hemisphere, it was the job of the United States to intervene and maintain order in this area whenever necessary. The wide police powers assumed by the United States under the Roosevelt Corollary to the Monroe Doctrine caused such ill will both in Latin America and Europe that this sledgehammer diplomacy was repudiated several administrations later. Meanwhile, the Roosevelt Corollary was first applied to the Dominican Republic when it defaulted in its financial obligations. The United States moved troops into the island and placed its customs service in American receivership.

A logical outgrowth of the Roosevelt Corollary was Taft's "dollar diplomacy," which he pursued with some success in Nicaragua (but which failed in the Far East). The relations of the United States and Nicaragua had been consistently tense. American investments there were substantial, and it was also an alternate canal route. Taft's technique to assure American economic and political control in Nicaragua was to transfer that government's debt from European banks to American banks, thus liquidating the cause for European intervention and, at the same time, promoting private American banking interests. In accordance with this policy an American loan was arranged in 1911, secured by control of the customs, the railway, and the Bank of Nicaragua. A revolt of resentful natives in 1912 was curbed by the United States Marines who did not finally depart until the 1930's. Secretary of State Bryan, in 1916, negotiated a treaty with Nicaragua which guaranteed the right of the United States to a canal route. Nicaragua received a cash award.

Although President Wilson repudiated the Roosevelt Corollary and "dollar diplomacy," he was forced to pursue similar policies when successive revolutions in Haiti endangered the interests of creditors. A force of Marines was landed in 1915 and made Haiti a "protectorate." Similar disorders in San Domingo brought similar intervention, and a government by United States Naval Officers was established in 1916, which lasted into the 1920's.

The Roosevelt Corollary was amplified in 1912 by the "Lodge Corollary," announced when Japanese interests were arranging to buy a fishing base in Lower California. The effect of the statement (which was enough to kill the deal) was to extend the Monroe Doctrine to non-European nations.

Mexico. All of these strains were troublesome enough, but the gravest series of Western Hemisphere crises occurred in the relations of Mexico and the United States. From 1877 to 1911 Mexico was ruled by the dictator Porfirio Diaz, who was generous to foreign investors. About half of two billion dollars of foreign investment came from the United States. Diaz was overthrown by the revolutionist Francisco Madero in 1911, touching off a series of diplomatic difficulties. Many investors lost their money, some their lives. The United States, in the interest of stability, recognized and supported Madero, but he was soon assassinated by order of a rival, Victoriano Huerta. Wilson, who now became President, was unable to grant diplomatic recognition to a government founded on assassination and offered American financial encouragement in return for free elections if Huerta were not to be a candidate. Huerta was not interested in the proposition. For the next year or so, an arms embargo to Mexico was laid, but was then lifted to allow weapons and munitions to reach Huerta's enemies. At the same time the port of Vera Cruz was blockaded to bar similar imports by Huerta.

In the spring of 1914, Huerta's troops arrested an American naval supply party in Tampico and refused to make the ceremonial amends demanded by their commander. In this tense moment, to prevent rumored landings from a munitions ship,

American naval forces shelled and occupied Vera Cruz. Mexicans supported Huerta as never before, and the two nations neared war. However, the "ABC" powers—Argentina, Brazil, and Chile—successfully mediated the dispute in a meeting at Niagara Falls, Canada. Huerta did not like the terms, resigned, and was succeeded by his foe, Venustiano Carranza.

Carranza was troubled by chronic brigandage, led by Pancho Villa who also posed as a political leader. His operations included raids into United States territory and General John J. Pershing was sent with fifteen thousand men, to pursue him. With America's entrance into World War I the unsuccessful force was withdrawn, and Carranza was recognized as President of Mexico.

Alaska, Newfoundland, and Canada. There were also a good many questions of relations with the neighbors to the north. The discovery of gold in the Klondike region brought up the question of the location of the boundary of Alaska. In 1903 Great Britain and the United States agreed to arbitrate the dispute. While the Commission was sitting, President Roosevelt hinted that he would use force if the award were not satisfactory. It was satisfactory. The Newfoundland fisheries dispute, dating back to the American Revolution, was finally settled by an Anglo-American Convention in 1912, in a manner to allow Newfoundland its proper local regulations. In 1911 the oceanic sealing question was reopened in a conference among the United States, Great Britain, Russia, and Japan. An American monopoly in the Bering Sea was accepted, in return for a share of the profits to be given to the nations which withdrew. A reciprocal trade treaty with Canada was negotiated in 1911 to prevent retaliation for the Payne-Aldrich Tariff (see page 166), but was rejected by Canada because some Canadians resented talk of the annexation of Canada in the United States.

The Trend toward Internationalism. In this same period the United States took part in affairs which might have been regarded as of primary interest to Europeans. Americans were present as delegates to the Hague Conferences of 1899 and 1907. The first Conference established the Permanent Court of International Arbitration (with only voluntary jurisdiction). The second adopted something like Argentina's "Drago Doctrine" in which the Argentine Foreign Minister had replied to the "Roosevelt Corollary" by asserting that international debts must not be collected by force. Americans were also present at the Algeciras

Conference in 1906, dealing with African affairs, through which
Roosevelt played a mediating part in differences between France
and Britain on one side, and Germany on the other. During the
years 1908–9, arbitration treaties were made by Secretary of State
Elihu Root with twenty-five nations. Secretary of State Bryan, in
1913 and after, negotiated about thirty more like treaties.

THE UNITED STATES AND THE FAR EAST

The American interest in the Far East had been chiefly a commercial interest before the conquest of the Philippines. Thereafter, it became an even more serious matter.

China: The "Open Door Policy." Chinese affairs absorbed
much attention from the United States. The decaying Chinese
Empire seemed ripe for the sort of partition which had been the
destiny of Africa. In the late 1890's Great Britain suggested an
Anglo-American guarantee of equality of business opportunities
there. The notion was carried forward by Secretary of State John
Hay who circularized the major European powers, as well as
Japan, with the proposition that the powers would not attempt
to block each other's trade in China. The answers he received
were evasive but—on the principle that silence gives consent—he
interpreted them as approving what then was announced in 1900
as the "Open Door Policy." That same year antiforeign Chinese
tried to expel all foreigners, in the "Boxer Rebellion." It was put
down by a joint military expedition. Although America urged
moderation, the governments concerned levied heavy damages
on China. Three-fourths of America's share of $25,000,000, how-
ever, was remitted and used to educate Chinese in American
universities.

America's Mediation of the Russo-Japanese War. The next
serious flare-up in the Far East was the Russo-Japanese War,
1904–5, which was started by Japan without warning, as a solution to rivalry over Manchuria. President Roosevelt wished neither side to be totally defeated because that would destroy the
balance of power in China. Japan, after winning a series of
victories, found itself near the end of its resources (a fact not
publicized, of course) and asked Roosevelt to offer his influence
as a mediator. He agreed. At Portsmouth, New Hampshire, in
1905, peace was signed between Russia and Japan. Japan secured

recognition of her place in Korea and Manchuria. The Japanese people, not knowing the narrowness of their margin of victory, resented Roosevelt's intervention, but the rest of the world's opinion was represented by the award of the Nobel Peace Prize to him in 1906.

Japanese-American Relations. Japanese relations with the United States had opened on a painful note in the 1850's when their doors had been forced open by Commodore Matthew C. Perry. From that time forward the Americans rather admired the Japanese, partly for their graphic arts and their architecture, and partly because they so flatteringly studied and adopted Western technologies. The only false chord in this rhapsody was the immigration question. The people of the western United States feared an overwhelming influx of Japanese. (The figures which had alarmed the Californians were these: Japanese immigrants into the United States, 1891–1900, 26,000; 1901–10, 130,000.) The Japanese government slowed emigration directly to the United States but could not do much about secondary migration of Japanese from nearby countries and territories to the United States.

In 1906 the San Francisco school board segregated oriental children. The Japanese were insulted but of course, the executive branch of the federal government could do nothing officially. However, Roosevelt persuaded the school board to rescind its order, in return for which he limited immigration by executive order. Next he dealt with the Japanese government and arrived at what has rather oddly been called the "Gentlemen's Agreement" (1907). Japan agreed to permit no more laborers to come to the United States. It was then announced that the offensive school-board order had been rescinded. The orders and exclusions, although dressed as "agreements," did not relieve ill will. From this time on, American display of contempt for Asiatics aroused genuine hatred for the United States in the only Asiatic nation that was industrially qualified to hurt the United States.

In 1908 the Root-Takahira agreement provided recognition of the status quo in eastern Asia and the "Open Door" in China. President Roosevelt sent the navy around the world, partly to show that the United States, as yet, had no reason to fear Japan. (The American Navy ranked second; the Japanese, fifth.)

THE FIRST WORLD WAR

In 1914 Europe divided itself into two armed camps and plunged into war. Germany, Austria, and Turkey as the Central Powers opposed Britain, France, Belgium, Russia, and Italy— the Allies. Eventually, America was drawn into this cataclysm and proved to be a leading power among powers. Having used her great resources to bring about peace, the United States, deaf to President Wilson's warning, refused to champion the preservation of that peace, rejecting membership in the League of Nations.

The Struggle for Neutral Rights. With Wilson's proclamation of American neutrality, the country immediately was engaged in controversy over neutral rights with both belligerents. Great Britain, in blockading Germany, had greatly lengthened the "contraband list." In spite of American protests about neutral rights on the high seas, the British clamped on a very tight blockade, even barring food shipments; by March 1915 the blockade was almost perfect.

Germany attempted to resist the blockade by the then novel means of submarine warfare (which some people thought to be sneaky and unfair). Submarine warfare became the central point around which neutrality controversies revolved. Because submarines were relatively defenseless on the surface, they dared not investigate ships or provide safety for the torpedoed crews. Therefore, the Germans announced that all enemy vessels in British waters would be sunk on sight. Inevitably, as unwarned, unexpected sinkings occurred, American lives were lost and American tempers were inflamed. The British blockade might be legally questionable, but it cost America little. Submarine warfare, as waged by Germany, cost American blood.

The first great German-American crisis came with the sinking of the British liner *Lusitania,* in 1915, with the loss of 124 Americans. American opinion veered sharply from the German cause for the most part thereafter. An exchange of notes with the German government ended with German-American relations distinctly frigid. When the British ship *Arabic* was torpedoed in August, 1915, the German Ambassador to the United States, Count von Bernstorff, promised that no more ships would be sunk without warning unless they tried to escape—a tactically impossible guarantee.

German-American relations were worsened in 1915 by the discovery of German spying and sabotage in America. Two members of the German Embassy staff were expelled.

This was about the slowest moving war since the siege of Troy. President Wilson sent his personal adviser, Edward M. House, on a tour of European capitals in the interest of a negotiated peace, in 1915. Although he was politely received, it was plain by the spring of 1916 that each side hoped to crack the military deadlock and smash through to victory by force of arms; the war went on at snail speed.

Early in 1916 the Germans announced that they would sink armed enemy merchant ships at sight. Fearing more American loss of life and the consequent growth of belligerent feeling in the United States, isolationist Congressmen supported a movement to give up neutral rights by warning Americans not to travel in armed ships. Another congressional proposal was to refuse passports to Americans who proposed to travel in the ships of nations at war. Wilson knew that if the United States did not preserve neutral rights the rights would die forever, and any warring nation could legally rule all seas. He and his helpers fought these congressional proposals to death in the Congress in 1916.

Unhappily the combatants gave neutrals little time to deliberate. Crisis followed crisis. The sinking of the unarmed cross-channel ship *Sussex*, in March, 1916, in which several Americans were injured, resulted in Wilson's announcement that German-American diplomatic relations would be severed after the next such incident.

The British were not without a capacity to irritate. In the summer of 1916 they published a "black list" of Americans doing business with the Central Powers, and refused to allow them to use British banks, ships, or cables. American protests and threats of reprisal caused a moderation of the policy.

American reaction to the war was not confined to notes of protest to the belligerents. A "preparedness movement" brought the beginning of officer-reserve training, under private auspices, in 1915, and the National Defense Act of 1916 provided for systematic enlargement of the armed forces. A Council of

National Defense was also established in that year to co-ordinate military and industrial preparations. The Shipping Act of 1916 provided for the expansion of the Merchant Marine.

The Election of 1916. The country thus faced a presidential election. The Democrats renominated Wilson, and the Republicans named Supreme Court Justice Charles Evans Hughes. The Democrats praised their record of neutrality and preparedness and lauded Wilson with the slogan, "He kept us out of war." The Republicans had no strong counter, but the electoral vote was the closest in decades, 277–254. California's choice of Wilson by the narrow margin of less than four thousand votes was dramatically decisive, since it was the last state reported. The Congress remained Democratic.

In 1916 there was still talk of peace by negotiation. Both the Germans and the Americans sent up "trial balloons." With German encouragement President Wilson proposed himself as mediator. The German government said it was willing to talk peace, but the Allies refused the offer unless Germany would first state her peace terms. This was not done. In December, Wilson requested both sides to state their terms. The statement of war aims by the Allies required restoring all conquered territory held by the Central Powers, plus the payment of damages. This was bound to be unacceptable to the Central Powers, the side which was "ahead." The best that Wilson could do was to advocate a "peace without victory," to be preserved by an international organization.

America's Declaration of War. After this flurry of pacific but fruitless notewriting, the march of maritime crises was resumed. Early in 1917 the Germans announced unrestricted submarine warfare as a military necessity. All ships in British waters would be sunk on sight. Regarding this as a violation of the earlier pledge, Wilson, on February 3, 1917, the day on which the American ship *Housatonic* was sunk, broke off diplomatic relations with Germany. Wilson hoped to discourage submarine attacks by arming American merchant ships. When a Senate filibuster delayed the program, the President went ahead by authority of a law passed in 1797. But the situation at sea worsened. In nine days, beginning on March 12, five American ships were sunk.

Simultaneously with this shattering series of disasters came the public exposure of the "Zimmermann Note" from German

Foreign Minister Zimmermann, promising territorial rewards if Mexico and Japan fought on the German side. The Mexicans were promised New Mexico, Texas, and Arizona if they persuaded Japan to enter the war, too.

On April 2, 1917, Wilson, on the unanimous advice of his Cabinet, asked the Congress to declare war on Germany, to make the world "safe for democracy." The resolution was completed in the Congress on April 6 (six Senators and fifty Representatives voted "nay").

Entrance into the war was certainly not a case of hastening to side with winners. Submarine warfare was at its most effective. Russia had collapsed into revolution and civil war. Italy had suffered military reverses, and the Allies were on the defensive on the western front. From the war's inception, American sympathy was for the Allies. The cultural ties with England could not be denied; American sentiment for the French had existed since the days of Lafayette. Economically, America was also tied to these nations. With the advent of war, American trade with the Allies increased enormously, while that with Germany decreased because of the effectiveness of Britain's blockade. Eventually, the huge purchases by the Allies created a need for money, and American bankers made substantial loans to them. Germany, on the other hand, could not buy so readily in the American market and thus had little need for our currency. Therefore, there was very little common cause with Germany. America had long feared German imperialistic ambitions in the Western Hemisphere; and Germany's invasion of Belgium, in violation of that country's neutrality, appalled most Americans. Later Germany's unrestrictive submarine warfare, in which so many American lives were lost, became the decisive factor in bringing the United States into the Allied camp.

Military Operations. In the next year and a half, the United States expanded its army from two hundred thousand to four million, almost two million of whom saw combat. The navy (half a million men), directed by Admiral William S. Benson, Chief of Naval Operations, convoyed, fought submarines, and helped block the North Sea, under the overseas command of Admiral William S. Sims.

The American Expeditionary Force (A.E.F.), under General John J. Pershing, arrived in France late in June, where an administrative argument was settled by forming the American army into a new army group instead of using it to strengthen existing Allied groups. The professional soldiers of the First Division were in combat by October 1. The A.E.F. soon had full membership in the loosely organized Supreme War Council of officers and civilians, which tried to co-ordinate military operations without giving up authority to any one commander.

In March, 1918, the Germans mounted a great offensive in the west. The time seemed opportune, partly because of the effectiveness of submarine warfare and partly because the collapse of Russia allowed the release of many divisions from the eastern front. In a little over two weeks they drove thirty-five miles into a wedge near the junction of the French and British fronts. A few thousand American troops served in this battle. Faced with catastrophe the Allies now adopted a system of unified command under the French General Ferdinand Foch. The Germans continued to move forward and by the end of May were about fifty miles from Paris. The American Second Division and parts of two others were thrown into the fight at Chateau Thierry, where the German advance was stalled, on the Marne River. In June the Second Division and a brigade of Marines recaptured Belleau Wood while the First Division took Cantigny.

The Allied counteroffensive was building up. A major German attack along the Marne, in late July and early August, was held up in a battle involving eighty-five thousand Americans. By this time a million American soldiers were in France, and Foch took the offensive late in July, along the Aisne and Marne rivers. In August the British attacked along the Somme River, in a continuous operation which lasted until the end of the war.

In September the first distinctly American operation, using over half a million men, began against the St. Mihiel salient. Wholly successful, the Americans took thousands of prisoners and hundreds of guns. Later in that month, over a million American troops pressed the bloody, stubborn Meuse-Argonne offensive, which was still victoriously in motion when the war ended (the battle having cost 120,000 American casualties).

Wilson's "Fourteen Points." During the course of the fighting, President Wilson had been developing his plans for a durable peace. In the Congress, in January, 1918, he announced a fourteen-point program, soon famous as the "Fourteen Points." In summary, they provided for open diplomacy, freedom of the seas, equality of international trade, disarmament, just colonial arrangements, fixing of the boundaries of Russia, Belgium, France and other nations according to nationality, and the establishment of a permanent League of Nations for the settlement of present and future differences. Except for the difficulty of identifying any specific "nationality," and the practical impossibility of conducting open diplomatic affairs (since Wilson did not repudiate the secret treaties among the European allies), there can be no doubt that this was a most advanced program for securing world peace.

And it was politically effective. It seemed to offer the Germans a chance to get out of the war without facing total destruction. Unlike wars before or since, this had been a war of attrition, as though two duellists had agreed to open their arteries and see who could longer survive the bleeding. Germany was bled almost to death by the fall of 1918. In October the German and Austrian governments requested a cease-fire or armistice, as a preliminary to a conference to discuss peace on the basis of the "Fourteen Points." Amid world-wide rejoicing the armistice was arranged for November 11, 1918.

The war had cost the United States over a hundred thousand lives and a direct expenditure of about twenty-two billion dollars, plus further billions loaned to the Allies.

A congressional off-year election had occurred on the eve of the armistice. Wilson feared that partisanship might hurt the prospects for success in the approaching peace conference. His method of avoiding it was not subtle, for he asked the voters to return a Democratic Congress, regarding such an appeal as a request for a vote of confidence and not realizing it was a negative attack on the Republicans. On election day the Republicans carried both Houses of the Congress. Still shortsighted, Wilson included no Senators and but one Republican in the delegation which he took to France to talk peace terms.

The War at Home. World War I, as it has since been named, was the greatest social and economic convulsion the American people had experienced since the Civil War. To secure a unified war effort great restrictions were applied to economic and civil liberty, which had the effect of making people more used to government controls than in any earlier generation.

Within days of the declaration of war the President established a Committee on Public Information, headed by George Creel, for the purpose of influencing public opinion to favor the administration's policy. In a few weeks the Congress enacted a draft law, not the first, but the first effective one in American history. Under this law twenty-four million men were ultimately enrolled, of whom almost three million were called. The Espionage Act of 1917 penalized intellectual opposition to the war (writing and speaking) and was strengthened in detail in 1918 by the Sedition Act. Lincoln had been equally repressive of civil liberty—but not so systematically nor effectively.

On the economic side the national effort was prodigious. The world's strongest industrial system was quickly and, for the most part, efficiently geared to military programs. The Liberty Loan Act of 1917 provided for borrowing directly from the public. Five great loans were floated in succession, bringing in over twenty billion dollars. In 1918 the War Finance Corporation was created to finance production. It loaned three billion dollars to war industries. The War Revenue Act of 1917 took advantage of the new Income Tax Amendment to secure these loans by raising an adequate revenue.

The War Industries Board, headed by Bernard M. Baruch, co-ordinated industry through a system of priorities, price fixing, and preclusive buying. A National War Labor Board was appointed to act as a kind of Supreme Court of labor disputes.

The consumer's position was regulated by the Food and Fuel Control Act, which was administered by Herbert Hoover, to direct the production and distribution of those commodities. Trade with the enemy was forbidden by law, and international trade was strictly regulated through a system of licenses issued by the War Trade Board. The railroads, under decentralized control, were unable to use their facilities as efficiently as desired. By presidential order William Gibbs McAdoo unified them under governmental control.

So well was the "home front" organized that the goal of total participation (set for 1919) was never reached. American industry and finance overmatched the strained Central Powers with relative ease—one might say, a year "ahead of time."

The Peace Treaty and the League of Nations. The peace conference opened at Paris in January, 1919. Wilson headed the

American delegation (which may have been a mistake because it seemed to commit him to every agreement and because participation in the daily arguments may have lowered his dignity as chief of the strongest state). There he was associated with the Prime Ministers of Great Britain, France, and Italy—respectively, Lloyd George, Clemenceau, and Orlando—each of them present to defend interests he regarded more highly than he regarded Wilson's plans for permanent peace. Particular goals were the punishment of Germany, financial damages, and territorial shifts.

Wilson insisted that priority be given to drawing up a plan for a League of Nations. The draft of the Covenant, as it was named, derived from American, British, and South African thinking. When it was ready, President Wilson thought his part of the job of the conference was pretty well finished and he returned to the United States. There he found opposition developing among Senators who published a statement known as the "Round Robin," attacking the League of Nations. After announcing that the League was an essential part of the settlement, Wilson returned to Paris.

By this time the Allies had formulated their demands. The French wished compensation for damage done by the Germans and either the occupation of the Rhineland or the creation of an independent Rhenish state. They accepted a temporary occupation of the Rhineland and the promise of an Anglo-Franco-American defensive alliance of which the latter was refused by the Senate.

The Italians demanded to be given a boundary at the Alps (which would mean the annexation of two hundred thousand German-speaking people) and the city of Fiume. Discouraged by Wilson, Orlando went home in anger.

The Japanese abstained from discussion of Western affairs but claimed the Shantung Peninsula, which they had taken from the Germans. Wilson gave in on this point, contrary to his expressed principles. The Western world missed a propaganda victory when it did not seize on Japan's suggestion of a racial-equality declaration.

In the course of discussions Wilson secured several modifications of the Covenant which were designed to appease the reluctant Senators. These were matters of exempting tariff, immigration, and regional agreements from League control. As appeasement, they did not suffice.

The Treaty of Versailles was completed early in May, 1919, signed by the Germans (with great distaste) late in June, and submitted by Wilson to the Senate early in July. It was a very long document which placed the blame for the war on Germany, reduced Germany's area, arranged to assess reparations against that country, and denied it any substantial army, navy, or air force. Part of the treaty was the League of Nations Covenant providing for an equally representative Assembly, a Council dominated by the stronger nations, and a separate Court of International Justice.

It now remained to be seen what reception would be given to the treaty in America. The critical question, of course, was whether the Senate would agree to it. In the Senate there were Wilsonians, who favored immediate ratification; moderates, led by Henry Cabot Lodge, who favored it with reservations; and "irreconcilables," who urged complete rejection. It was the League which made the difficulty as a new wave of the old isolationist tradition swept the country. With the benefit of hindsight we can now see that had Wilson yielded to the Lodge group, compromising on the reservations, he still would have salvaged a good deal of value. But he did not follow that policy. Instead, he embarked upon a long speaking tour to rouse the people to his side. This might have been successful except that his health failed in September, 1919, and he never fully recovered. In the Senatorial crisis Lodge submitted his reservations but lost to a combination of irreconcilables and Wilsonians. Then, on unconditional acceptance, the treaty failed of two-thirds ratification—although, if the Wilsonians and reservationists had joined forces, a modified treaty would have been ratified.

The Senate went ahead to end the war without the treaty. To evade Wilson's veto, the war was legally ended only after he left office. Peace treaties with the Central Powers were concluded in October, 1921.

The Democrats hoped that popular support for the League could be aroused in the presidential campaign of 1920, but their candidate, James M. Cox of Ohio, was crushingly defeated by Warren G. Harding, also of Ohio, in a campaign which saw the winning party straddle the League issue.

14

The Twenties

From 1898 to 1920 the United States had been steadily more active in international affairs, but with the end of the war and the election of 1920 a revulsion of feeling appears to have overcome the public. The country was tired of international turmoil and domestic reform and responded enthusiastically to Harding's campaign speech calling for a return to "normalcy"—a return to the pre-Wilsonian days of complacency, nationalism, and isolationism. Such was the temper of the entire decade.

THE HARDING ADMINISTRATION

Warren G. Harding established the policies of re-encouragement of laissez faire and withdrawal from foreign affairs, but the President's sudden death left the fulfillment of these policies to his successors. The Harding administration, itself, is best remembered for a series of spectacular scandals, which even surpassed those of the Grant era.

Postwar Depression. The first universally felt experience of Harding's administration was regrettably painful—the brief depression of 1921, which was the effect of readjustment from the "abnormalcy" of the business conditions known during the war years. Thousands of businesses failed and millions of people were unemployed, but, except for the farmers, the blight was brief and recovery rapid.

Corruption. President Harding's term of office was cut short by death in 1923, twenty-nine months after he took office. Mysterious and sinister conjectures regarding the cause of his death have been made, but none have been adequately documented. He was succeeded by Vice-President Calvin Coolidge.

A moral storm followed the President's passing when colossal corruption was found in the executive branch, involving the Departments of Justice, the Navy, and the Interior, the newly formed Veterans' Bureau, and the Alien Property Custodian. The chiefs of the latter two agencies were both sent to prison. (Charles R. Forbes, head of the Veterans' Bureau, squandered and stole two hundred million dollars of the money appropriated for veterans.) The notorious "Teapot Dome" scandal was uncovered in the Department of the Interior. Naval oil reserves were first transferred to the Interior Department and then secretly leased to oil operators Harry F. Sinclair and Edward L. Doheny, by Secretary Albert B. Fall. A Senate investigating committee under Senator Thomas J. Walsh discovered that Sinclair and Doheny had "loaned" Fall a total of $125,000 without security. The leases were cancelled, and Fall went to jail; but Doheny and Sinclair were acquitted of bribery, although Sinclair was punished for contempt of court. Attorney General Harry M. Daugherty was accused of criminal conspiracy. Specific allegations against him arose from the lax enforcement of liquor laws and failure to prosecute suspects in the Veterans' Bureau. He was acquitted, but President Coolidge requested his resignation.

Foreign Affairs. Harding's administration was, in a sense, born out of a reaction against the international-mindedness of his predecessors. It was, of course, impossible for the country to be wholly detached from foreign affairs, but it is hard to see any event of Harding's term as permanently influential in American diplomatic history.

The event which attracted the most attention was the Washington Conference of 1921, which met to discuss naval disarmament. The head of the American delegation, Charles Evans Hughes, proposed to scrap certain existing ships and to limit the size of future navies. The five leading powers present—the United States, Great Britain, Japan, France, and Italy—agreed to a ratio of the tonnage of battleships (expressed in the above order) of 5:5:3:1.67:1.67. Certain problems of the Far East were temporarily settled at the same time, most important of which was a nine-power agreement to guarantee China's territory and independence and to respect the "Open Door" policy.

A pressing problem of international relations was that of the war debts owed by the Allies, the largest being those of Britain, France, and Italy, owed to the United States. There was also much owed to Britain. British leaders offered to cancel what was owed to Britain if the United States would do the same for them. The Americans refused, but the point had been established in European minds that the principal debtors could not or would not pay unless they, in turn, could collect from *their* debtors.

In 1922 the figures were set. The British were to pay more than four billion dollars in sixty-two years, plus interest at a little more than 2 per cent. Cuts were made in the French and Italian debts of 60 and 80 per cent, respectively, and the interest was reduced. Although no final solution was ever reached, the war debts remained as a source of psychological poison and were joined to the German reparations problem in later years (see pages 196–197). American popularity declined abroad, and isolationism increased at home. It is an interesting speculation given the system of international trade, whether the gold supply of the world could be manipulated so as to allow these payments without destroying the world economic system. Certainly the United States would damage its own industry if it had to spend vast amounts abroad for manufactures, to keep the gold from accumulating in one place out of reach of the debtors.

POSTWAR SOCIETY

From late 1918 until the end of the decade of the 1920's, the American people passed through an abrupt change of mood, from the earnestness of the war years to a frivolity not otherwise known in the country's experience of the twentieth century.

An example was the ratification of the Eighteenth Amendment, prohibiting the sale or transport of alcoholic beverages, and the quick defiance of the laws enacted to enforce it. This paradox can probably be explained by the rural dominance of the ratifying legislatures of industrial states, since the most spectacular defiance occurred in large cities where the profits of illicit sales, called "bootlegging," made crime brazen.

The following year (1920), the Nineteenth Amendment eliminated the criterion of sex as a qualification for voting. This amendment was the culmination of a long campaign by suffragettes and other reformers. Some had expected it to "clean up" politics, but except for increasing the number of voters, it has had no appreciable effect on the election process.

The interest of people was not in regular politics. The two most theatrical episodes in the political history of the time were rather outside the current of the American political tradition. The first of these was the Big Red Scare of 1919–20 when police arrested thousands of political eccentrics and a few communist subversives. The other was a home-grown fascist movement called the Ku Klux Klan, organized as an anonymous instrument of terror against Catholics, Jews, and Negroes. After a few years, during which it exerted a good deal of political power in some states, common sense and a few prosecutions caused its decline.

The nationalism of the time was imbedded in the country's law by a succession of immigration statutes. In 1924 immigrants ineligible for citizenship were barred. This was applicable to the Japanese, many of whom were deeply angered by it. After four presidential vetoes, illiterates were barred from entering the United States in 1917—a provision which, if enacted earlier, would have kept out many who became eminent Americans. A bias against eastern and southern Europeans was written into the "quota laws" of 1921 and 1924 which fixed national quotas of annual immigration at percentages of those present in 1890, an arrangement which made it clear that the framers favored northern and western European immigrants over all others, as it was these people who had predominated in early immigration.

The great number of inventions since the Civil War had cumulatively worked a social revolution by the 1920's. Interchangeable parts and mass production removed the making of everyday items (clothes and food products) to the factory. Lowered prices created a consumer society.

The nation was more closely knit by improvements in communications. Rapid printing presses, typesetting devices, and page-plate processes made printed matter more widely accessible. The telephone simplified person-to-person communication. The phonograph, the silent motion picture, the radio, and the sound-picture for the first time made auditory and visual impact simultaneously possible over the whole country and had the inevitable, and perhaps undesirable, effect of establishing a trend to national conformity in thought and feeling. One could call this revolution the nationalizing of thought and taste.

Improvements in transportation made all parts of the country less remote from each other when measured by the time required to go from one place to another. Bicycles and trolleys (both urban and interurban) put the nation on wheels. Then the automobile brought a demand for better highways and provided speed and the mobility so dear to Americans. By the 1920's automobiles, especially cargo trucks, were beginning to cut into railroad revenues, and the latest wonder, the airplane, was a fairly common sight.

The transport revolution was made possible by the development and perfection of new engines and motors. The internal combustion engine, using gasoline or oil, could be built in compact power units admirably suited to automobiles, aircraft, and boats. The use of electricity, generated by water power or coal-burning plants, simplified the problems of mechanical power for industrial use and made electrical illumination commonplace in cities, indoors and out. Electricity was also rapidly applied to domestic appliances.

Looking back, one can see that, as technology advanced, the arts and morals declined. The only vigorous, fresh art form of the twenties that still has its millions of devotees was jazz music, which appeared simple but was a deceptively sophisticated and refined art requiring a remarkable self-discipine for its practice. Much has been made of the moral decay of the "tawdry twenties," in recent treatises. Statistical studies seem to show that the sex-moral standards of women were sharply lowered to the masculine level. Accompanying and contributing to the general immorality of the time was the rise of racketeering and gangsterism in the big cities.

In 1926 two sensational trials, one civil and one military, attracted great attention.

The civil trial was that of John Scopes, a Tennessee schoolteacher, who was indicted for teaching the doctrine of evolution. The prosecution was aided by William Jennings Bryan. Scopes was defended by Clarence Darrow. Scopes, although convicted, was almost forgotten in the interesting struggle between fundamentalist Bryan and sceptic Darrow, who were debating the Old Testament.

The military trial was the court-martial of Colonel William Mitchell, an army flier, who outspokenly condemned American military policy as blind or backward-looking in its failure to put more reliance on air power. He was found guilty of conduct harmful to order and discipline. When suspended from the service, he resigned his commission. Considering the data available to him in the early years, his conclusions had an element of brilliant guesswork, but his long-range vision was clear.

The coincidence of these two episodes in one year symbolized the social revolution which had happened by the decade of the 1920's; a downgrading of older values of the spirit; and an excitement over the advances and the future of the new material technologies.

THE AGE OF COOLIDGE

President Calvin Coolidge, heir of Warren Harding in 1923, is still affectionately remembered by some for his reserve, for his quiet humor, and as a symbol of the last carefree age in American history—carefree, if rather graceless. But in regard to Coolidge as a political figure, little that is memorable can be associated with his name except a concept of economy in government, no longer admired in practice. He did not lead. At most he suggested and withdrew. This may have been a virtue but more probably was a permissive cause of disasters to come. He reached the vice-presidency partly because, while governor of Massachusetts, he denied in stirring language the right of policemen to strike. The occasion was a police strike in Boston, an issue he took up only when the strike was pretty well settled.

Coolidge's First Administration. As President one of his first attention-getting acts was to veto a veterans' bonus bill (an act of courage) which was then passed over his veto in May, 1924. Except for his veto of a farm bill, this was about the extent of the significant record by which he could be judged in the presidential campaign of 1924, for which he was easily renominated by the Republicans.

The Election of 1924. The Democrats had serious trouble in their convention, when Alfred E. Smith and William G. McAdoo were deadlocked for 102 ballots. Compromise and fatigue brought the nomination, on the next ballot, of the able and colorless "Wall Street Lawyer," John W. Davis. The effect of nominating two such conservative gentlemen was to produce a relatively strong third party, the Progressive party, which nominated Robert M. LaFollette on a social-democratic platform. Democrats had hoped the "Harding Scandals" would strengthen them; but Coolidge was elected in a genuine landslide, seven and a half million votes ahead of Davis, and eleven million ahead of LaFollette, who carried only Wisconsin.

Coolidge Prosperity. In the next four years the Coolidge administration practiced economy by cutting taxes twice and also reducing the national debt. (The federal budget was then about one-twentieth of its present size.) They were not rewarded at the polls, for the Republicans lost seats in the Congress in the off-year election of 1926. Probably the most "newsworthy" event of the term, so far as domestic affairs were concerned, was President Coolidge's announcement, in 1927, that he did not "choose to run" in 1928. He also took a less dramatic but very grave step when he faced up to the farm issue. In 1924 he had vetoed the McNary-Haugen Bill for selling farm produce at fixed prices at home and at free prices abroad, the losses, if any, to be made up by the producers. In 1928 he vetoed it again. The feeling which eventually brought passage of these bills was generated by the continuing agricultural depression which had now lasted since the slump of 1921. Certain it was that farmers did not share in the otherwise general prosperity. Prosperity to Coolidge, as well as to Harding, was dependent upon the growth of business interests. Both administrations fostered that development by means of a high protective tariff; income tax reduction; and the withdrawal of federal intervention in, and regulation of, business. Thus, when President Coolidge announced, "The business of government is business," he rather concisely, but truthfully, summed up the domestic policy of the decade.

The Election of 1928. The presidential campaign of 1928 was one of the less pleasant chapters of the American story. The Republicans chose Herbert Hoover over the claims of several other contestants. As a relief administrator and director of civilian consumption during World War I, he had gained much respect. He was Coolidge's Secretary of Commerce. The Democrats nominated Alfred E. Smith, with little opposition. The campaign seemed to hinge on prohibition and the fact that Smith was a Catholic. Actually, it now seems that the voters saw no reason to expel the party which took the credit for prosperity. If Smith's religion played a part, it probably nullified rural resentment over the Republican failure to cope with the farm problem—

the rural regions being the great bastions of American Protestantism. Smith's frank disapproval of the Prohibition Amendment probably was equally damaging among farmers. The vote was a repetition of 1924, as Hoover won by an enormous plurality.

Foreign Affairs. We tend to think that the United States had no diplomatic history during the Presidency of Calvin Coolidge. Actually, the administration made a shining, but impermanent, record. Althought the United States had not joined the League of Nations, it took part in a number of conferences and maintained offices at the League's headquarters. Several Americans were appointed to the panel from which the judges of the Court of International Justice were to be selected in case of need. Throughout these years the United States stood at the verge of joining the Court, apart from the League, but never did so. In 1927 the United States sent delegates to the Geneva Naval Disarmament Conference (on the subject of smaller ships) which broke up without agreement. In 1927 Secretary of State Frank B. Kellogg circulated a "treaty" to outlaw war. Sixty-two nations signed it, without any provision whatever for enforcement. It is significant that although America could not remain completely aloof from foreign affairs, those measures that she did take did not saddle her with international responsibility.

Mexican relations posed problems which were treated somewhat more realistically. The Mexican Constitution of 1917 proclaimed that Mexican mineral rights had never been saleable; however, in 1923 it ruled that earlier oil-land acquisitions were to be respected. The next administration was unfriendly to American and other foreign developers, and it took strenuous efforts by United States Ambassador Dwight H. Morrow to reconfirm the arrangement.

Insurrections in Nicaragua kept American troops busy there in 1927 and 1928. By this time it was apparent that such activity by the United States was extremely distasteful to Latin-American leaders. The tide of disfavor built up by the Roosevelt Corollary and by numerous interventions on its behalf began to ebb. The specific turning point was the "Clark Memorandum," by Reuben J. Clark, who spoke for the State Department in 1928 and officially repudiated the Roosevelt Corollary.

Another considerable problem which the Coolidge administration had to wrestle with was the problem of German reparations and American war debts, two subjects so intertwined that European leaders swore they could not be separated. (European thought was to pay war debts from the collection of reparations.) The Allies had finally set German reparations at 132 billion gold marks. By 1923 the Germans were in default, and the French "foreclosed" by occupying the industrial Ruhr Valley. A settlement was arranged by Charles G. Dawes in 1924 (the "Dawes Plan") which provided a new monetary system for Germany and some financial credit. Again, in 1929, the Germans were bailed out by the "Young Plan," which reduced the payments and extended the time. In 1932, however, 90 per cent of the amount due was cancelled. It was a victory for simple arithmetic and for the old-fashioned view of money as a medium of exchange, not a thing valued for itself.

In 1930 the Congress passed the highest protective tariff in American history, the Smoot-Hawley Act. Fearing paralysis of world trade, hundreds of economists protested, but the President signed the bill.

THE UNFORTUNATE MR. HOOVER

When Herbert Hoover took office, the only obvious cloud on an otherwise sunny horizon was a persistent "farm problem." American agricultural prosperity had reached an intoxicating level in 1918 and continued to increase until 1921. Thereafter, it slumped steadily and became a chronic source of discontent and, perhaps, a warning of a storm to come.

Agricultural Legislation. Shortly after his inauguration the President called a special session of the Congress to deal with agricultural and tariff problems. The members of Congress from agricultural states—the "farm bloc"—were ready with a plan similar to the McNary-Haugen bills, now called the "export debenture plan." It was passed by the Senate but was beaten three times in the House and died under threat of a presidential veto if it were to be passed. Instead, the Agricultural Marketing Act of 1929 was enacted that provided for "orderly marketing" through public agencies and for a certain amount of public financing. The Federal Farm Board spent $180,000,-000 in two years but was blown away in the later economic storm.

The Stock Market Crash. Except for agriculture, the economy appeared to be in excellent condition if a boom may be regarded as healthy. Construction and factory production began to decline in 1927, but the boom continued, fed by happy speculation in securities—a speculation in values not much related to reality. The miserable days of reckoning came in October and November, 1929, bringing a collapse of the securities markets. The market value of listed stocks fell seventy-five billion dollars by the summer of 1932. The depression that followed was a traumatic experience for the American people equaled only by the Civil War, and it still strongly affects American behavior.

The Days of Depression. President Hoover's initial reaction was to urge private and state voluntary relief programs for the steadily growing hordes of unemployed. This relief was assisted by a small federal program of public works. The President adhered to the economic view of his predecessors—that prosperity of the nation's business enterprises culminates in national prosperity. Hoover's advisers and sympathizers do not appear to have believed in measuring national prosperity by using the national income as a standard, nor to have given much thought to the notion that mass production cannot long continue without mass consumption. As filtered through the commonplace minds of their local interpreters in newspapers and luncheon clubs, the exhortations of the leaders to work hard, to take confidence in the future of the country, and to support individualism seemed not economic thinking but rather the platitudes of a morality which was more often talked about than lived.

The public's opinion of the government's views was clearly revealed in the congressional election of 1930, when the Republicans lost the Senate and held the House by an unreliable majority of only two seats.

The President then advocated a program of generous credit to railroads and financial institutions, which was written into law by the Congress in the Reconstruction Finance Corporation Act of 1932, providing up to two and one-half billion dollars for such loans. However, this stratagem never captured the public imagination, even when its resources were enlarged in order to provide loans to local governments for public works. By the Glass-Steagall Act of 1932 part of the government's gold reserve was put to work to support the credit of businesses. At about the same time the President vetoed a bill to expand the federal employment service on the ground that it would invade states' rights. This was the sort of thing to be remembered by the voter. The Federal Home Loan Bank Act of 1932 came closer to satisfying individual wishes by establishing a system for supporting the risks of the lenders of home-mortgage money so that pressure to foreclose on defaulters would not be so great.

To many veterans the possibility of paying off their "adjusted compensation" certificates (insurance policies awarded to veterans in 1924 and worth, on the average, a thousand dollars each) in cash seemed a sensible way to encourage purchases and to relieve those in distress. In 1931 the Congress (over President Hoover's veto) provided that 50 per cent of the value could be borrowed. Pressure to pay all of the bonus was rapidly built up. To influence the Congress thousands of veterans gathered as a "Bonus Expeditionary Force," in shacks and abandoned buildings in Washington. When a bill to that effect was beaten in the Senate, most of the veterans went home. The rest were driven out by troops, after four lives were lost.

Foreign Affairs. Foreign affairs were a constant and frustrating distraction. A naval conference at London worked out ratios for ships below the battleship class by which the Japanese ratio was slightly increased. The President tried to halt the relapse of central Europe into economic chaos by proposing a one-year moratorium on war debts and reparations. But even more serious troubles were at hand that year as the Japanese Empire sent its armies marching into Manchuria in violation of all major understandings on China among the world powers. Secretary of State Henry L. Stimson told both Japan and China that this country would recognize no territorial changes made in that fashion. But, while the West wrote, conferred, and scolded, Japan continued on its march down the bloody road to ruin.

15

The New Deal

The presidential campaign of 1932 was one of a crucial half-dozen in American history which clearly mark sharp turns in the stream of events. President Hoover was renominated, without difficulty, on a platform that excited almost no one. The Democratic nomination, for the first time since 1920, seemed a real prize. On the fourth ballot it went to Franklin Delano Roosevelt, popular governor of New York. In his acceptance speech he promised "a new deal" for the forgotten man. The Democratic platform was not very prophetic of the country's future but did mention concrete social legislation and promised to repeal the Prohibition Amendment.

Mr. Roosevelt's optimistic campaign speeches were based on the analyses of college professors and expert advisers—the Brain Trust—and his radio manner and voice captivated millions. By contrast, Mr. Hoover seemed to be making a negative appeal, with charges of dangerous radicalism against the Democrats. The election went to Roosevelt in a reversal of the 1928 Republican landslide. Roosevelt carried forty-two states. The President's inaugural address was brief and breezy. Although thin in content, it had an optimistic tone that was felt deeply by millions of almost desperate listeners.

"The Hundred Days." Following the election the depression deepened and stagnation spread until the banking system was clogged and still. In the weeks after the election (just before the President's inauguration) practically every bank was closed. Among Roosevelt's first acts was a call to convene the Congress. He also declared a "bank holiday" and put rigorous temporary controls on currency. About three-fourths of the banks were reopened, by federal permission, in a few weeks.

The Congress assembled on March 9, 1933, in the session that became famous as "the hundred days." It inaugurated the New Deal by enacting the "three R's"—relief, recovery, and reform. The President's emergency banking program was approved and extended. The Economy Act was a premature flourish that cut about a quarter of a billion dollars of conventional expenses. In anticipation of the repeal of Prohibition, the permissible alcoholic content of beverages was raised to 3.2 per cent, thus gratifying farmers, revenue collectors, and victims of the fourteen-year drought. Soil problems and juvenile delinquency were both attacked by the Civilian Conservation Corps (CCC) which enrolled hundreds of thousands of unemployed young men at thirty dollars a month. The Federal Emergency Relief Act (FERA) provided outright grants to local authorities for work relief, under the direction of administrator Harry L. Hopkins.

In a deliberately inflationary move the United States abandoned the gold standard (which many European nations already had done) and cancelled the gold clause in contracts. In later litigation the Supreme Court held this action constitutional and legal but improper and unbecoming.

The Agricultural Adjustment Act (AAA) proposed to restore farmers' purchasing power by curtailing production of certain staples in return for government subsidies to be financed by a tax on processors of agricultural commodities. Farm credit was also liberalized. (The tax and controls were ruled unconstitutional in 1936.)

The Tennessee Valley Authority (TVA) was established to reorganize the entire economic life of a depressed geographic unit, in continuous consultation with its inhabitants. The program proposed an integrated plan of flood control, prevention of erosion, and industrial development by hydroelectric power. It has served as a standard for determining fair rates of privately owned utility companies, and it provided the power to make the first atom bomb.

The Federal Securities Act compelled honesty in the marketing of stocks and bonds. In 1934, enforcement of this law was assigned to the Securities and Exchange Commission (SEC). The United States Employment Service (USES) was established wherever states would co-operate. The Home Owners Loan Corporation (HOLC) refinanced home mortgages at low interest rates for about a million families who probably otherwise would have been foreclosed, and it made a profit. The Federal Deposit Insurance Corporation (FDIC) insured bank accounts, a policy which ended the destruction of banks by the "runs" of panicky small depositors. Farm mortgages were refinanced by the Farm Credit Act, and, later, all agricultural financing was consolidated in the Farm Credit Administration (FCA). The Emergency Railroad Transportation Act created the office of Co-ordinator of Transporation to stave off the economic disaster facing most railways.

The National Industrial Recovery Act (NIRA) was believed to be the crown of the structure of the New Deal. It intended to promote recovery by industrial self-regulation to prevent unfair competition, each industry making its own code. The supervisory agency was the National Recovery Administration (NRA). To offset the monopolistic flavor of the industry codes, labor was given the right to organize and bargain collectively without interference by management, by the famous "Section 7(a)." Another part established the Public Works Administration (PWA), headed by Interior Secretary Harold L. Ickes, with several billions to spend. Much of the NIRA was later invalidated by the Supreme Court.

Except in wartime there has never been a busier Congress. Oldsters have called it "revolutionary," but most people have accepted its program as one of patching, mending, propping up, and renovating the institution of private property and America's own specific brand of capitalism.

The New Deal at Zenith. After the first mighty spasm of the "hundred days," the New Deal settled down to a steady program of relief, recovery, and reform. Its activities from the middle of 1933 to the end of 1936 fall into two phases which might be called (1) the end of the beginning, and (2) the "Second New Deal."

Agriculture continued to receive a major share of attention on the ground that it was the part of the economy most neglected in the past and most needed for recovery in the present. Under the Agricultural Adjustment Administration (AAA) the Commodity Credit Corporation was established to lend money to farmers, on their crops, so that they could hold them off the market and await a favorable price situation. The Farm Credit

Administration (FCA) was authorized to do a similar task under the Crop Loan Act of 1934. Other acts extended benefits to farmers of an increasing list of crops, providing further protection against farm foreclosures and relief for farmer-bankrupts.

The problem of money, in the broadest sense, engaged a great deal of the administration's attention. The RFC was instructed by the President to buy and sell gold in such a way that the United States would control the value of gold. The initial price was set above the world price, and it was thereafter increased. This action devalued the dollar, known in the jargon of the day as the "commodity dollar," but did not raise commodity prices very much, although it annoyed foreigners and increased the pressure for favors to the silver interests. The Gold Reserve Act of 1934 gave the President power to manipulate the value of the dollar to cause an increase in prices. He set the value at fifty-nine cents in gold. The "silver bloc" in the Congress won a complete victory for their mineowners by the Silver Purchase Act of 1934 whereby the federal government buys, at an artificially high price, all silver offered. The relation, if any, of this act to other New Deal acts is invisible. It greatly profits the owners of silver mines and may have ruined China by draining the silver reserves of the Orient.

The Constitution received some remodeling, also. In 1931 the Wickersham Commission had presented a confused report on the effectiveness of the Prohibition Amendment, not recommending repeal but showing that some change was required. In 1932 the Democrats promised to repeal the amendment and this was done by means of the Twenty-first Amendment, ratified in December, 1933. The Twentieth, or Lame Duck Amendment, had been ratified earlier in 1933. It abolished the old requirement that a Congress meet after its successor had been elected, and it changed the date of presidential inaugurations from March 4 to January 20.

Other reforms continued the now familiar pattern. The Civil Works Administration (CWA) was a temporary proliferation for work relief in the hard winter of 1933–34. The Federal Communications Commission (FCC) assured the regulation of all interstate and foreign communications systems. The Federal Housing Administration (FHA) insured private mortgage lenders against loss. A number of acts extended the power of the Department of Justice agents to intervene in enforcing the law in matters of interstate crime.

Popular opinion of the government's course so far was shown by the congressional elections of 1934, in which the Democrats gained ten seats in each house.

The "Second New Deal," so-called, began in 1935 with the special aim of benefiting laborers and small farmers. In a sense it was a tactical political operation designed to disarm rising groups of radicals, both leftist and rightist, by curing the grievances they were exploiting. Among these people was Francis E. Townsend, who gained followers by promising two hundred dollars a month to all persons over sixty years old. Another was Huey P. Long, Governor of Louisiana, and later a Senator, who proposed to guarantee every family an income of five thousand dollars a year. A third was the Reverend Charles L. Coughlin, who addressed huge radio audiences in the interest of his National Union for Social Justice, which attacked monetary practices (and later declined when accused of anti-Semitism). The popularity of these men and their programs made it plain in 1935 that there were still serious grievances abroad.

The greatest single blow ever struck at incipient radicalism in American history was the Social Security Act of 1935, which provided a pension plan for the aged who had worked in "covered" industries, or their surviving dependents. It also provided assistance to co-operating states in caring for the blind and for dependent children. Having dulled the grievance of the "Townsendites," the Administration blanketed the sails of the share-the-wealth followers of Senator Long by the passage of the Revenue Acts of 1935 and 1936, which sharply raised personal and corporate income taxes in the upper brackets and, also, raised taxes on large inheritances. From these two acts dates the bitter hatred of Roosevelt which long persisted among many rich people.

Other changes created the Works Progress Administration (WPA) to provide work for persons previously on "relief," the Rural Electrification Administration (REA) for electrifying the rural areas through co-operative associations (large numbers of farms were not served by the utilities), and the National Youth Administration (NYA) for aiding young members of "relief" families to secure education or manual training.

Organized labor was given its NRA gains of "7(a)" in the Wagner (or National Labor Relations) Act, which guaranteed collective bargaining in general, and was the most favorable legislation to labor in a long time. During this period the labor movement grew; in 1936 John L. Lewis established the Committee for Industrial Organization, within the American Federation of Labor, to try to bring in the unskilled or low-skilled workers. Internal dissension led to its separation from the American Federation of Labor in 1938 as the Congress of Industrial Organizations. In time its chief strength lay in previously unorganized "mass industries," principally automobiles, aviation, and steel. The organization began with the theatrically successful but widely denounced "sitdown strikes," 1936–39. The Public Utility Holding Company Act limited holding companies to administratively responsible size, to prevent use of the device for purely speculative purposes. The principles of the NRA were modified and‑ applied to one industry, the bituminous coal business, in the Guffey-Snyder Act. When some members of the Congress doubted its constitutionality, President Roosevelt aroused adverse criticism by advising them to leave that question to the courts. (The courts later invalidated it.)

It will be seen that the "Second New Deal" was really a more profound change than that of the "hundred days." In the beginning the New Deal had been a patchwork of mixed temporary and permanent actions designed to keep the wheels going around. In the next few years grave changes were made which affected the structure of society. Most New Deal controversy has arisen from the acts of 1935 and 1936.

The Election of 1936, the Popular Test. The Republicans named Governor Alfred M. Landon of Kansas, largely because he had survived growing Democratic strength there. The party platform denounced the New Deal as anticapitalist and unconstitutional but made no promises to change anything except the income taxes. Roosevelt was jubilantly renominated by the Democrats, whose platform was the record of the New Deal. The "anti" forces joined in the "Union Party," in which Townsend and Father Coughlin were interested, to nominate William Lemke, a North Dakota Republican Congressman.

The campaign was very hard fought. The Republicans labeled the New Deal as bureaucratic and un-American; and some said

it was Russian inspired. Landon dismayed some of his supporters when he said he favored a change in the Constitution
to validate some of the New Deal labor legislation which had
been thrown out by the Supreme Court.

Measured in votes the election of 1936 was the closest to
unanimity since that of 1820. Postmaster General James A.
Farley, who managed Roosevelt's campaign, predicted that
Landon would carry only Maine and Vermont. That was the
precise result. By an electoral vote of 523 to 8 the American
voters had enthusiastically endorsed the Roosevelt program.

The End of the New Deal. President Roosevelt was never as
influential in his second term as in his first. This was partly
owing to a growing preoccupation of the public with making our
legendary "isolation" a fact (contrary to Roosevelt's wishes) as
European dictators seemed to lead the world ever nearer to
war. It was also probably caused in part by the enormous congressional majority of the Democrats (77–19 in the Senate,
328–107 in the House) which was almost too large to be instilled
with party discipline. No doubt the constant adverse criticism
of an almost unanimously anti-Roosevelt press proved the adage
that constant dripping wears away stones. And finally, the
President suffered two serious tactical defeats which showed
the opposition that he was by no means invincible. These two
defeats were the rejection of his plan to reorganize the judiciary,
and the failure of his attempts to influence the selection of a
favorable Congress in the off-year election of 1938.

In his inaugural address of 1937 the President began, in his
familiar vein, emphasizing certain social legislation which he
thought necessary, and asserting that a third of the people were
"ill housed, ill clad, ill nourished."

Part of the blame for the condition of the country he put on
the Supreme Court, early in February, when he sent a plan to
the Congress for reorganizing the judicial branch. The sore point
was the series of court decisions which declared some of the most
important New Deal legislation unconstitutional. Although the
proposal covered many aspects of reorganization of the judiciary,
the great controversial crux was the recommendation to empower
the President to add another Supreme Court Justice (up to a
maximum of fifteen) for each one who reached the age of seventy
without retiring. The suggestion was perfectly constitutional but

just as certainly impolitic and, in spirit, probably opposed to the tradition of an independent judiciary. The implication of the President's proposal was that the elder judges were the prisoners of prejudices acquired in the nineteenth century and were paralyzing the executive and legislative branches.

The Chief Justice, Charles Evans Hughes, denied that the Court was behind in its work. The huge Democratic majorities in the Congress split on the issue. Senate leader Joseph T. Robinson died in the midst of his battle to put the program across. The court upheld several important New Deal acts in the following weeks (causing cynics to remark that "a switch in time saves nine"). In the end the President got a few lesser reforms of the judiciary, a divided party, and publicity for the fact that he had been successfully defied. (Ironically unpredictable deaths and resignations in a few years gave him a "Democratic" court.) The bitter fruit of this last seed was harvested in the special session of late 1937 when a coalition of Republicans and southern Democrats denied him every major piece of legislation he asked for, just a little over a year after the triumphal election of 1936. And the Revenue Act of 1938 scaled down the tax rates which had been so objectionable to the well-to-do.

Roosevelt fought back by selecting several members of Congress to be eliminated in the off-year election of 1938 and personally interfered in New York City and in several states. His safari into local politics netted but one lone Representative.

Some statutes which could be called New Deal measures were passed. The United States Housing Authority (USHA) was established to co-operate with local governments in slum clearance. The Agricultural Adjustment Administration was remodeled and became an agency for maintaining the farmer's purchasing power at or near parity with his cost of living. It also provided a crop-insurance program. The business "recession" of 1937 was met by enlarging the rolls of the Works Progress Administration (WPA), increasing Reconstruction Finance Corporation (RFC) loans, and loosening credit restrictions generally.

The Temporary National Economic Committee, guided by Senator Joseph C. O'Mahoney of Wyoming and economist Leon Henderson, was organized in 1938 to study the steady centralization of financial and economic power. Its ominous findings were disregarded in the growing excitement over foreign affairs.

The last really significant statute that can properly be called a New Deal act was the Fair Labor Standards Act of 1938, more commonly known as the Wages and Hours Law, by which minimum hourly wages and maximum weekly hours could be set for businesses in interstate commerce. It thereby practically solved the child labor problem because child workers were not worth the minimum wages required. Hourly rate minimums have been periodically increased since then. Other so-called "New Deal acts" since 1938 have almost all been modifications of earlier policies.

A kind of symbolic seal was set on the end of the New Deal by the Hatch Act of 1939, intended to reform political abuses in the WPA, which barred federal civil servants from party politics.

Evaluation of the New Deal. Although the social and economic legislation of the New Deal was practically all on the books by the end of 1938, its chief author and its symbol, President Roosevelt, lived on in office until 1945. Recollections of the New Deal commonly embrace the whole of his Presidency and many evaluators tend to estimate the New Deal solely in terms of the man who led it.

As for the New Deal as a legislative program, its adverse critics, who have had freer access to the press than the defenders have had, indict it for the following reasons. It was a program to centralize power in a federal bureaucracy at the expense of state and local government, and it encroached on areas of life which had been traditionally free of the cognizance of law. It created class cleavage by aggrandizing organized labor and making minority groups arrogant in their new-found over-protection. It increased federal taxes to a point where private initiative was discouraged and private property rights endangered—indeed, sometimes destroyed. Its wasteful economic policy—intended to promote "recovery"—actually prolonged the depression. Whether deliberately or not, until checked by courts and Congress, its so-called "reform" program was leading the country into Marxian Socialism. Its relief agencies were administered by corrupt or incompetent directors in the interest of promoting the political advantage of the administration, and with the effect of pandering to the lazy and debauching the moral fiber of the energetic.

Defenders of the New Deal say that it redressed the balance of interests between the rights of property and the liberty of human beings by undertaking necessary reforms of the American system which had been neglected by all governments, whether local, state, or national. These reforms gave hope to millions who had been hopeless of benefiting from American life and who might easily have been inflamed into supporting a Fascist or Communist revolution, as in Europe. The relief program came just at the time when local governments and voluntary agencies had exhausted their resources; and the unemployed (and their families) were facing serious malnutrition and grave hardships, if not actual starvation and exposure, in a country where food and clothing were lying unsold in huge supply. The recovery program put industry's machines in motion once again by raising purchasing power through the building of productive public facilities. The reforms of the program were really repairs of a weakened and damaged private enterprise system which was able to function healthily when its abuses were corrected. This attitude toward the New Deal sees it as an essentially conservative program which enacted prudent and necessary legislation to preserve "the American way of life" because it was in danger of collapse after decades of shortsighted mismanagement.

During the years when the New Deal was a political issue, however, its opponents gained more support on the editorial pages than in the polling places.

In recent years the oversights and limits of the New Deal have become more apparent. Although the New Deal won the support of northern black voters, its actual programs encouraged segregation in federal housing and intensified the desperate plight of southern sharecroppers and tenant farmers (many of whom were black). The new social security system had built-in inequalities in benefits between men and women, and was based on the assumption that men were the breadwinners. Social security did not at first cover the occupations most often filled by women or blacks (teachers, household help). In the areas of racial relations and women's rights, the brightest spot of the New Deal was Eleanor Roosevelt, who as First Lady carved out an active role for herself by concentrating on these areas.

16

The Second World Upheaval

As President Roosevelt was enacting an enlightened foreign policy toward Latin America and United States dependencies, storm clouds were gathering in far places. The Japanese had just resigned from the League of Nations; and fascist parties debauched the public life of Italy and Germany, led by war-praising Benito Mussolini and Adolf Hitler. As these men ravaged Europe, the United States, steeped in isolationism, proclaimed its neutrality. But as war continued unabated, America, realizing the Axis threat, became increasingly unneutral in thought and deed. With the infamous Japanese attack on Pearl Harbor, America plunged headlong into war and helped bring it to a successful conclusion. This time the United States became a leading factor in the establishment of a postwar international organization to maintain the peace. Wilson's ideal was finally brought to fruition; and America, at long last, recognized herself as a responsible member of the family of nations.

FOREIGN POLICY IN THE DEPRESSION

President Roosevelt's principal diplomatic attention in his first term was directed to the establishment of good relations with the Latin American states by means of his "Good Neighbor Policy." After turbulence in Cuba had been mediated by Sumner Welles, the Platt Amendment, offensive to most Cubans, was rescinded in 1934; and a reciprocal trade treaty helped both nations stabilize the sugar market. Armed forces were withdrawn from Haiti in the same year, and Panama was somewhat conciliated by the President's unsuccessful attempts to improve its treaty relations with the United States. At the Montevideo Conference of 1933 the United States delegation repeated its denial that any nation could interfere in the domestic concerns of another, and, in later conferences, the United States worked to establish a solidarity among sovereignties in the Western Hemisphere. Mexican relations were threatened by further expropriations of lands owned by foreigners, but careful negotiations brought an amicable settlement by which Mexico reimbursed former owners, at least partially.

The United States had problems in its own household—the possessions and territories—where the application of a kind of "good kinsman" policy might be useful. Philippine Independence was finally given a definite scheduling (see page 174). The government of the Virgin Islands (purchased from Denmark in 1917) was improved, and its economy benefited from the repeal of Prohibition. Puerto Rico, in abject poverty, was not immediately helped, but its problems began to receive attention. Only the full-fledged territories of Hawaii and Alaska had their basic demands—statehood—ignored.

An early New Deal move to encourage foreign trade was the founding of the Export-Import Bank to finance it. Of even greater importance was the Trade Agreements Act of 1934, by which many reciprocal trade treaties were made.

An odd by-product of the demand for expanded markets was the diplomatic recognition of Russia in 1933, a fruitless move, economically speaking, but one applauded by most Americans at the time.

THE PERIOD OF ISOLATIONISM

In the 1930's the American people seemed to show a profound distaste and distrust of foreign nations. In applying this mood to day-to-day situations, they took steps to cut themselves off from membership in the community of nations so far as possible. Usually under such circumstances a nation develops a strong nationalist feeling, builds up its armed forces and glories in their might, but not so the United States. The mood united isolationism and pacifism. The element of pacifism developed partly because the high promise of World War I to make the world safe for democracy had not been kept. The world was in turmoil with drums and trumpets sounding, and, at home, the depression had convinced many that the wine of American life was down to the lees and dregs.

Isolationist Thinking. The isolationist feeling was rationalized in the Senate investigation of the munitions industry, begun in 1934 and directed by Senator Gerald P. Nye of North Dakota. The Senate Committee showed that the munitions industry and the group collectively lumped together as the "international bankers" had made large profits from World War I. A conclusion drawn and believed, but not proved, was that men with a financial interest in the outcome of the war had somehow tricked the American people into that squalid business by prostituting the elevated idealism of the country. Military institutions declined in esteem. Reserve Officer Training Corps units were dissolved in some colleges. Peace societies multiplied. As Americans have always done, some began to press for legislation in the present to cure real or imagined evils of the past.

A continuing grievance was the failure of European nations to pay their war debts. European resentment of America's terms was communicated to Americans whose counterresentment (even before the Nye Committee's work) produced the Johnson Act of 1934, which forbade loans to any country in default of its war debt to the United States. The purpose, of course, was to prevent the creation of an American financial interest in the survival of any foreign power and, in a mild way, to punish default, which was almost as if to say, to punish world monetary conditions.

The Neutrality Acts. In 1935 the Italian dictator Benito Mussolini pushed his normally pacific and sensitive citizens into a brutal war of aggression against the semiprimitive Empire of Abyssinia (Ethiopia). This was the first serious war in the Western world since the early 1920's and civilized society was naturally agitated. The reaction of the United States was the passage of the Neutrality Act of 1935, which enabled the President to declare the existence of war and then to prohibit the export of arms to belligerents. The act did not prohibit the export of materials from which arms could be manufactured. Thus it unintentionally discriminated in favor of industrial nations. This act also forbade Americans to travel on the ships of belligerent nations except "at their own risk." This was a gratuitous surrender of an ancient right (of neutrals) which, previously, America had fought to preserve. In 1936 the act was extended to early 1937, and provisions were added to prohibit any financial aid to belligerents. This could operate in favor of wealthy nations with flourishing banking systems and to the disadvantage of the kind of nation which the aggressors chose to assault first—Ethiopia, China, Albania.

International affairs were more sadly confounded by the outbreak of civil war in Spain in 1936. The earlier neutrality acts applied to international wars only. If neutrality legislation was a "good thing," American neutrality legislation needed broadening. In 1937 a special act was passed, specifying Spain by name and forbidding the export of munitions to that country (a detriment to the "Loyalists" because the rebels had most of the Spanish army, hence the better supply of war materials). A few months later the rules were broadened by another act delegating to the President the enumeration of what might and might not be exported. When China was attacked again by the Japanese in 1937, application of the act, officially a neutrality law, would have aided Japan, because Japan, being heavily industrialized, was better able to supply herself than was China. This was the President's position, and he refused to exercise his delegated power on the ground that such "neutrality" would aid an aggressor. Also, he refused to declare the existence of war in this area so that an arms embargo would not be enforced against China. Indeed it is hard to see how any of these neutrality acts could have operated with clear impartiality, unless in a contest between nations which were "identical twins"—an absurdity, of course.

The domestic dream of ignoring foreign affairs found its most extreme practical expression in a proposal of Representative Louis Ludlow of Indianapolis to amend the Constitution so that a declaration of war could only be determined by a national referendum (except in the event of invasion). This was a popular suggestion and came close to passage in the House of Representatives.

Roosevelt's Challenge to Isolationism. The President resisted his country's pacifist isolationism so far as resistance was fruitful, even at the cost of losing support in the interior states, particularly in the Missouri Valley, the archbastion of isolationism. In 1934 the Vinson Act provided for rebuilding the American navy up to treaty strength, but the Congress did not appropriate enough money for the work. In 1936 a system of

Merchant Marine subsidies was enacted. In 1938, as the skies over Europe darkened, the second Vinson Naval Act presented the famous concept of the "two-ocean" navy to be built over a ten-year period and appropriated enough money to make an effective beginning. Thus when the great crisis came, the country was at least "tooled up" for naval warfare. It is a singular coincidence that the country may well owe its survival to the work of two Presidents Roosevelt, both former Assistant Secretaries of the Navy, who together, more than any other men, popularized the navy.

In the face of the bold, unashamed praise of war as an instrument of national policy by Adolf Hitler, Benito Mussolini, and the Japanese war lords, President Roosevelt tried to organize American opinion in his "Quarantine speech" (Chicago, 1937) by calling for collective international ostracism of aggressors. The pacifist-isolationist mood was at the moment too strong for him.

THE DEEPENING WORLD CRISIS

Relations with Japan were very poor. Japanese planes sank the American gunboat *Panay* in December, 1937; and late in 1938 the Japanese shrugged the Open Door policy out of existence.

In Europe the Germans were moving from triumph to triumph in a series of military actions announced in advance in Adolf Hitler's book, *Mein Kampf*—occupation of the Rhineland (1936); alliance with Japan and Italy (1936); annexation of Austria (1938); acceptance of the Czechoslovakian Sudetenland, surrendered by the Munich Pact as an appeasement gift (1939); annexation of the rest of Czechoslovakia (1939); and even the signing of a nonaggression treaty with Russia (1939). Between these latter hounds, Poland had become a stag at bay.

President Roosevelt's message to the Congress in January, 1938 urged increased military and naval appropriations. About 14 per cent of the budget of 1939 was marked for defense purposes, and the President, in the months immediately following, twice asked and received additional military appropriations. The total appropriated in 1938 and 1939 was a little under two billion dollars.

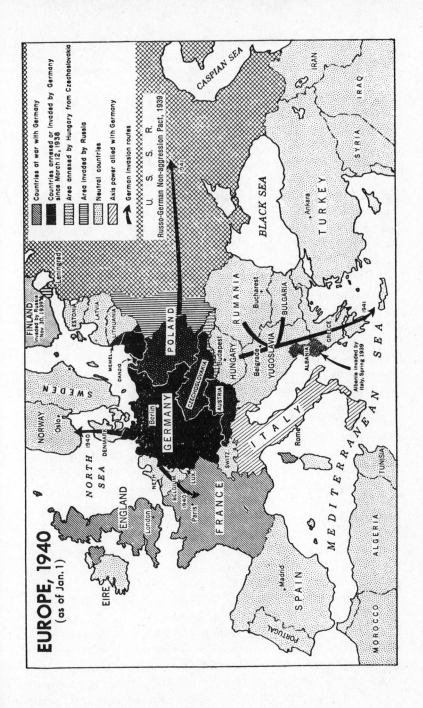

EUROPE, 1940
(as of Jan. 1)

Legend:

Countries at war with Germany

Countries annexed or invaded by Germany since March 12, 1938

Area annexed by Hungary from Czechoslovakia

Area invaded by Russia

Neutral countries

Axis power allied with Germany

German invasion routes

Russo-German Non-aggression Pact, 1939

U. S. S. R.

CASPIAN SEA

IRAN

SYRIA

IRAQ

BLACK SEA

TURKEY

• Ankara

FINLAND
Invaded by Russia
Nov 30, 1939

• Leningrad

SWEDEN

NORWAY

• Oslo

NORTH SEA

ESTONIA

LATVIA

LITHUANIA

MEMEL

DANZIG

POLAND

RUMANIA

Bucharest •

BULGARIA

Belgrade •

YUGOSLAVIA

GREECE

ALBANIA

Albania invaded by Italy, Spring 1939

1941

MEDITERRANEAN SEA

Budapest •

HUNGARY

CZECHOSLOVAKIA

AUSTRIA

GERMANY

Berlin •

1940

DENMARK

NETH.

BELG.

1940

LUX.

SWITZ.

FRANCE

Paris •

ITALY

Rome •

TUNISIA

ALGERIA

MOROCCO

EIRE

ENGLAND

London •

SPAIN

• Madrid

PORTUGAL

The momentum of German aggressions carried them successfully into an assault on Poland in September, 1939. Britain and France declared war on Germany within days but could offer no practical help to the Poles, who were crushed by the German armor and air force in four weeks.

The immediate American reaction was to ask, "How can we stay out?" President Roosevelt proclaimed neutrality and called a special session of the Congress. The United States joined the other American powers south of Canada in announcing a neutrality zone to surround the American continents. The special session of the Congress repealed the embargo on military materials and allowed cash-and-carry sales of arms, in the Senate by a 2:1 vote, in the House by 3:2—votes a long way from unanimity.

After a curiously quiet winter in Europe—a period called the "phony war"—the German forces erupted into Norway and easily repelled weak British aid to the Norse. Weeks later the Germans thrust at France through neutral Belgium and Holland, crushing them promptly and almost trapping the entire British army at Dunkirk. It became apparent that Hitler's European opponents were no match for him, unaided. American opinion veered sharply in support of the British, and the President shipped surplus arms and planes to them. The German forces continued their stunning successes, and France capitulated on June 22, 1940. A French "collaborationist" government was established at Vichy; other Frenchmen rallied to their General Charles de Gaulle in Britain.

American precautions were intensified. The Cabinet was made bipartisan, and the Congress levied an additional billion dollars in taxes marked for defense. The Smith Act was passed to prohibit diffusion of the doctrine that the government should be overthrown by force. National Guard units were called into the federal service. Fifty antique destroyers were given to Britain in exchange for defense bases on the island perimeter from Newfoundland to British Guiana. In September the country's first peacetime draft law, the Selective Service Act of 1940, was enacted. A four-billion-dollar naval program was also voted.

The fall of France was followed by aerial warfare, now named the "Battle of Britain," in which the Royal Air Force beat back the German Luftwaffe, destroying enemy planes at a rate of two German for one British. In October the Germans and Italians (who entered the war as France fell) moved into the Balkans. The British countered by landings on Crete and other Greek islands, and, beginning in November, punished the Italian navy and pulverized the Italian army in North Africa.

Absorbing as the European and African spectacle was, the United States had its own peculiar problems in its relations with Japan. In the spring of 1940 Secretary of State Cordell Hull had cautioned the world against tinkering with the Dutch East Indies; in September, he made a similar statement about French Indo-China directly to Japan, which was even then on the verge of a formal military alliance with Germany and Italy. President Roosevelt forbade the shipment of oil or scrap iron outside the Western Hemisphere, except to Britain; this prohibition angered Japan.

Against this tumultuous background the American people went through a presidential campaign. After a sphinxlike silence Roosevelt let himself be nominated for an unprecedented third term. On the Republican side a classic "dark horse," Wendell Willkie, was nominated against the wishes of conservative party managers. He was an Indiana-born New Yorker and an inter-national-minded amateur in politics. Roosevelt later said that the blunt, straightforward Willkie was the only one of his op-ponents who alarmed him as a possible victor. Politically the two men were not far apart, except on some domestic issues. Willkie ran more strongly than Landon had in 1936, carrying ten states, but, of course, Roosevelt's victory was clear and could be inter-preted as a rousing endorsement.

The program of aid to lonely Britain was enlarged early in 1941, when the President recommended "lend-lease" in his famous speech extolling the "Four Freedoms": freedom of speech and worship, freedom from want and fear. In March, over strong, isolationist opposition, the Congress passed the Lend-Lease Bill and authorized seven billion dollars for materials to be traded, loaned, leased, or given to the antitotalitarian nations. American naval forces assumed the protection of shipping in the western half of the Atlantic. Anglo-American military conversations were held secretly in Washington.

In the war theaters the enemies of Germany saw their situa-tions deteriorate. The dashing Erwin Rommel recouped the Italian losses in North Africa by thrusting the British back to Egypt, and German troops rolled over the Balkans and Greece. A British attempt to hold Crete ended in disaster. Like clockwork the German machine turned its power against Russia. While agonizing to the Russians, this was a relief to the West which had been expecting every successful German operation to be followed by an invasion of Britain. The United States organized assistance to the retreating Russians, beginning with a billion dollar helping of lend-lease. The British, who had feared a German flanking movement in the north, were relieved by the American occupation of Iceland in July.

The war was now almost two years old and American precautions were not yet complete. A massive propaganda blow was struck in August by the promulgation of the "Atlantic Charter," a joint statement of war aims by Roosevelt and British Prime Minister Winston Churchill guaranteeing, so far as they could, a decent, nontotalitarian world. Ironically, the Russians promptly endorsed it. Two days before the publication of the Atlantic Charter, the House of Representatives had approved a one-year extension of the Selective Service Act by a margin of *one vote*. In September the President ordered American naval vessels in the western Atlantic to sink any German or Italian vessels there. Three American destroyers had fought small battles with submarines by the end of October.

Meanwhile, the Far East was rumbling and troubled. The United States and the Japanese had come to a deadlock with discussions at a standstill. A Japanese carrier force was noted absent from its home base by American intelligence. The best American guess was that it was headed for Singapore or the Philippines. Instead, it attacked the Pearl Harbor naval base of Hawaii on Sunday morning, December 7, 1941. The following day Congress declared war on Japan, and three days later the Axis powers declared war on the United States.

THE SECOND WORLD WAR

Even before the involvement of the United States in the war it had been understood in Washington that, if war came, Germany was to be disposed of first before finishing off Japan. However, during most of 1942 the Allies were on a grim defensive everywhere, and upon its success rested the outcome of the war.

The Year of Survival, 1942. Not for centuries had Western civilization come so close to destruction as it did in 1942 when the blackest months of the war were experienced. With the Japanese in full cry and the Germans at their greatest territorial extension early in the year, it was almost too much to hope that their blades would be blunted and their hordes and fleets proved vulnerable before the year was out. The year 1942 must be placed among the memorable dates in the course of world history.

Following the very successful blow at Pearl Harbor, the Japanese invaded Thailand and Malaya, took Singapore, landed in the Philippines, and took Wake and Guam. From January to early May the Americans and Filipinos fought defensively, finally surrendering Bataan and then the island fort of Corregidor. General Douglas MacArthur went to Australia to organize the Allied forces in the Southwest Pacific. Still the Japanese pressed on, taking the Netherlands East Indies and giving the United States Navy its second worst thrashing, in the Battle of the Java Sea, at the end of February.

But, unknown to all, the Japanese had about reached their fullest spread. In the two days after Corregidor fell, May 7–8, the Japanese navy was held in the Battle of the Coral Sea, a battle wholly of planes against ships, which stopped their advance on Australia. A month later the Japanese attempted to take Midway Island and met bloody ruin, retiring with the loss of four carriers, the prey of American naval aviation. The chance to take the Hawaiian Islands, best on December 8, 1941, had steadily receded, and now it was entirely gone. In the following weeks the Japanese landed on the chill misty Aleutians but the strategic consequence was negligible, and in the summer of 1943 they withdrew from those Alaskan islands under heavy American pressure.

Early in 1942 in North Africa the German General Rommel's Afrika Korps broke up a British counterattack and reached the Egyptian border. While plans were being made to evacuate Allied noncombatants to the far upper reaches of the Nile, General Bernard Montgomery revived the British Eighth Army and smashed the Afrika Korps back at the climactic battle of El Alamein, turning point of the African phase.

The German armies (and the armies of several less eager satellites) pressed into the military jelly called Russia on the longest battlefront in recorded history. From the frozen north to the subtropical Black Sea "Riviera," colossal masses of troops moved convulsively in the most massive, but not best managed, military operations ever known. By the early winter of 1941–42 the Germans had reached the outskirts of Moscow. In mid-winter the Russians counterattacked and made slight gains, "slight," that is, in relation to the size of the land mass involved. But when the spring sun dried the boggy plains, the Germans moved forward again. They entered the Caucasus and drove toward the Volga. A week before the end of summer they entered Stalingrad, on the Volga. And there they stood, unable to gain a mile, fighting through a long and dreadful winter while the town fell to rubble. This was the high flood of Germany.

Thus the year 1942 ended with the Japanese and Germans defeated decisively at the extended limbs of their power—Coral Sea, Midway, El Alamein, and Stalingrad. Light began to creep back into the West.

The War Against Germany and Italy. The geography of the globe required that every great power in the war except Russia had to fight a two-front war. At the beginning the American fronts were the Atlantic and the Pacific, against German submarines and all forces the Japanese chose to detach from their struggle against China.

Except for a continuation of the British air offensive and the antisubmarine war in the Atlantic, there was not much Allied activity in the north in 1942. The great theater of operations in that part of the world was the Mediterranean and its coasts, especially North Africa. Once the Germans were routed in Egypt, as they had been at El Alamein in November, 1942, they could not find a defensible position east of Tunisia, to which place they were steadily driven by General Bernard Montgomery's British Eighth Army. A surprise was being prepared for the enemy. Four days after the victory at El Alamein, a joint Anglo-American force under General Dwight D. Eisenhower landed in the west of North Africa and also raced for Tunisia. With the British pressing from the south and the Americans from the west, the Germans in Tunisia fought fiercely with their backs to the sea until they surrendered a quarter million men in May, 1943. In two months the Allies floated to the shores of Sicily which was conquered in five weeks of fighting. In less than four weeks more the British were on the "toe" of Italy's mainland and pushing north. The Americans landed at Salerno a few days later, one day after the Italian government surrendered (on September 8). Mussolini escaped to the north, and the Germans took over as the effective rulers of most of Italy. The Anglo-American armies fought slowly north in a miserable and costly winter campaign.

Affairs on the Russian front portended disaster for the enemy. To the pain of the Germans the Russians fought a winter campaign in 1942–43, re-entering Leningrad and wholly capturing the German armies whose ill fate it was to have entered Stalingrad. The Germans tried to recover their losses by a summer campaign and suffered a series of unmitigated defeats in the second half of 1943. In January, 1944, the Russians were back in Poland.

All this time the German people and their industry were suffering the intensified horrors of aerial bombing, progressively worse than the attacks they had earlier inflicted upon the British population. In Britain, which had become the world's greatest air base, General Eisenhower and his allied colleagues had begun to plan the invasion of Europe from the west, with the code name "Operation Overlord." Meanwhile, in Italy, Rome was liberated; in Russia, the Black Sea coast was cleared of Germans.

The invasion of western Europe, on the Norman coast, was the largest amphibious operation in the history of the world. The American contingent was under General Omar N. Bradley. On June 6, 1944, the assault was made along sixty miles of shore line. A month later about a million men had gone ashore and half that many tons of supplies. The German resistance was mismanaged. Instead of a mass, stunning counterattack, German troops were fed into the struggle piecemeal, as they came to their commanders' hands. The invasion of France was supported from the south when General Alexander M. Patch brought an army ashore on the Mediterranean coast in mid-August. West of the Rhine for the rest of that year the Anglo-Franco-American armies performed prodigies in liberating France, Belgium, and Luxembourg. For example, General George S. Patton's Third Army, including an "unblooded" reserve infantry division, the Ninety-Fifth, took Metz by assault, something never done before in ten centuries of military history. From September to December various elements of the attackers were operating in Germany. Aachen, the first large German city taken, fell at the end of October.

Meanwhile the Russians were advancing steadily, entering East Prussia, Warsaw, Budapest, and Belgrade by January, 1945.

In the middle of December the Germans launched the kind of offensive they might better have used in June, when a massive surprise attack was made on the thinly held Ardennes front, with the Belgian ports as the objective. They rolled for fifty miles before they were broken and beaten in the last week of the month. This was the last serious German offensive (now known as the "Battle of the Bulge"). From February through April the Allies battered the Germans, who began to collapse with greater rapidity. The Russians entered Berlin toward the end of April; with their approach Adolf Hitler committed suicide. The British took Bremen; American and Russian troops met at the Elbe River. In Italy Mussolini was lynched a few days before the Germans there surrendered. Surrender in Germany came on May 4, effective May 8. The "German race" had missed its rendezvous with a millennium of greatness, as earlier promised by Hitler.

The War Against Japan. After the decisive battles of the Coral Sea and Midway, the Americans moved always on the offensive in the Pacific and Far East. Step one was the clearing of Guadalcanal in the Solomon Islands, a bitter, nasty little war of six months, accompanied by four sharp naval battles. Guadalcanal was rid of Japanese in February, 1943. The great island of New Guinea was the scene of fighting from January, 1943 until early 1945, by which time resistance had mostly ended there. Meanwhile, the second half of 1943 saw the clearing of Japanese from the other Solomon Islands, and American landings in New Britain. In these engagements naval surface and aviation forces, the Marine Corps, and the army were all seriously involved.

Admiral Chester W. Nimitz, commander of the United States Pacific Fleet, envisioned his line of advance as a progress from the Solomons to Tokyo via all the island chains between. The long, tortuous movement began with assaults on Tarawa and Makin late in 1943. These initial battles showed that the cost would be high. The names of successive island battles in 1944 run together like a hoist of bloody flags: Kwajalein, Eniwetok, Saipan, Guam, Peleliu, and others.

The year 1944 also saw advances in the Southwest Pacific,

with decisive battles fought at the Admiralty Islands, Hollandia, and Dutch New Guinea. Farther west, on the mainland of Asia, Allied forces in northern Burma were able to fight their way far enough to establish a base for an aerial route to China. The campaign to retake the Philippines began with the summer. The battle of the Philippine Sea, like that of the Coral Sea, was entirely an affair of naval aviation. The crushing defeat of the Japanese shook their government and cleared the way for MacArthur's dramatic return to the islands. The Battle of Leyte Gulf, in October, was the funeral of the Japanese navy and assured the reconquest of the Philippines. Manila fell in February, 1945.

The war moved closer and closer to the Japanese home islands, as Iwo Jima was taken in a month's fighting at the price of twenty thousand Marine Corps casualties. The distance to Tokyo was now measured not in thousands but in hundred of miles. And the remaining distance was cut in half by the conquest of the Ryukyu Islands in a battle lasting from March till June, 1945. The Japanese air force spent its men as projectiles in suicide dives, causing great damage and many casualties in the American sea force. The Ryukyus, with their chief island Okinawa, cost almost fifty thousand American casualties.

The Japanese power of resistance was steadily dying, partly because of the long string of defeats abroad, and partly because of the paralyzing and frightful bombardment of the home islands. Early in 1942 General James Doolittle led a fleet of bombers to Japan primarily for morale purposes, but the systematic, strategic bombardment began in June, 1944 and was steadily increased in violence and intensity until it was furious and deadly by the summer of 1945. Allied participants were the Twentieth Air Force of the United States Army, plus British and American naval aviation. Terrible effects were achieved by the incendiary bombing of the flimsy, inflammable Japanese cities.

When the Japanese rejected a surrender ultimatum, on July 29, 1945, unknown to them they called forth a flame that extinguished the sun on their flag and still commands man's fearful awe. Their refusal to surrender was followed by the atomic bombing of Hiroshima (August 6), the most frightening fact of history. Russia, anxious not to be too late, declared war on Japan. Another bomb was dropped on Nagasaki (August 9), and on the next day the Japanese offered to surrender. Terms were accepted on August 15. The worst and greatest war of all was over.

The War at Home. Never before had a people exerted so much strength at such remote distances from their home base. The organization of that exertion is a principal part of the story of the war.

First there were the people, to be trained and led to co-operate in military and civil life. Selective Service was at work before the war began, and by 1945 almost ten million men had been inducted into the military. On the civilian side the War Manpower Commission was put in charge of all recruiting and training. In 1943 all war workers were "frozen" in their jobs. The work week was lengthened to forty-eight hours, with extra pay for the extra eight hours. Able-bodied men were released for more strenuous assignments by the organization of female auxiliaries of each of the armed services.

For the specific problems of labor, the War Labor Board was established. Although an anthology of difficulties could be composed, the working force produced the goods and received the military's thanks at the close of the war from General Eisenhower. Wage increases were controlled, unions (by secret ballot) were allowed to maintain union membership clauses, and labor organizations were represented on the War Labor Board. The eastern coal mines were taken over by the government to avoid a strike; and the railroads were also seized for a brief period. To utilize human abilities most efficiently, the Fair Employment Practices Commission was established in 1941 to thwart discrimination in employment on federal contracts because of race. Several states enacted the idea in statutes.

Equally important, of course, was the organization of the material production needed for war, a task involving the control of materials, manufacturing, and distribution.

Preclusive purchasing abroad of critical materials was practiced to forestall enemy buyers. The very dangerous shortage of rubber (since the Japanese had overrun the sources of supply) was relieved by rigid control of distribution and the encouragement of the use of substitutes. Both liquid and solid fuels were conserved by government administrators appointed for the purpose. These measures were felt, and generally accepted, by the public in rationing or downright absence of formerly familiar products.

The war proved expensive, costing about 200 billion dollars more between 1940 and 1946 than came in through taxes. The deficit was financed through the sale of "Defense" and "War" bonds. The debt incurred placed about the same burden on Americans as had the Civil War, requiring about 3 per cent of national income to pay the interest on bonds.

The war's most obvious effect on civilians was an end to unemployment. Women entered heavy industry. Cities became engorged with war workers, many of them blacks, young people, and women. The results were racial tensions leading to riots in Detroit and Los Angeles and newly found economic independence for marginal groups. Housing problems increased in the cities, reaching crisis stage in some areas.

Manufacturing was the province of the War Production Board, which cut nonessentials out of American life and promoted the conversion of factory facilities to the war effort. The effect was to harness the world's greatest productive capacity for military purposes. Psychologically it was not a difficulty for most manufacturers since costs and profits were guaranteed.

With labor and production equipment having been put to work, it remained to try to distribute the civilian share of the products as fairly as possible. To this end, scarce commodities were rationed and all prices were controlled, under the direction of the Office of Price Administration (OPA).

To protect the country from internal attack the Federal Bureau of Investigation was greatly enlarged. Six Nazi saboteurs were executed in 1942. Under the Smith Act of 1939, Communist activities were scrutinized but, because the Russians were allies, only some Trotzkyite or out-of-season Communists were imprisoned. More than a hundred thousand Japanese-Americans were moved from the west coast states to interior concentration camps for "reasons" chiefly emotional, since their war record was exemplary.

The calendar inexorably required political action. Although the Democrats retained control of the Congress in the election of 1942, their margins were narrowed. In the presidential election of 1944, Roosevelt was renominated for a fourth term against the Republican candidate Thomas E. Dewey of New

York. On the Democratic side the only contest had been on the decision to substitute the name of Senator Harry Truman of Missouri for that of Vice-President Henry Wallace.

The campaign saw the emergence of the Political Action Committee of the Congress of Industrial Organizations (PAC-CIO) in active support of friendly candidates, mostly Democrats. At times it was difficult to tell the difference between campaign statements of the two major parties, except by labels. Most notably, both promised support for some kind of peace-keeping world organization to be created at the end of the war. The voting showed a clear majority for Roosevelt, Dewey having carried only twelve states, with 99 electoral votes to Roosevelt's 432.

In January of 1945 the President's friends noticed that his health appeared to be declining. In April, without other warning, he died at Warm Springs, Georgia, of a cerebral hemorrhage. Thus, on the edge of victory, passed the most beloved and hated American of his generation, longest tenant of the White House, and most unashamedly mourned in the streets.

Wartime Diplomacy. Military alliances during the war years required constant maintenance and repair, which were accomplished by means of the "conference." The numerous conferences held between 1941 and 1945 planned, first, to achieve military victory and, second, to make victory permanent through political means.

Two weeks after Pearl Harbor, Prime Minister Winston Churchill visited President Roosevelt in Washington. They agreed to concentrate on victory in Europe first. A product of their talks was also the "Declaration of the United Nations" by which more than two dozen allies promised to live by the principles of the Atlantic Charter and to make war and peace together (January 1, 1942). In the following summer the first Moscow Conference informed the Russians that western Europe could not be invaded that year. After a firm footing on North Africa was established, the Casablanca Conference of January, 1943 discussed but reached no final decision on the invasion of western Europe. However, the participants did agree to the invasion of Sicily and Italy and adopted the "unconditional surrender" of the enemy as the primary war aim. In Washington a few months later, the "Trident Conference" set May 1, 1944 as the date for the invasion of Europe at Normandy. In August, 1943 President Roosevelt traveled to the Quebec Conference, which refined plans for the invasion of Europe and agreed to intensify the war in southeastern Asia. In November, Roosevelt and Churchill conferred with the Chinese leader, General Chiang Kai-shek, in Cairo and assured him of their intention to persist at war until the Japanese were crushed. Still traveling hard, Churchill and Roosevelt met the Russian Dictator Joseph Stalin at Teheran in the same month and explained their plans for the assault on Europe in the following spring. The last great military conference was held at Potsdam after the European war. (President Truman now represented the United States.) It was there that the ultimatum of July, 1945 was drawn up to be sent to Japan.

Far more complicated, delicate, and difficult to assess were the more strictly political meetings. The military conferences produced orders to be obeyed. The political meetings produced policies to be submitted, sooner or later, for the approval of world public opinion.

In 1943, at Moscow, the Foreign Ministers declared the "necessity of establishing a general international organization" and took up the vexing and tragic problems of the Polish government-in-exile and the question of a postwar policy toward Germany. Scant is the word for their success. More successful was the almost simultaneous erection of the United Nations Relief and Rehabilitation Administration (UNRRA), under Governor Herbert H. Lehman of New York, to try to restore a decent minimum level of material life in the desolated theaters of operations.

The Teheran Conference of 1943, in addition to its more urgent military decisions, gave some time to the consideration of a postwar international organization. In that same year Congress endorsed a resolution, favoring an international institution to keep the peace. In July, 1944, delegates from more than forty nations met at Bretton Woods, New Hampshire, and agreed on the establishment of an International Monetary Fund and an International Bank for Reconstruction and Development, as steps to postwar economic stability. At Dumbarton Oaks, Washington, D.C., beginning in August, the major powers agreed on a draft statement which could be used as a basis for the discussion of a United Nations charter.

Other conferences took up specific regional problems. At

Quebec in September, 1944, the postwar occupation of Germany was planned. The Yalta Conference, in the Crimea in February, 1945, attended by Roosevelt, Churchill, and Stalin, promised Japanese territory to Russia, a zone in Korea, and "rights" in Manchuria and in two Chinese cities (formerly Russian) as an inducement to war on Japan. A boundary of Poland was agreed upon, and Russia promised to assist in founding a democratic Polish government. German reparations were also discussed. All liberated states were to have free elections. Inasmuch as Russian help was not needed to defeat Japan, and Russia broke her promises to promote democracy in eastern Europe, the Yalta Conference has provided political ammunition, of a rather low explosive power. Although the British and American negotiators seem, on the surface, naive, the fact is that Russia could not have been defied and challenged except at the risk of encouraging a new Russo-German alliance against the rest of the world. Such an alliance was and is an economic and political "natural." German technology, Russian natural resources, and a mutual taste for dictatorships could yet, in combination, destroy civilization.

The Establishment of the United Nations. In the spring of 1945, shortly after Roosevelt's death, the United Nations (UN) was founded at San Francisco. The Charter provided a General Assembly of all member nations, a Security Council composed of the major powers (China was classed as "major") and six rotating memberships, and a permanent Secretariat, as well as a number of other agencies. To secure unanimity it was necessary to give each major power in the Security Council a veto over action which might be proposed to settle international disputes.

The UN, as a very loose confederation, has not given perfect satisfaction; however, it has some major settlements to its credit and serves as a forum for the thorough airing of international public grievances.

17

The Man of Independence

The responsibility of deciding momentous issues was inherited by Harry S. Truman of Independence, Missouri, upon the death of President Roosevelt. The decision to use the atomic bomb was but the first of constant, complex, and commanding judgments to be rendered in both domestic and foreign affairs. In foreign policy President Truman met with notable success, but such good fortune eluded him at home.

DOMESTIC PROBLEMS

In 1945 President Truman announced that he would continue his predecessor's policies. But unlike the New Deal program, which was readily accepted, very little of Truman's proposed legislation was enacted into law. The continuing "cold war" in Europe heightened the public's fear of communism and to this problem the President also directed his attention. But the immediate domestic issue facing Truman, upon his inauguration, was that of inflation.

Inflation. As World War II drew to a close it was thought by many to be necessary to take steps to counter its inflationary influences. Early in 1946 Chester Bowles of Connecticut was put in charge of the Office of Economic Stabilization. Price controls on nearly all commodities and services were ended in 1946, prematurely from the point of view of persons interested in combatting inflation. In 1948 a special session of the Congress failed to meet Truman's request for anti-inflation legislation. The President opposed an income-tax reduction bill on the ground that it would contribute to inflation, but it was passed in spite of his veto.

Defense and Governmental Reorganization. "Selective service," which had lapsed, was renewed in 1948 and continued the policy of peacetime conscription. To increase military efficiency, the army, navy, and air force were united under a Secretary of Defense in 1947. The organization of both the Congress and the Executive Branch was changed after studies of their procedures, the executive study having been undertaken by former President Herbert Hoover. Also at Truman's suggestion was the adoption of a new Presidential Succession Act in 1947, providing for descent, after the Vice-President (there was none at the moment), to the Speaker of the House and then to the President pro tempore of the Senate. A Constitutional change was made with the passage of the Twenty-second Amendment, initiated in 1947 and ratified in 1951, limiting presidents to two terms. This has been interpreted as a Republican measure to prevent the tenure of a latter-day Roosevelt.

Labor. After the war, labor responded to inflation by striking for higher wages. Never before had America experienced so many strikes in one year (1945–46). Although labor received its demands (and the country continued in the cycle of higher wages-higher costs-higher prices), the wave of strikes contributed to the enactment of the Taft-Hartley Law, passed (over the President's veto) by the Congress in 1947. Some of its provisions were the outlawing of the closed shop, secondary boycotts, jurisdictional strikes, and refusal to bargain in good faith. It also required that union bargaining officers sign a noncommunist affidavit.

The Election of 1948. The presidential election of 1948 was an unusual one. Two minor parties splintered from the Democrats. The "Dixiecrats," supporting Strom Thurmond of South Carolina gained strength for their candidate in several southern states. The Progressive party, behind Henry A. Wallace, proposed a very liberal domestic program and more amicable relations with Russia. The Republicans again nominated Thomas E. Dewey, and his victory was predicted by all "well-informed" commentators. Yet, although he lost electoral votes to Thurmond and failed to carry New York because the Wallace interest cut into the Democratic party's strength, Truman won 303 electoral votes to Dewey's 189 and Thurmond's 39. "Old Guard" Republicans said Dewey's campaign was too gentle or too "new dealish."

The "Fair Deal." Truman, bolstered by his unpredicted election, attempted to advance his "Fair Deal" program, but the conservative elements in both parties united to block much of his proposed legislation. He was defeated on repeal of the Taft-Hartley Act, rigid supports of farm prices, and more federal power projects. Effective lobbying by the American Medical Association killed his national health insurance program, and the South filibustered his civil rights proposals. However, some measures were approved: the increase of the minimum wage level, the extension of social security benefits to more people, and the allocation of federal funds for slum clearance.

Internal Security. The practical existence of the "cold war," a psychological contest of diplomacies and military rivalries (against Russia, a power avowedly devoted to world revolution by means of subversion) posed some hard problems of reconciling national safety and the Bill of Rights. In 1947 President Truman introduced a "loyalty check" on federal employees. The investigations which ensued thereafter brought forth the indictment (and later conviction) of a former State Department official, Alger Hiss, for perjury in connection with testimony on political relations with an admitted communist, Whittaker Chambers. The Supreme Court upheld the "loyalty check" and made other important decisions in these matters. It ruled that the Congress could make it a crime to conspire to teach the revolutionary doctrine of Marx and Lenin (1951), but the Court ruled out a state's noncommunist oath (for public employment) which did not excuse ignorance of the subversive character of a "communist front" organization (1952). During these years congressional investigating committees dug deeply and furiously, and with much fanfare. They reported that several Communists or "fellow travelers" held important places in government, although not the highest places. Practically all of them had joined the movement during the time of the national mood of despair or cynicism in the 1930's. The search for them was conducted by the investigating Senators and Representatives as though by a grand jury inquiring without the restrictions of privacy. Most press attention went to the cold but theatrical junior Senator from Wisconsin, Joseph McCarthy. A fruit of the interest in the matter was the conviction of eleven leaders of the American Communist party, after prosecution by Truman's Department of

Justice, for conspiracy to teach violent revolution. Several Americans were convicted of espionage, that is, specifically, revealing secrets of atomic research to the Russians. Two were sentenced to death.

The problem of internal security also resulted in the passage of the McCarran-Nixon Act of 1950, over Truman's veto, which in its terms required organized communism to act in the light of rigorous publicity. Objectors said it encouraged communists to become an underground organization and made public "repentance" psychologically more difficult. Others said the weakness of the threat of American communism made the rigor of the act disproportionate.

Fear of subversion affected the United States immigration policy and resulted in the McCarran-Walter Act of 1952 (passed over the President's veto), which prohibited totalitarians or ex-totalitarians from entering the country.

The Charge of Corruption. As the election of 1952 neared, the President was harassed by the great emphasis placed on the peccadilloes of some minor officials, matters magnified into an effort—probably unsuccessful—to identify the President with corruption in the public mind.

PROBLEMS ABROAD

With the war at an end, serious problems of reconstruction lay ahead. Economic systems and political institutions required repair or replacement. At the same time, international affairs were further complicated by the dissolution of the wartime alliance between the East and the West.

Economic and Political Reconstruction. The economy of the globe had been largely directed to war ends. Now it needed the help of the United States to be adjusted to conditions of peace. American help was given partly as a matter of simple justice and partly as a political expedient to forestall the exploitation of human miseries by those who planned world revolution. At the end of 1946 President Truman could report that lend-lease arrangements were practically terminated. The United States had contributed about fifty billion dollars. Other nations, through reverse lend-lease, had contributed about one-seventh as much. Measured by the standards of ability to pay and benefits received, the proportions seemed fair enough, except in the case of the Russians who have been suspiciously reluctant to return useful materials.

In 1947 Secretary of State George C. Marshall (retired five-star general) announced a plan of American aid in reviving the economics of the desolated nations. Russia and her satellites refused to participate. President Truman requested seventeen billion dollars from the Congress. Many more billions were appropriated in the next few years. The plan has been criticized from the "right" for its original invitation to the Russians and for its weight in the American public budget. Critics from the "left" have complained that it stabilized extremely conservative and unjust national economic systems. However, it seems certain that the "Marshall Plan" (sometimes called the European Recovery Plan) not only hampered the growth of communist parties in the nations of western Europe, but also enabled those countries, in a short time, to regain their prewar level of agricultural and industrial production.

Political reconstruction was undertaken through the UN and by means of military alliances. The UN began to function as such late in 1945 and was fully organized by the following spring. In 1946 Bernard M. Baruch, for the United States, offered a plan for the internationalization of atomic energy, including an international inspection program and a prohibition of the further manufacture of atomic bombs. The Russians in 1957, eleven years later, accepted part of the international control and inspection features.

Although the UN made important settlements in cases involving Iran, Greece, Indonesia, and Israel, before 1949, the conflicting claims of Communist China and Nationalist China were not resolved. Unless the United States had kept its armies intact in 1945 and sent them to fight the Chinese communists, it seems doubtful that the communist triumph there could have been prevented.

The conduct of some German and Japanese elements during the war was literally so atrocious that an outraged public opinion was appeased by the trial and execution of numerous leaders and the punishment of about a half a million lesser offenders. The precedent has been criticized for reviving a punitive notion of victory, dead since the seventeenth century, which could bear hard on future losers if the victors held a non-Western view of "law."

From 1945 to 1949 six major conferences were held by the great powers to agree on settlements with the defeated. The meetings solved small problems, but large problems such as the unification of Germany remained unsolved. The basic reason for the lack of harmony was the steadily increasing intransigency of the Soviet Union.

The "Cold War." With the war completed, the Russians tended to revert to their old suspicion and hostility. The result has been a series of crises, called the "cold war." The first great response of the Western world to Soviet hostility came in 1947 when the British found they could no longer bear the strain of continuous military support of Greece and Turkey against possible (even probable) Russian aggression. President Truman seized the opportunity to announce the "Truman Doctrine" by which the United States assumed that burden, and he further promised to assist in the defense of the rest of Europe. Both Houses of the Congress endorsed the policy by votes in an approximate ratio of three to one.

In April, 1948 Russian relations with western Europe worsened as the Soviets attempted to starve the Allies out of occupied Berlin, by closing off all ground communications. The Allies supplied Berlin by air for eleven months and refused to flinch at the prospect of Russian aerial attack. In the end the baffled Russians backed down at a considerable cost of prestige in Europe.

The increasing tension between East and West led to the formation, in 1949, of the North Atlantic Treaty Organization (NATO), which in time combined every principal North Atlantic, Baltic, and Mediterranean nation that dared to join a military alliance of joint defense against Russia. The organization was given substance by the establishment of an international army; General Eisenhower was its first Commander-in-Chief. This was the first permanent military alliance ever entered into by the United States.

The Korean "Police Action." The principal test of the United Nations was the defense of South Korea against the aggression of North Korea and Communist China. As the richest and strongest of the sincere members of the UN, most of the burden of the Korean "police action" was carried by the United States.

At the end of World War II, Korea, north of the 38° parallel, was occupied by communist troops; south of that line, by United States and Allied forces. The temporary line gradually became a semipermanent boundary as each group insisted it had the right to organize the whole. The communist elements refused to participate in free elections supervised by the UN in 1948, following which the Republic of Korea was established under President Syngman Rhee. In 1949 American troops were withdrawn.

In June, 1950 the North Koreans, using Russian equipment, invaded South Korea. The action was denounced by the UN, which adopted the cause as its own. President Truman ordered American forces into Korea, under command of General Douglas MacArthur.

At first greatly outnumbered, American forces were almost driven off the peninsula, but they accumulated strength and secured their Pusan beachhead. Against the North Koreans alone, the issue could no longer be in doubt. In September a perfectly executed amphibious operation was performed by the Americans at Inchon and within ten days the capital of the Republic, Seoul, was liberated. American and Republic of Korea troops advanced northward, with strong naval and aerial support, taking the North Korean capital, Pyongyang, and pressing toward the Manchurian border. At this moment Chinese communist troops entered the war and drove the UN forces back to the thirty-eighth parallel. Contrary to the policy laid down in Washington, General MacArthur urged and threatened an attack on China proper, whereupon he was summarily relieved by President Truman and replaced by General Matthew B. Ridgway. Armistice negotiations began in July, 1951 and dragged on inconclusively until they were left "in the air" late in 1952.

American opinion generally applauded the intervention but later divided on whether the gains had been sufficiently exploited to justify the casualties of almost 125,000 men of the UN forces killed, wounded, and missing. However, the "police action" seems to have put a stop to communist aggression by direct attack, which was Truman's primary purpose. The exercise of presidential power in committing U.S. troops to combat without a declaration of war would all too soon be cited as another precedent for action in another area of Asia.

18

They Liked Ike

The Republicans, ranked behind the very popular General Dwight D. Eisenhower, returned to power in the election of 1952. The Republican standard-bearer was opposed by the somewhat reluctant Democratic candidate, Governor Adlai E. Stevenson of Illinois. Eisenhower showed enormous strength, polling 442 electoral votes to Stevenson's 89 and winning a popular plurality of six and a half million votes. The Eisenhower victory owed a good deal to a feeling that the Korean military action was being mismanaged and that a military hero might be the one to conclude it properly. Republicans also exploited the idea that the previous Democratic administrations had been "soft" on domestic communism, and they linked this idea with a word-picture of a party twenty years in power, stale, weary, and somewhat corrupt. More positively, the prestige and nonpartisan past of the Republican candidate united factions within the party and probably inspired local leaders to get out the vote more strenuously than in the two Dewey campaigns. As for the Democratic candidate, Stevenson won the fierce loyalty of some, but his wayside audiences were numbered in the hundreds where the Eisenhower name drew thousands, and it really did not seem to matter much what either man said.

THE SCENE AT HOME

Once in power, the new administration showed itself not much different from its Democratic predecessors so far as deeds were concerned. Its public language seemed to favor the business community rather more than had the spokesmen of the executive branch in the years immediately before 1953, and many high appointments went to businessmen who had been loud in their blame of the Roosevelt and Truman administrations, but the domestic program of the new Congress was not much more conservative than the programs supported by the coalition of Republicans and southern Democrats which had usually dominated the Congress since the late 1930's.

State and Private Control of Natural Resources. The field of the conservation of natural resources was the field in which the new administration broke most sharply with the recent past. Western Republicans and southern and southwestern Democrats in the Congress had for a long time been attempting to change the traditional national conservation policy so as to lessen the power of the federal government and increase the control of natural resources by state governments. To judge by the three hundred and fifty-year history of American land speculation, of which this new development is merely an episode, it is impossible to avoid the conclusion that the change in policy was urged because it might be easier for private persons to acquire these resources from state governments than from the federal government. This judgment is not invidious. There is a body of opinion which says that it is better, both morally and economically, for natural resources to be developed privately for present profit than to have them held by the nation as a legacy for posterity.

The first victory for the localist and present-minded viewpoint was the passage by the Congress of a bill giving the states the title to submerged coastal lands (May, 1953). This law was passed in order to overturn earlier decisions of the Supreme Court, which had ruled that the United States had the "paramount right" to these lands and that title could only be transferred by act of the Congress. At stake was a vast supply of oil which lay under the sea off the coasts of Florida, Louisiana, Texas, and California, and which could now be exploited under leases granted by these states. The opposing argument of conservationists that these oil lands ought to be retained as a national endowment—perhaps for the benefit of education—was ignored or dismissed as "socialistic."

In 1954 a contract was negotiated for the construction of a private power plant to be built by the Dixon-Yates financial group in order to provide power for sale to the Tennessee Valley Authority and re-sale to the Atomic Energy Commission. Fearing a weakening of the locally popular Tennessee Valley Authority, the city of Memphis, Tennessee, elected to relieve the demand upon the Authority for power by building its own municipally-operated plant. This construction would make the private works unnecessary and the contract for the private plant was cancelled by President Eisenhower, but not before the political opposition had raised an uproar over the close tie of the Bureau of the Budget with the private power interests.

The President vetoed, in 1956, a bill to abolish federal regulation of natural gas production, not because he opposed the bill in principle but because of what he called "highly questionable" lobbying in favor of the bill. One of the lobbyists representing the oil industry had offered $2,500 to a Senator as a campaign contribution from the "personal funds" of an oil company president.

Several attempts to promote the private development of electric power on public sites failed in the Congress, chiefly because of the organized opposition of conservationists who feared what they called the "give-away" of invaluable scenic and historic public parks and monuments.

Beginning in 1955 there was launched a program to make atomic energy available for mechanical purposes under private management, and one such plant was officially inaugurated. A great deal of experimental work looking to that end followed. What might be expected in the future had been shown by the launching of an atomic-powered submarine, the *Nautilus,* in 1954. Somewhat similar power plants could be made available for pacific purposes.

Agriculture and Labor. Under the direction of Eisenhower's Secretary of Agriculture, Ezra Taft Benson, of Utah, the administration began to undo the fixed farm price support policy of the previous administrations. The Republican majority in the Congress enacted the Agricultural Act of 1954 which provided for flexible price supports for the basic commodities, corn, wheat, cotton, and peanuts, ranging from 75 per cent to 90 per cent of parity, according to the discretion of the Secretary. ("Parity" may be simply defined as the price level where the farmer's crop-dollar equals the value of the dollar he must spend for farm equipment and supplies.) This program has since been hotly controverted by a minority of farm spokesmen who claim it will destroy the family-size farm. Apologists for the program have said that fixed price supports create unmanageable and depressing farm surpluses, and that they reward and perpetuate unbusinesslike farming practices. They say we can do without the small farmer, with his high unit-costs, who must be subsidized to survive. President Eisenhower resolutely supported Benson in every contest with his opponents.

In 1955 the American Federation of Labor and the Congress of Industrial Organizations agreed to merge. This was accomplished "at the top" in 1956, with the choice of George Meany to head the consolidation. There had been no great change in national labor policy since the passage of the Taft-Hartley Law by the Eightieth Congress but, in 1957 and 1958, a Senate Committee conducted investigations into financial mismanagement and other abuses in national labor unions. The investigation had a disastrous effect on the careers of several high union officers who had been prominent in the leadership of the American Federation of Labor before the merger. Those industrial unions which came under close scrutiny were praised for their accounting and electoral procedures; attempts to inquire into their conduct of strikes ended in indecisive exchanges of accusations and counteraccusations.

The St. Lawrence Seaway. In 1954 the United States joined with Canada in an agreement to canalize the St. Lawrence River drainage system, a program which enables large ships to sail directly from the Great Lakes to the Atlantic Ocean and will probably make seaports of the Great Lake ports, slow the growth of New York Port, and make northeastern railroads less important.

Internal Security. President Eisenhower expanded the security program concerning federal employees. Reasons for dismissal from federal service now included (in addition to disloyalty) alcoholism, narcotic addiction, and immorality. Despite other pressing problems, much of the public's attention was drawn to congressional investigations of past subversive activity in the United States. The most publicized of the interrogators, Senator Joseph McCarthy of Wisconsin, was so carried away by his role that he allowed himself to antagonize three-quarters of his fellow Senators and was "condemned" for unbecoming conduct toward them, by a vote of sixty-seven to twenty-two, late in 1954. He died in 1957 after losing most of his prestige.

The Elections of 1954 and 1956. Since the Congress which was elected with Eisenhower had a Republican majority, it came as a surprise in the mid-term election of 1954 that the Democrats recaptured both Houses of Congress and took eighteen of the thirty-three governorships which were at stake. The President was proved to be far more popular than his party.

The national political scene was twice temporarily clouded by serious illnesses of the President, first, a coronary thrombosis (1955) and, second, an intestinal ailment requiring major surgery (1956). However, he agreed to offer himself for a second term, thus saving the Republican party serious embarrassment and, probably, internal strife. As far as candidates were concerned, the election of 1956 was a repeat of the 1952 Eisenhower *versus* Stevenson contest. Eisenhower campaigned on the record of his administration—"peace and prosperity"—while Stevenson found it even harder to excite a following than in 1952. His most memorable criticism was an attack on the administration's tests of atomic weapons on the ground that they produced a dangerous fall-out of radioactive materials, but his opponent's disclaimers apparently satisfied the listeners. The President had established himself as a personage apart from the Republican party and in the voting Eisenhower ran even better than he did in 1952, but his party did not recapture the Congress, which remained in the hands of a Democratic majority. One could only speculate on this remarkable phenomenon—the President's pronouncements often seemed more "Democratic" than "Republican." Perhaps he was the first nonpartisan President since John Quincy Adams.

ECONOMIC AND SOCIAL DEVELOPMENT

The economy of the United States after 1952 was the economy of a well-fed, almost fully-employed people. Despite occasional alarms the country escaped any postwar liquidation and lived in a state of "boom." The history of extraction, production, and distribution had therefore been almost nothing but a statistical table reflecting prosperity. An economic survey of the year 1955, a typical year of the 1950's, may be illuminating as illustrating the decade. The national output was valued at about 10 per cent above that of 1954 (1955 output estimated at 392 billion dollars). The production of manufacturers was about 40 per cent more than it had averaged in the years immediately following World War II. The businessmen of the country spent about 30 billion dollars for new factories and machinery. National income available for spending was almost a third greater than it had been in 1950. Consumers spent about 256 billion dollars, that is about 700 million dollars a day, or about twenty-five million dollars every hour, all around the clock. Sixty-five million people held jobs and only a little more than two million wanted jobs but could not find them. Only agriculture complained that it was not sharing in the boom. To some observers this was an ominous echo of the mid-1920's. As the farmer's share of his product declined, marketing costs rose. But there were few pessimists among the observers of the national economy. Those few seemed to fear that the prosperity was based on government pump-priming on a stupendous scale. Federal budgets were being drafted by Republicans who had denounced the Democrats as wasteful spenders, yet they were running six, seven, and eight times as high as the largest New Deal peacetime budgets. Most of the government's income, of course, was going to military expenses, past, present, and future.

Historically considered, probably the most significant economic change since the end of World War II was in the character of the labor force. For the first time in history, "white collar" workers outnumbered manual workers. The remarkable increase in industrial productivity required an increasing number of accountants, salesmen, engineers, designers—just to keep up with the capacities of the "blue collar" worker. The rise of the birthrate required more teachers and school administrators. The lengthening of the life span employed more doctors, dentists, nurses, recreational suppliers, and so on. Clerical workers increased a thousand per cent in the twentieth century, while the American population only doubled. There were even more service employees than farmers—that is, more cooks, waiters, bartenders, bus boys, and hotel maids than there were tillers of the soil. From a population which was 95 per cent rural under President Washington, the United States had shifted its base until only a tenth of the people depended on farming in the 1960's.

Outstanding social achievements were accomplished in the fields of civil rights, health, and welfare.

In 1954 the United States Supreme Court ruled that the segregation of pupils in the public schools according to race was unconstitutional. This voided a long series of precedents to the general effect that separate but equal facilities for education were sufficient for the states to meet their legal obligations to Negro pupils. Two facts stood out immediately. First, the Court, with several members born and bred in the South, was unanimous. Second, the Justices leaned heavily on the recent findings of sociology and psychology for the data which guided their opinion. In the following year the "border" states began to abandon segregation in education. In several southern states, legal expedients and, more rarely, intimidation, were used to bar such proceedings. The legal expedients were generally of the sort rendered obsolete by the Civil War. The opposition received most of the publicity, but impartial factual surveys showed education integration proceeding at a glacial rate. It would take federal intervention and troops, first in 1957 and throughout the 1960's, to open reluctant school doors.

The nation's health was better than ever before. Beginning with the discovery of sulfa drugs in the 1930's and then antibiotics, penicillin, and vaccines for poliomyelitis, mumps, and measles all prolonged life, with the result that more people died from degenerative diseases, such as cancer and heart problems.

Growth in the 1950's brought new problems to urban areas. Housing was most available for the middle class in suburbs, removed from city services and transportation. The cities filled with fleeing rural poor. The nation began a massive superhighway system which relieved traffic problems but caused increased dependence on cars and separation of the poor from the rest of the population.

Social security benefits were extended in 1955 to millions of people not previously "covered." The categories of employment to which the new legislation applied were mostly in the general fields of religion, domestic service, and clerical work. In 1956 women were permitted to begin to draw retirement benefits at age sixty-two, and members of the armed forces were made eligible under the program for the first time. Social security, first instituted as a national reform measure of the 1930's, had become an accepted national institution. By 1956 over eight million persons were receiving money payments under the Old Age and Survivors Insurance program, the basic but not the only important part of the program. In addition, the federal government had committed itself, through the Social Security Administration, to programs of disability insurance, death benefits (an odd phrase, surely), maternal and child health, and unemployment insurance and services. These latter projects usually are shared by the state governments. Apart from the psychological effect on the people, it seems likely that social security benefits might well be an important brake on a decline of purchasing power in future economic downturns.

Continuing government interest in social welfare was evinced by the establishment (in 1953) of the Department of Health, Education, and Welfare, with Cabinet rank.

THE SCENE ABROAD

Foreign affairs had never loomed so huge in American life at a time when the world was professedly at peace. From eastern Asia around to western Europe, the United States found itself involved in a permanent crisis not of its own making.

The Korean Armistice. When General Eisenhower was running for office, in 1952, probably one of his most potent vote-getting promises was his assertion that if elected he would go to Korea to get the stalled armistice talks in motion. He went in December, 1952, and negotiations were renewed. Finally, in July, 1953, terms were arrived at with the North Korean and Chinese Communists. Democrats grumbled that they had rejected the terms which the administration accepted because the terms did not include repatriation of certain American civilians held in China, but critics were ignored in a general rejoicing at home. In effect the armistice stopped the fighting and left the situation much as it was when the trouble started. Early in 1954 delegates of nineteen nations met in a conference on Far Eastern affairs, at Geneva. The unification of Korea was part of the agenda but was defeated by communist opponents.

SEATO. With the success of the communist rebels in northern French Indo-China, the United States took the lead in setting up the South East Asia Treaty Organization (SEATO) in 1954, a defense alliance of all friendly nations with interests in that part of the world. Unlike the NATO it was not given body by the erection of a military establishment.

Russo-American Relations. The dictator of Russia, Joseph Stalin, died in 1953, apparently not much lamented, even at home. His successors put the office of dictator "in commission," so to speak. Some tactical changes in Russian policy were noticed, which encouraged western optimists to hope for a softening of Russian foreign attitudes and some melting of the "cold war." But relations with Russia entered a more sombre phase when it was announced by the United States in 1954 that the Russians had exploded their own "hydrogen bomb," a new and worse atomic weapon which the United States had already developed. The announcement was confirmed by the Russians. There remained now only the perfection of methods, on both sides, for delivering the new weapons in self-propelled missiles across oceans. This would place it within the power of either Russia or the United States to destroy the human race without the possibility of a successful defense by the attacked. In 1955 and 1956 it was urged that the continued testing of atomic devices was adversely affecting the future of the race. Scoffers said the fear was exaggerated; the others said the maximum amount of dangerous radiation in the atmosphere which should be tolerated was none.

In 1955 Russian talk of coexistence led the West to hope that conciliation might be effected. In this encouraging atmosphere President Eisenhower and other Western leaders met with the Russians at Geneva in July, 1955. The major objectives of disarmament, unification of Germany, and settlement of Asiatic problems were unfulfilled; but the conference did produce a lessening of world tensions, and it was hoped that this spirit would prevail. In 1956 further encouragement of this hope was derived from learning of denunciations of Stalin's terrorist record by several of his leading political heirs. Concessions to small and heretofore rigorously terrorized neighbors accompanied this remarkable about-face. However, at the end of 1956 it was once more clear that Russian persistence in diplomatic vice was still a habit not easily to be shaken off by the Communists. Late in

1956 a violent rebellion in Hungary was harshly repressed; on the other hand, a more pacific adjustment in Poland was successfully carried off without Russian interference. The moral seemed to be that satellites might reorganize so long as their deeds did no harm to the prestige of the Russian army.

It was with a feeling of shock that the American people learned in October, 1957, of the launching of the first artificial moon by the Soviet astrophysical scientists. This launching was a part of the observance of an "International Geophysical Year," a world-wide co-operative effort among scientists to learn more about the earth. The Russian launching was not unexpected by other scientists. However, it came much earlier than had been expected even by the well-informed and seems to have been a total surprise to the American public which had entertained the myth that the Russians were mostly shoeless, turnip-eating, oppressed peasants whose few scientists acquired most of their knowledge from foreign publications or from spies in Britain and America. Four more artificial earth satellites were soon orbiting around the earth, one of them Russian and three American, but the Americans continued to be depressed because the Russians were "first," and their satellite by far the largest.

In a sense the shock was probably good for the people because it provoked a re-examination of the American educational system, and something of a revulsion against occupying good youthful minds with curricular trifles instead of the red meat of the liberal arts and sciences necessary to the advancement of knowledge.

The military meaning of the Russian "Sputnik," as the satellite was named, was the subject of much sober thought. Perhaps the nation which could first learn to bring down an automatically-armed satellite through the earth's atmosphere to a designated target could rule the world by terror alone.

Events in 1959 hinted at a thaw in the cold war. However, a scheduled Summit Conference in Paris (May, 1960) was wrecked by Soviet leader Khrushchev, who refused to attend unless the United States apologized for spy plane flights over Russia. Though Khrushchev intimated that he would try to reshape or ruin the United Nations, he had in fact no particular influence on its structure or function.

The Middle East Crises. Next to Korea, the most troublesome part of the world, from an American viewpoint, was that known variously as the Near East or Middle East, which lies between India and the Mediterranean. Once smoothly policed by the British Empire, as an essential link of its eastern and western parts, it had been abandoned, more or less, by Britain because the British people simply could not carry the economic burden of such policy any longer. Americans did not rush in where Britons could not afford to tread, except to guarantee Turkey. This left a power vacuum which was tempting to the Russians and to some rather unpromising types of Arab "nationalist" leaders. After World War II the new state of Israel was founded there, mostly financed by American private gifts. Neighboring Arab states dedicated themselves to its extermination at some undefined but early date. At the same time western Europe became increasingly dependent on Near Eastern petroleum which came via the Suez Canal. In 1956 the dictator of Egypt seized the canal and barred Israeli shipping. Israel, Britain, and France, in succession, attacked Egypt. The attack was halted by order of the United Nations, but none of the problems which led to the outburst were solved. The world looked to the United States expectantly, and it was thus forcibly pointed out that in the middle of the twentieth century the United States occupied a position in the world analagous to that of the British Empire in the previous two hundred years. In March, 1957 the Congress adopted a formal military policy, at the request of President Eisenhower, concerning the Near East, called the "Eisenhower Doctrine." According to this declaration the President was authorized to use armed force to assist any nation or group of nations which asked for help against the aggressive attack of a communist country.

The United States would have liked to put the costly and vexing burden on the United Nations but the effective part of the United Nations, the Security Council, was impotent while the cold war lasted. Old-fashioned diplomacy offered little hope. Diplomacy among equals required agreement on moral premises. The communist fraction of the world denied the moral tradition of Western society and had thereby insulated itself against it. It is hard to see how two halves of a world without a common moral denominator could come to terms. Meanwhile, the peace of exhaustion, if not of order, was continued.

19

Kennedy and Johnson

At the turn of the decade the United States had grown by the addition of Alaska (1958) and Hawaii (1959). The sixties began with tensions in foreign affairs, momentous space explorations, and a presidential election and new administration. The census estimate for 1970 calculated 205 million Americans, an increase of 24 million in ten years; 60 per cent lived in metropolitan areas and 5 per cent on farms. The median age declined to 17.7 years. Americans seemed to believe their country was an invincible republic of virtue which could direct the course of history. Their faith would be attacked in the coming decade.

THE ELECTION OF 1960

By 1959 the Republican nomination was assured for Vice-President Richard M. Nixon. The Democrats nominated Senator John F. Kennedy of Massachusetts on the first convention ballot. Kennedy chose Senator Lyndon B. Johnson of Texas as his running mate.

As the campaign evolved, Kennedy said that the economy was unhealthy and that American strength and prestige had declined since 1952. Nixon campaigned defensively. A novelty of the campaign was a series of televised debates between the candidates, which proved less important for their content than for their revelations of the contending personalities. Many Republican party officers blamed Nixon's defeat on the debates, saying that he was too reserved in contrast to the dynamic

Kennedy, but the Republican Party Chairman said that Kennedy won by greater skill in appealing to black voters, who supported him 8:1. Kennedy narrowly defeated Nixon by a popular plurality of one-fifth of 1 per cent, although the Electoral College vote was a decisive 303–219. Kennedy's victory made him the youngest American (43 years old) ever elected President. The Democrats remained in nominal control of Congress.

AFFAIRS AT HOME

At the end of 1963 few of President Kennedy's most warmly endorsed domestic projects had been written into law. Although the Congress raised the minimum wage and gave more generous Social Security benefits, a coalition of Republicans and southern Democrats had blocked medical care under Social Security, federal aid to education, a cabinet Department of Urban Affairs, stiffer controls of farm production, and economic powers to combat future depressions. Legislation to protect blacks in public accommodations, education, and voting was moving very slowly through the Congress. The business community's chronic suspicion of the President became acute hostility. The public, however, appeared to approve the administration in the mid-term election of 1962, which made no appreciable change in the congressional party balance. In 1963 the Equal Pay Act passed, offering some relief to blacks and more especially to women.

Constitutional Amendments. During the term for which Kennedy was elected, the Constitution was twice amended. The Twenty-third Amendment gave three electoral votes to the District of Columbia. The Twenty-fourth Amendment abolished tax-paying as a statutory requirement for voting in federal elections.

The Racial Dilemma. The flaming issue in American life was the race question. American blacks, with a new militance, determined to translate the emancipation of the 1860's into a reality of the 1960's. Classic forms of violence erupted: terrorism by whites against blacks and against whites who sided with blacks in attempts to secure their rights and their human dignity. There also were riotous crimes against property by blacks. Of several score killed, the majority were black, although blacks form but a tenth of the population. The Department of Justice disregarded popularity in enforcing the applicable laws, but state and local governments frequently appeared inept at peace-keeping.

WORLD PRESSURES

The United States was militarily stronger than Candidate Kennedy had said, although its military policy overemphasized atomic weapons at the expense of conventional arms so that the nation seemed committed to atomic war or nothing. President Kennedy effected a balance of arms, and by the end of 1963, the United States had the strongest and most flexible forces in all history. America is more military than it admits to itself; the century's twenty-ninth foreign military operation was about to begin.

Cold War. War loomed chillingly close in 1961 when the East German government walled off East Berlin to dam the river of refugees. Kennedy reacted with strong assurances to West Berlin and sent additional troops.

In an internal revolution in Cuba, Fidel Castro took power on January 1, 1959. He was welcomed as a democratic leader, but his regime soon took on the property-seizing, firing squad accoutrements of a dictatorship and showed special unfriend-liness to the United States.

No one was much surprised when Castro announced his communism and wove close ties with the Soviet Union and Red China. In April, 1961, an invasion of Cuba by American-backed refugees from the Castro revolution failed at the Bay of Pigs.

In the fall of 1962 atomic war seemed near as President Kennedy demanded the removal from Cuba of Russian missiles with a range covering half of the United States. The Russians removed the missiles, but Cuba remained a gall to the United States. In response to Communist Cuba, the United States began a policy of economic aid to Latin America, but this so-called Alliance for Progress was too little, too late.

Test-Ban Treaty. A treaty to prevent the pollution of the planet by atomic fallout from atmospheric or oceanic tests of nuclear devices was signed in Moscow by the United States, Great Britain, and the Soviet Union in September, 1963. Infant mortality, abnormal since 1951, dropped annually after testing stopped. If Kennedy is remembered as an effective President, the nuclear test ban may be his principal monument.

WAR IN VIETNAM

Southeast Asia presented an agonizing panorama. A 1962 treaty created a neutral Laos in which the Communists were the strongest element. But it was events in neighboring North and South Vietnam that would tragically involve Americans in the next decade.

Partitioned Vietnam. After eight years of French-Vietnamese warfare an international conference at Geneva (1954) accepted division of Vietnam, pending free elections in 1956. In 1955 the International Control Commission said that the Geneva terms were being observed. Although pressed, President Eisenhower refused to help South Vietnam with more than a few dollars and some military advice. President Diem of South Vietnam, with American approval, prevented the scheduled election and repressed his opposition, thereby stimulating the growth of existing guerilla forces. As Eisenhower said, "possibly 80 per cent" would have voted for the Communist Ho Chi Minh—who led the victory over France. Diem's opponents were a mixed bag of Buddhists, Communists, and Nationalists, whose outside help came from Communist nations.

From 1955 to 1960 South Vietnam endured a home-grown guerilla war, until North Vietnam called on the Communist "National Liberation Front" (commonly referred to as the Viet Cong) to lead the struggle. This seemed to American leaders to threaten a Communist takeover of the area. So President Kennedy hazardously, covertly, and without consent added force to counter the Viet Cong, until by late 1962, there were 15,500 American troops in unpublicized combat in Vietnam and the Viet Cong cried, "Imperialism!" Thus came undeclared war, with no UN sanction or predictable end, only later (1966) justified by invoking the equivocal SEATO treaty.

AN END AND A BEGINNING

The administration of the "thousand days" came to a bitter end when President Kennedy was shot to death by rifle fire on

November 22, 1963, while riding in a motorcade through the streets of Dallas, Texas. A suspect was arrested and, in turn, was assassinated in the Dallas police station even before arraignment. With assurance Vice-President Lyndon B. Johnson assumed the awful burden of the office. The constitutional system had survived another serious test.

JOHNSON'S GREAT SOCIETY

President Johnson assumed responsibility for the stalled domestic programs of Kennedy and in 1965 announced his own program for a "Great Society." Johnson's dream appeared to fit the aspirations of his generation, as public and congressional support materialized to secure passage of acts designed to effectuate practically every plank in the Democratic platforms of 1960 and 1964. In 1965 and 1966 President Johnson exerted more forcible and successful peacetime legislative leadership than any President since Roosevelt during his "hundred days."

Race and Law. The Congress passed the Civil Rights Act of 1964 after a 75-day Senate filibuster. Although it was not so extensive as black leaders wished, the act prohibited the use of race as a criterion for employment, public accommodations, voting, and vocational training. It also forbade discrimination by sex in employment but did not specify enforcement procedures. The public accommodations clause had aroused most opposition, but in December, 1964, the Supreme Court unanimously upheld its constitutionality under Congress's broad power to regulate commerce.

In some areas blacks' demands continued to meet violent resistance. In June, 1964, three civil rights workers were murdered in Mississippi; their buried bodies were found two months later.

The civil rights movement received worldwide attention when the Reverend Martin Luther King, Jr., of Atlanta, leader of passive resistance to segregation, was given the 1969 Nobel Peace Prize. In 1965 the Congress passed the Voting Rights Act, permitting the use of federal voting registrars in states that still used literacy tests and where less than half the adults were registered voters.

Presidential Election, 1964. Republican party leaders were so sure that Senator Barry Goldwater of Arizona could not win the Republican nomination that they made no concerted effort to thwart his harvesting of delegates in advance. But Goldwater won the nomination on the first ballot and then purged his opponents from high party offices. His exuberant followers rushed into the campaign as if it were a crusade.

President Johnson won an easy nomination and waged a low-key campaign. Johnson's choice of Hubert H. Humphrey as a running mate pleased liberals, who equated Goldwater conservatism with McCarthyism and a reversal of fifty years of social legislation. Adopting a middle-of-the-road stance, Johnson won the election by a popular vote of 42.7 million to 26.9 million. The electoral vote was 486–52. Goldwater carried South Carolina, Georgia, Alabama, Mississippi, Louisiana, and Arizona. His showing in the Gulf States was attributed to anger at the racial views of the Democratic leadership. Goldwater's platform and overeager followers had alienated descendants of recent immigrants, blacks, and the poor. He lost many Republican votes, but if he had held all the declared Republicans, he still would have had but 44 per cent of the popular vote.

War on Poverty. In Johnson's first State of the Union address, he declared an "unconditional war on poverty" and asked the Congress for money to wage the war on several fronts, including rehabilitation of depressed areas and retraining of workers technologically unfitted for employment. The great migration of agricultural blacks to industrial centers multiplied the economic problems. The country needed a $40 billion annual increase of the gross national product to absorb the growing labor force, even allowing for an unemployment rate of 4 per cent.

Heeding Johnson, the Congress passed eighty-six major acts, including Medicare, which partly subsidized medical care for the aged. Its cost has been high, but neither patients nor taxpayers have shown satisfaction. Cities decayed faster than they were renewed, and suburban flight continued. Although Edward Brooke became the first black Senator since Reconstruction, and Thurgood Marshall became the first black Supreme Court Justice, both Newark and Detroit endured fiery, bloody slum riots in 1967. For each black moving into a city there were several whites who moved out. Remaining whites showed a growing resentment of black people who wished to change their ancient subculture.

FOREIGN AFFAIRS

Traditional Western friendships endured except for French chilliness and brief American occupation of the Dominican Republic in 1965. Russian relations were only as civil as interdependent survival required.

Eastern Affairs. Russo-Chinese relations had cooled steadily following the death of Stalin in 1953. Mao Tse-tung, leader of Red China, accused Khrushchev of deviating from the orthodox Leninist-Stalinist program of world revolution by violence. He so annoyed the Soviet chief that Khrushchev withdrew Russian technological assistance from China. The sudden, mysterious fall of Khrushchev from power in 1964 elevated two internationally unknown leaders, Leonid Brezhnev and Alexei Kosygin, to the posts of Secretary of the Communist Party and Premier of the U.S.S.R., respectively. Soviet explanations of the ouster were obscure, but the relations between China and Russia continued frigid and remained so at a time when NATO's strength waned.

In October, 1964, China complicated the problem of arms control by exploding a small atomic bomb. The achievement heightened Chinese prestige among Asian countries, and the specter of Chinese intercontinental missiles spurred United States military spending.

American Vietnam Involvement. The war in Vietnam pervaded life like a spreading stain. In 1963 dissension over policy led to the killing of President Ngo Dinh Diem in a military coup. Years of chronic instability followed in which South Vietnam had twelve governments, none with a proved popular base. South Vietnam's army had lost 25,000 dead and at least 100,000 deserters by 1965. As a fighting force it was finished. President Johnson had a choice between phasing out or pressing harder. He chose to send 125,000 American troops and to risk bombing North Vietnam (China's friend), which would at least improve South Vietnamese rulers' morale. The Vietnam question became a long-range international crisis of the utmost gravity. Even the intensification produced only an unsatisfactory stalemate.

North Vietnam sent leaders, weapons, and some troops. American generals advised punishing the enemy severely, and Johnson claimed that he was preserving the confidence of small nations in America's ability to protect them.

In 1964 the Senate's "Tonkin Gulf" resolution gave Johnson a free hand to prevent further aggression by North Vietnam. Beginning in February, 1965, the United States bombed targets in North Vietnam and then intermittently stopped to see what the response would be. American draft calls increased 100 per cent in 1965, and young men flooded the nation's colleges to avoid the draft. In an eight-year period the American army doubled in size, its cost trebled, and bombing and chemical warfare defoliated and destroyed much of the country the United States was "protecting."

American numbers in Vietnam grew astonishingly. Dates and totals tell the story: 1963, to 17,000; 1964, to 22,000; 1965, past 75,000; 1966, to 375,000—and on to a peak of 542,500 in February, 1969. (Seventh Fleet navy men are not counted, but Marines are.) The maximum estimate of the Viet Cong, alive and dead, was 330,000, of whom 63,000 were infiltrators from the north. The use of atomic bombs against an agrarian population was tactically unpromising and would have threatened the end of mankind.

There was great cost in blood and life. For what they are worth, the estimates of all troop deaths on both sides total 750,000, two million additional wounded, plus civilian dead and wounded uncounted. Civilian casualties can only be guessed as a greater, horrendous total.

Opposition to the Vietnam War. Senatorial and popular opposition to the war became outspoken in 1966. The psychology of warfare makes it hard to change fruitless tactics, but even Defense Secretary Robert McNamara admitted in 1967 that the bombing had not cut North Vietnam's infiltration into the south. A reputable poll in 1966 showed two-thirds of the American people favoring compromise peace. What troubled many was that the military seemed a fourth branch of the government, possessed of independent policy authority.

The Vietnam War, fourth bloodiest in American history, was a presidential exercise about which the citizenry was not consulted. American policy was not based on clear long views of all implications of successive steps. No force then fighting could demonstrate popular support in Vietnam. Although intentions were originally benevolent, tactics hurt both friend and foe, and fierce attack stiffened an unfree subject people who had no alternative except to show endurance.

The Vietnam deadlock was emphasized by an attack in January, 1968, in which United States and allied troops were surprised in thirty-five urban places and lost their precarious control of many rural areas. Refugees, abandoning their hamlets and pouring into cities, numbered about 350,000. The Americans seemed to be helping a cause for which the Vietnamese cared little.

"Peace Talks." After long disagreement on a site, "peace talks" began in Paris, May 10, 1968, between South Vietnam, North Vietnam, and the United States. The discussions at first seemed only to illustrate the gulf separating the parties involved.

THE ELECTION OF 1968

In November, 1967, Senator Eugene J. McCarthy had accepted leadership of a movement to shift the national policy from war to peace and announced his candidacy for the presidency. His cause seemed forlorn until he defeated an administration slate in the New Hampshire Democratic primary. After this evidence of voter discontent, Senator Robert F. Kennedy also entered the contest. In March, 1968, President Johnson announced his withdrawal from presidential contention to devote his time to negotiating an end to the Vietnam War. (He faced probable defeat in the next week's Wisconsin presidential primary.) Vice-President Humphrey then announced his candidacy.

Hoping that presidential politics was the way to peace and to domestic tranquility, amateurs flocked to aid McCarthy and Kennedy, who between them harvested large majorities in Democratic primaries. Their chief obstacles (excepting each other) seemed to be the regular party commitment to Humphrey and the possibility that antiblack voters might react against any Democratic nominee by either voting Republican or supporting the independent candidacy of George C. Wallace of Alabama, who hotly opposed federal intervention to cool racial frictions.

Then Kennedy was assassinated, like his brother before him, in Los Angeles in June (the murderer was caught and convicted).

At the Republican convention, Richard M. Nixon was nominated on the first ballot, overcoming opposition from Nelson Rockefeller and Ronald Reagan. At the Democratic convention the party showed deep cleavage on the Vietnam question, refusing in the end clearly to repudiate presidential policy. Convention officers seemed very heavy-handed, and about ten thousand young demonstrators battled Chicago police in what investigators later called a "police riot." Hubert Humphrey received the nomination on the first ballot.

Nixon opposed the war but discussed it little, while wooing southern voters. Humphrey moved slightly away from presidential policy, but whether it helped or hurt him is debatable. Johnson stopped American bombing of North Vietnam on October 31 (but 300 planes were lost over Laos thereafter). The popular vote was painfully close: Nixon, 43.4 per cent; Humphrey, 43 per cent; Wallace, 13.6 per cent. The electoral vote was 301, 191, 46. The fragmented Democrats "controlled" the Congress. Wallace had carried five states. Humphrey lost all eight states which had presidential primaries, excepting Massachusetts. The Democratic coalition of 1932–64 had collapsed; only its black membership remained faithful.

THE STALLED SOCIETY

The patterns of American life seemed strangely awry. The annual gross national product neared $800 billion. But unemployment in the black ghettos remained at intolerable levels, and inflation threatened continuously, while the dollar strained in an imbalance of foreign payments. Men and planes poured into Vietnam but only increased the number of casualties. The hopes of the poor met frustrations in the actual workings of the Great Society programs. The response was turbulence: peace demonstrations by well-fed collegians, the looting of shops by lads on welfare pittances. A dramatic illustration of the malaise was the carefully planned assassination of Martin Luther King in April, 1968, followed by days of ghetto rioting in 125 cities. Caught after an international hunt, James Earl Ray pleaded guilty to the murder, received a life sentence, and forestalled open explanations. Seven years later, claiming innocence and blaming venal lawyers, he asked for a retrial.

THE 1960'S IN RETROSPECT

The 1960's were years of affluence for most, and obesity was one of the chief health problems. Consumer spending increased over 60 per cent. Passports issued for pleasure travel in 1968 were six times as numerous as in 1950. Consumer debt doubled from 1960 to 1969, while the national income grew about 75 per cent. Farms were larger, farmers fewer; farm income was 6.25 per cent of the whole. Jobs open to the unskilled decreased two-thirds.

The booming economy leveled off in 1966, except that prices continued climbing. The United States spent $57 billion more than received, and 40 per cent of federal spending was unproductive, i.e., military. The federal budget more than doubled in the years 1961–69, twice the growth rate of national income. Nonproductive overspending depreciated the consumer's dollar 17.5 per cent from 1959 to 1969, so that higher wages bought less in 1970 than in 1965. Simultaneously there was measurable undernourishment in scattered poverty areas.

In foreign affairs the United States and the Soviet Union kept their unspoken agreement to coexist. In 1967, after talking at Glassboro, N.J., President Johnson and Premier Kosygin were said to have agreed not to be driven into nuclear war. But weapons systems multiplied.

Overriding all other foreign questions was the harsh national debate on Vietnam, where the substitution of simple slogans for new ideas may have killed two million. The argument was cloudy because the Congress did little but ratify executive action with money. The President was politically inept in not noticing that the hydrogen bomb threat made the first mass peace movement in American history psychologically possible. Air power proved overrated, and conscripts were no match for guerillas. Revulsion against doctrinaire war divided Americans dangerously.

In the two decades ending in 1969, blacks advanced economically more than whites, but statistics were deceptive. By

1967 blacks achieved the purchasing power of whites of 1947; meanwhile whites, although gaining less rapidly, were far, far ahead. And as campaigns for integration moved northward, northern white sympathies decreased so sharply that some young blacks despaired of accommodation and organized for violence. Southern racial activism had been church-centered and loving; northern activism was street-centered and less pacific. Before 1960 most black reformers accepted American values, asking only for equal membership. By 1970 a few very articulate leaders demanded reformation or separation, and racism seemed to govern white America's outlook.

Calmed by Eisenhower, then excited by the brief Kennedy interlude, Americans of every faction found a great gap between their dreams and reality. The whole spectrum demonstrated. In politics the 1960's were the decade of the streets.

A Chinese curse is "May you live in interesting times." The 1960's were manic times. Theorists competed in shocking to get attention. Incivility and abuse impatiently replaced fervor and satire. Television made every issue visible and brought the Four Horsemen into the house. Rich young whites labeled themselves revolutionaries but dressed like eccentric royalty. They had known no world without affluence, nuclear fear, TV, and antibiotics. They idolized leisure and suspected office hours as debasing. In the lower schools attendance doubled, 1950–68, while costs (but not quality) septupled. Colleges enrolled nearly 4 per cent of the whole people, the largest and most complaining studentry ever, which rioted periodically throughout the decade. Pursuing pleasure as happiness, rebels added marijuana, heroin, and hallucinogens to the already accepted repertory of nicotine, caffeine, and alcohol.

Such social seething might be temporary, but the demographic profile of the United States made a sharp turn. The "baby boom" of the 1950's was followed by a "baby bust" in the later 1960's as young people chose small families and praised zero population growth. Compared to 1946, 33 per cent more women had 4 per cent fewer babies. In 1973 the births per thousand for women of childbearing age broke a low record set in 1936. Meanwhile the population bulge of young adults strained the American economy's ability to absorb new workers.

20

From Nixon to Carter

President Richard M. Nixon assumed office in January, 1969, to face an unhealthy economy, an unhappy society, a deteriorating environment, and the problem of keeping his promise to end the Vietnam War.

THE ECONOMY AND SOCIETY

In the war-fevered economy, production, profits, and employment all worsened in 1969, but prices rose (except in securities markets). Economists expected both production and unemployment to increase. "Tight money" brought lofty interest rates, fewer housing starts, and a shelter shortage unknown since 1950. Government had tools to prevent a 1930's type deflation, but this recession was strangely inflationary.

The number of identifiably poor people increased in 1969–70. Nixon proposed to raise conventional Social Security benefits but retracted promises to complete tax-deductibility for medical costs of the aged. However, he did recommend minimum income guarantees.

Americans gave much attention to institutional schooling, to which they attach a sacred importance. Schools were obviously unable to urbanize the massive agrarian influx. Printing presses and vocal cords were overworked discussing integration, which filled court dockets, made governors threaten defiance, and pro-

voked violence against children by supporters of "lawnorder."
The most despairing young blacks said that they were not
dropouts but pushouts from whites' culture and felt threatened
with extermination by private weapons in the world's most
heavily armed society.

Candidate Nixon had proposed "black capitalism," that is,
incentives to lure businesses to ghettos. Labor leaders called this
apartheid; black critics said ghettos could not support business.
The 1969 "Philadelphia Plan" was designed to bring blacks into
building trades by quota at a sure but very slow rate.

PLANET EARTH

From 1957, when Yuri Gagarin became the first human being
to orbit the earth in a space capsule, to 1961, the U.S.S.R.
garnered a series of firsts in space exploration. Beginning in
1958, the United States sponsored both a communications
satellite system and a space exploration program that culminated
in 1969 with the first manned moon landing. Other landings
followed, but Americans lost interest and complained that their
regular television shows were being preempted by news of the
space flights. As costs rose, the United States switched to un-
manned probes, space relay stations, and even cooperation
with their former rivals, the Russians.

About three decades after urgent warnings by biologists that
we were poisoning and gassing ourselves toward extinction, the
need for preserving space-vehicle Earth was felt. Both great
life stabilizers, the oceans of air and water, showed measurable
damage, mostly due to profligate use of fossil fuels. With the
present strength of nationalism, no certain remedy appeared,
although the world's white people produced 98 per cent of the
strain, and that mostly by Americans. In the early 1970's the
United States did dust off laws left over from the Progressive
period and made a few steps toward cleaning up air and water,
but remedies were expensive.

THE SCENE ABROAD

Americans could only view the world scene with alarm and
despair as Nixon assumed office. In his search for peace Nixon

stunned the American people with several controversial moves. By the end of his first term of office, however, some measurable easing of the tension had occurred.

China. In public view, President Nixon's most noticeable foreign policy change was toward Red China. The ban on travel to China was lifted, and in election year 1972 Nixon made a headlined trip to Peking. United States official policy finally began to admit that the world's most populous country existed. After the thaw, the Chinese mainland inevitably replaced the Taiwan government in the United Nations.

"Vietnamization." Campaigner Nixon promised to tell his Vietnam peace plan when elected. President Nixon announced it as "Vietnamization," i.e., turning most of the fighting over to the South Vietnamese. However, he ordered troops to strike positions in Cambodia to buy time for withdrawal. Americans reacted with mass peace demonstrations which led to a tragic incident in May, 1970, at Kent State University in Ohio. National Guardsmen killed four students during an antiwar demonstration.

The Armed Forces. After 1969 the selective service system began using a draft lottery procedure by random drawing of birthdates; young men were eligible at nineteen or when college deferments expired. Although this procedure lessened complaints of bias, the reform was not enough for a people sick of undeclared wars fought by "peacetime" draftees. By 1972 the armed forces were adjusting to an all-volunteer recruitment.

Peace Settlement. Vietnamization would not solve the problem of Americans known or presumed to be prisoners of war. The peace talks in Paris finally began to bear fruit, and in October, 1972, American negotiator Henry Kissinger prematurely announced, "Peace is at hand." The United States resorted to massive bombing of North Vietnam in December to speed the agreement. In January, 1973, a truce was arranged. Three months later the prisoners of war (only a quarter of those who had been listed missing) came home. UN observers soon found that the Vietnamese had no intention of stopping their war, and the killing continued, to the frustration of the peacekeeping mission. The Americans, however, had mostly gone. The Congress forbade military aid to Southeast Asia as of August 15, 1973. Henry Kissinger and Le Duc Tho of North Vietnam jointly won the Nobel Peace Prize for their peace efforts, although Le Duc Tho refused it as events deteriorated in Vietnam. America's longest war was over, and within two years it ended for the Vietnamese as well, with victory by North Vietnam.

POLITICS AND POLICIES

Congressional opposition waned throughout Nixon's first term. The President made friends by proposing to clear the welfare jungle; he ended complaints about the draft; and he spent ten times more to feed the destitute than had been spent in 1968. His nomination of Warren Burger as Supreme Court Chief Justice (1969) met no obstacle, although two choices for Associate Justices were rejected by the Senate. President Nixon's veto of the 1970–71 Health, Education and Welfare Department budget was upheld. Attorney General John Mitchell won the conviction of seven radicals accused of conspiring to incite riots during the Democratic National Convention, although it was a bizarre and politicized trial. The convictions were reversed on constitutional grounds in 1972.

Constitutional Changes. In 1971 two proposed constitutional amendments received strong support. Amendment Twenty-six, lowering the voting age to 18, quickly passed state ratification in 1971. The other amendment became the center of emotional controversy. After languishing in the Congress for half a century, the Equal Rights Amendment, forbidding discrimination by sex, emerged and went to the states with Nixon's endorsement. By early 1975 ratification was still short four state votes, and many women's groups had made the amendment an issue. The Congress began hearings on an amendment to outlaw abortion after the Supreme Court ruled in 1973 that state abortion laws violated a right to privacy.

Civil Rights Issues. The new administration had a narrowed view of liberty, supporting the jailing of persons who *might* commit crimes and legislation permitting surprise searches of private dwellings. The Attorney General tried to delay enforcement of the desegregation law, and the Supreme Court ruled that busing across school district lines solely for racial balance was not required. Vice-President Spiro T. Agnew censured the news media for "instant analysis" and inherent bias. Investigations later revealed that the Nixon administration had allowed the C.I.A. to spy on people inside the United States and that the F.B.I. had engaged in widespread clandestine wiretapping.

The Election of 1972. The Republican Party easily renominated Nixon and Agnew. Nixon bypassed the party's national committee, and John Mitchell resigned as Attorney General to head the nonparty Committee to Re-Elect the President (CREEP). The Democratic Party, operating under new convention rules requiring age, sex, and race distribution in delegations, chose Senator George McGovern. McGovern, who had been a last-minute peace candidate for the nomination in 1968, made the continued American involvement in Vietnam a major campaign issue.

McGovern first chose Senator Thomas Eagleton as a running mate but replaced him with Sargent Shriver after reporters revealed that Eagleton had previously received psychiatric care including shock treatment. When Kissinger announced on the eve of the election that peace was near, McGovern's ineffectual campaign was further undermined. Nixon captured the electoral votes of all states but Massachusetts and the District of Columbia. The Republican Party, treated as an orphan during the campaign, did not share Nixon's success. Democrats remained a majority in the Congress.

Domestic Ills. From 1972 to 1974 Nixon lost most of his goodwill in the Congress and the nation. The welfare reform plan was abandoned. Nixon vetoed budgetary increases and dismantled the agencies left from Johnson's "War on Poverty." The administration was plagued with instability of the dollar and by inflation. The Congress authorized Nixon to institute wage and price controls, but the population resented the controls and bureaucracy. Nixon slowly backed away from the controlled economy in a four "phase" maneuver. The inflation continued unabated. The administration added to the rising cost of food by negotiating a large grain sale to the Soviet Union.

War in the Middle East and manipulations by major oil companies caused a fuel crisis in 1973–74. Some states rationed gas for the first time since the 1940's. Although Americans bought fewer and smaller cars and cut their travel, most resented any change in their fuel-wasting habits. The shortage eased but threatened to return unless Americans made a stronger commitment to conservation. The people, however, seemed more willing to satisfy greed for fuel by undoing environmental protection measures.

Resignation of Agnew. On October 10, 1973, Spiro Agnew became the second Vice-President to resign. Agnew pleaded no contest to charges of income-tax evasion stemming from his years as Governor of Maryland and agreed to the release of evidence implicating him in bribery and kickbacks. Nixon thus became the first President to implement the Twenty-fifth Constitutional amendment (ratified in 1967) providing for a President to appoint a Vice-President with congressional approval when a vacancy occurs. Nixon's choice was the popular and widely respected House minority leader Gerald Ford.

Foreign Policy Successes. While Nixon's position eroded at home, his foreign policy under special assistant Henry Kissinger (Secretary of State after September, 1973) was brilliant. Following the outbreak of war in the Middle East, Kissinger persuaded Egypt, Syria, and Israel to agree to a truce and long-term negotiations. Nixon's visits to the Soviet Union in 1972 and 1974 added the word "détente" to the public's vocabulary, warmed relations with Russia, and produced some trade agreements but not the hoped-for arms treaty.

SCANDALS AND SCAPEGOATS

On June 17, 1972, James McCord, Jr., security chief of CREEP, and four other men were caught breaking into the Democratic National Committee's office at the Washington, D.C., Watergate complex. The burglars carried bugging and camera equipment and a number of $100 bills traceable to CREEP funds. White House consultant Howard Hunt was soon identified as the channel through which campaign funds had reached the Watergate burglars. By October it was clear that the burglary had been part of a widespread espionage and political sabotage plan sponsored by CREEP. The Congress deferred investigation of the matter until after the election.

From the end of 1972 to August, 1974, the smudge of scandal spread through the Nixon administration. Counsel to the President John Dean turned state's evidence when he realized that he was to be the White House scapegoat. By January 1, 1975, when prosecution ended, fifteen members of CREEP and Nixon's staff were convicted, on charges ranging from burglary to perjury and obstruction of justice. Nixon sacrificed his top aides in an attempt to appear blameless after Americans became incensed at the administration's effort to cover up its involvement.

Constitutional issues arose when both special Watergate prosecutor Archibald Cox and the Senate Select Committee on Presidential Campaign Activities subpoenaed tapes of conversations between Nixon and his aides, and Federal Judge John Sirica ordered that the subpoenaed tapes be made available to him for a decision on whether to turn them over to a grand jury. Nixon responded to Cox's suit by ordering him fired, whereupon Attorney General Elliot Richardson and Deputy Attorney General William Ruckelshaus resigned in protest. The press labeled the incident the "Saturday Night Massacre." Nixon's new appointees, special prosecutor Leon Jaworski and Attorney General William Saxbe, renewed the subpoena request and pressed the Watergate investigation. The House Judiciary Committee also subpoenaed a number of tapes when considering impeachment resolutions. Nixon refused all requests on grounds of executive privilege but finally released edited transcripts as a "compromise" with the House committee. In July, 1974, the Supreme Court ordered that the tapes be turned over to Judge Sirica. The Supreme Court decision (8–0 against with Rehnquist abstaining) admitted the constitutionality of executive privilege but ruled it not applicable in a case involving possible criminal conspiracy. The release of the last of the tapes implicated Nixon directly in the cover-up of the Watergate break-in.

What most Americans could not understand was why the burglary and sabotage ever took place. Nixon had a comfortable lead in the polls and needed no illegal help to win. The administration's paranoia proved its undoing. Not only did Nixon's amoral advisers violate civil rights during the campaign, but with Nixon's approval they tried to prevent a full investigation. More interested in protecting itself than the country, the "law and order" administration became a victim of its own lawlessness.

By late 1974 the stench of political scandal covered all Washington. Disclosures of illegal campaign contributions by corporations to both parties and liberal use of funds by milk producers to ensure higher milk prices took the scandal to congressmen.

RESIGNATION AND SUCCESSION

After the release of the final tapes, Nixon faced certain impeachment by the House. The House Judiciary Committee had already voted three Articles of Impeachment, which charged Nixon with obstruction of justice in the Watergate case, refusal to comply with House subpoenas, and abuse of power by such activities as wiretapping and income-tax audits. Rather than prolong the agony, Nixon resigned on August 9, 1974, the first American President to do so. Gerald Ford thus became the first American President not elected by the people. Ford promised to pursue Nixon's foreign policy and to "bind up the internal wounds of Watergate."

Ford's early actions inflamed the wound instead. With what seemed undue haste he announced an unconditional pardon of Nixon before any charges were pressed. By announcing a conditional amnesty program for Vietnam draft evaders and deserters at the same time, he made the two appear part of a trade. The great majority of draft evaders rejected Ford's program of alternative service, but several thousand deserters turned themselves in to clear their records.

THE FORD ADMINISTRATION

The President slowly appointed his own administration. He turned for guidance to the liberal wing of the Republican Party, choosing Nelson Rockefeller as Vice-President and retaining several Nixon advisers, including Henry Kissinger as Secretary of State.

Domestic and Foreign Problems. The Kissinger-style shuttle diplomacy continued to produce results, including an arms limitation agreement with the Soviets, Middle East peace talks at Geneva, and improved relations with France and Japan. Americans paid little attention to Asia except when Ford ordered a quick raid to recover the crew of the Mayaguez captured by the Vietnamese when the American ship ventured into territorial waters. Ford's frequent flights abroad, intended to improve his image, left resentment that he had ignored domestic issues.

Domestic problems abounded. Only two months after Ford had

taken office, elections produced a two-thirds Democratic Congress. This Congress and the President were continuously at odds. Watergate would not go away. In 1975 four of Nixon's closest advisers were convicted of offenses related to Watergate, and Nixon filed suit to recover the papers and tapes he had left behind. In September, 1975, there were two attempts to shoot Ford. New revelations of CIA involvement in domestic spying and attempted coups abroad and of FBI efforts to embarrass feminists, student leaders, and civil-rights advocates further tarnished the office of the President.

Economics brought the worst news to President Ford. New York City neared bankruptcy, and despite pleas from urban leaders, Ford did not intervene. Instead, he accused New York of fiscal irresponsibility. While New York's crisis brought little sympathy from suburban and rural America, all were panicked by the sudden rise in unemployment to 8.5 per cent in 1975 and by continued inflation. Ford refused to cooperate with Congress to create temporary jobs, arguing that this would fuel inflation. By the time inflation and unemployment slowed in 1976, the consumer dollar brought only one-half of what it had in 1967. The young and blacks still had unemployment rates well above average. Ironically, bettering economic conditions in the summer of 1976 encouraged new job seekers (mostly women) and led to a rise in unemployment.

From 1975 to 1978 record cold, rising fuel prices, drought, and slowed population growth all hurt the economy. Severe shortages of fuel in the winter of 1976–77 plagued the changeover in administration. Industries serving the young were hit hard by the low birth rate. Schools built only ten years before were now empty and teachers laid off. The high cost of fertilizer and equipment coupled with bumper crops left farm income short of expenses. The fuel crisis and handling costs, however, kept consumer food prices high.

THE ELECTION OF 1976

The presidential campaign of 1976 was the first under a new campaign financing law that partially funded candidates while limiting the size of individual contributions. The gloom of the economy hung over the hotly contested primaries. When the dust cleared, the front runners in a tight race were Ford for the GOP and the former governor of Georgia, James E. (Jimmy) Carter for the Democrats. Each won his party's nomination on the first ballot. A strong campaign by conservative Ronald Reagan had pushed Ford to the right to secure the nomination. Ford symbolically chose conservative Robert Dole as his running mate. Jimmy Carter, who had campaigned as a modern populist, calmed liberal fears by naming Walter Mondale as his prospective vice-president.

Both campaigns were marred by slips of the tongue and notable only in that Ford became the first incumbent to agree to televised debates with his opponent. Despite (or perhaps because of) Carter's status as an outsider, he led Ford in the polls, but the gap narrowed throughout the campaign. The 51 per cent popular vote for Carter indicated that he had restored the old New Deal coalition of labor, urban areas, blacks, and the South. In crucial southern states, the high black vote for Carter turned the tide. To forge this coalition the new President had to promise a balanced budget, government reorganization, jobs for the unemployed, and a "moral" foreign policy. Carter had claimed he was free from the power brokers of Washington and their corporations. Now he would have to work with them to forge new ties to implement his policies.

A NEW FACE IN WASHINGTON

The national mood was changing. Traditionalists opposed human rights statutes that protected homosexuals, and some organized to combat women's liberation, even capturing several delegations to the 1977 International Women's Year meeting in Houston. Former student radicals surrendered to law officials to face old charges and start anew. The Supreme Court took an increasingly conservative stance, upholding employer practices that excluded pregnancy from medical insurance and forced unpaid leaves upon pregnant stewardesses. Highly organized protesters pressured Congress and state legislatures to stop payments for abortions. Allen Bakke's charge that affirmative action programs were a form of reverse discrimination reached the Supreme Court, garnering some support from liberals. Even the NAACP favored deregulation of natural gas, which would hurt the poor black consumer.

Domestic Stalemate. Carter made little headway on his campaign promises in the first year. The President's hopes of a balanced budget faded with continued inflation and high unemployment. Congress, preoccupied with its own scandals and concerns, proved obstinate. Carter's various constituencies, especially farmers, blacks, and labor, became increasingly restive. The head of the Urban League openly denounced the administration's insensitivity to black unemployment. Striking farmers organized tractor parades to Washington D.C. and Carter's home at Plains, Georgia. Labor lobbied for higher tariffs and was disappointed in 1978 when Carter finally intervened during the nation's longest coal strike by invoking the Taft-Hartly Act. The miners refused to comply but eventually reached a settlement. However, Carter's opposition to the B-1 bomber and to numerous waterway projects and his deferral of the neutron bomb encouraged liberals.

The President's plans for the executive branch also stalled. He had appointed a balanced cabinet including experienced members, Georgians, blacks, and women. He symbolically cut the staff by one-third, but a year later asked for congressional authorization to hire a staff potentially twice its current size. Congress defeated Carter's plans for a Consumer Agency, but approved a general law giving him power to reorganize the executive branch. Carter's proposal for a new Department of Education and a plan for civil service reorganization got a cool reception in Congress. Election reform met the same fate when Congress killed Carter's proposal for voter registration at the polls and buried (in committee) a constitutional amendment to eliminate the Electoral College.

The economic situation continued to plague Carter as it had Ford. Weather extremes again disrupted the economy. Inflation slowed a little by 1978 and unemployment settled at 7 per cent. Carter first proposed a tax rebate to aid the economy and then backed down when the economy improved slightly and Congress seemed obstinate on the rebate. Carter stressed energy conservation as necessary for national survival (even delaying a trip abroad to convince Congress), but his proposals stalled in the legislature until, in the spring of 1978, the houses agreed to a compromise bill which would slowly deregulate natural gas.

Washington could not shake its corrupt image. Budget Director Bert Lance, a close friend of the President, had to resign when Congress investigated his questionable banking practices in Georgia. Revelations that Tongsun Park, a Korean businessman, had a cozy arrangement with some Congressmen swapping campaign contributions for favors affected many, including party leaders. Several former Congressmen were indicted.

Congress did not lack controversial issues. The social security system neared collapse, and the legislature staved it off by raising social security taxes and deferring the mandatory retirement age to seventy, thus delaying the start of benefits for some while increasing revenue. The measure was unpopular in an election year, and within six months the House Ways and Means Committee voted to reduce the tax increase by financing from general funds. After months of disagreement between the Senate and the House, federal funding for Medicaid abortions was ended and the Supreme Court allowed the ban to stand. (A similar law passed by the previous Congress had been stayed by the court.)

Foreign Policy Issues. The Senate narrowly ratified two treaties that guaranteed the neutrality of the Panama Canal and gradually returned control to Panama. However, Senate amendments guaranteeing the right to intervene militarily led to Panamanian protests and nearly undid the efforts of the administration to create a favorable image in Latin America. The support and opposition to the treaty was bipartisan. Negotiations had begun under the Republicans, but conservative Americans claimed the Canal Zone was American soil.

Carter promised and delivered a new foreign policy stressing human rights and closer ties to Arab nations and black nationalists in Africa. His emphasis on human rights may have warmed the hearts of libertarians, but it delayed the negotiation of an arms limitation pact with the Soviets and cooled relations between the U.S. and Brazil. Andrew Young, new ambassador to the U.N. and a veteran civil rights leader, became the Carter spokesperson to the third world. The administration spent much time reinterpreting some of Young's more abrasive statements, but Young did gain the respect of black African leaders. Carter's proposed sale of military planes to Egypt and Saudi Arabia, as well as to Israel, encountered resentment in Israel and opposition in Congress. Carter's most successful venture into diplomacy was the end to the ban on travel to Cuba and the beginning of informal relations with the Castro government.

The Political Scene. By early 1978 Republicans were gleefully pointing to polls that showed that the President's popularity had slipped greatly. The Republicans had done well in the by-elections caused by Carter appointments and the GOP had more funds than the Democrats. Conservatives and liberals struggled for leadership of the Republican Party without any strong contenders emerging. Congress feared facing the voters after increasing social security assessment and Carter added to their unease by pushing for a national health plan before the fall elections. However, the Democratic majority in Congress was large enough to weather a moderate comeback by Republicans. The public was impatient for action. The seeds of dissatisfaction had been planted by the expectations raised in Carter's campaign.

Index